# Forty Years
## in the
# New Mexico Roundhouse

# Forty Years
## in the
# New Mexico Roundhouse

## David Abbey

SUNSTONE
PRESS

SANTA FE

Sunstone books may be purchased for educational, business, or sales promotional use.
For information please write: Special Markets Department, Sunstone Press,
P.O. Box 2321, Santa Fe, New Mexico 87504-2321.
Printed on acid-free paper
∞
eBook: 978-1-61139-771-0

Library of Congress Cataloging-in-Publication Data

Names: Abbey, David, 1952- author
Title: Forty years in the New Mexico Roundhouse / David Abbey.
Description: Santa Fe : Sunstone Press, [2025] | Includes bibliographical
   references and index. | Summary: "A description of New Mexico finances
   and budget development and a modern legislative and fiscal history in
   order to account for the state's relatively low social and economic
   rankings"-- Provided by publisher.
Identifiers: LCCN 2025023309 | ISBN 9781632937551 paperback | ISBN
   9781632937568 paperback | ISBN 9781611397710 ebook
Subjects: LCSH: New Mexico. Legislature--History--20th century | New
   Mexico. Legislature--History--21st century | New Mexico--Politics and
   government--20th century | New Mexico--Politics and government--21st
   century
Classification: LCC JK8066 .A23 2025 | DDC 320.9789--dcundefined
LC record available at https://lccn.loc.gov/2025023309

WWW.SUNSTONEPRESS.COM
SUNSTONE PRESS / POST OFFICE BOX 2321 / SANTA FE, NM 87504-2321 /USA
(505) 988-4418

# CONTENTS

# Acronyms Used in this Book

ACE: Act on Compensation Equity

AGA: Accountability in Government Act

AG: Attorney General

ARPA: American Rescue Plan Act

ARRA: American Recovery and Relief Act

AP: Associated Press

BAR: Budget Adjustment Request

BIA: Bureau of Indian Affairs

BNSF: Burlington Northern Santa Fe Railroad

BoF: Board of Finance

CARES: Coronavirus Response and Relief Supplemental Appropriations Act

CFO: Chief Financial Officer

COLA: Cost of Living Adjustment

CPA: Certified public accountant

CRS: Congressional Research Service

CYFD: Children Youth and Families Department

DD: Developmentally disabled

DFA: Department of Finance and Administration

DoH: Department of Health

DOT: Department of Transportation

DPS: Department of Public Safety

ECECD: Early Childhood and Education Department

ED&T: Economic Development and Tourism Department

EMNRD: Energy, Minerals and Natural Resources Department

EPNG: El Paso Natural Gas Company

ERB: Education Retirement Board

FCD: Financial Control Division

FCI: Facility Condition Index

FPL: Federal poverty level

FIR: Fiscal Impact Report

FMAP: Federal Medicaid Assistance Participation

FY: Fiscal Year

GAA: General Appropriation Act

GASB: Governmental accounting standards board

GOB: General Obligation Bonds

GSD: General Services Department

GRIP: Governor Richardson's Investment Partnership

GRT: Gross receipts tax

HAFC: House Appropriations and Finance Committee

HED: Higher Education Department

HR: Human resources

HSD: Human Services Department

HTRC: House Taxation and Revenue Committee

IT: Information technology

JTIP: Job training Incentive Program

LANL: Los Alamos National Laboratory

LASL: Los Alamos Scientific Laboratory

LCS: Legislative Council Service

LEDA: Local Economic Development Act

LESC: Legislative Education Study Committee

LFC: Legislative Finance Committee

LGPF: Land Grant Permanent Fund

MBO: Management by Objectives

Mcf: thousand cubic feet of natural gas

MCO: Managed care organization

NAEP: National Assessment of Educational Progress

NAFTA: North American Free Trade Agreement

NCSL: National Conference of State Legislatures

NEA: National Education Association

NMFA: New Mexico Finance Authority

NMHU: New Mexico Highlands University

NMSU: New Mexico State University

PARCC: Partnership for Assessment of Readiness for College and Careers

PCG: Public Consulting Group

PED: Public Education Department

PERA: Public Employees Retirement Association

PFM: Public Financial Management

PIT: Personal income tax

PRC: Public Regulation Commission

PSCOC: Public School Capital Outlay Council

PSFA: Public School Facilities Authority

RFP: Request for Proposals

RIF: Reduction in Force

RIP: Rest in Peace

RLD: Regulation and Licensing Department

SEG: State Equalization guarantee

SFC: Senate Finance Committee

SHARE: Statewide Human Resources, Accounting and Management Reporting Enterprise System

SHTD: State Highway and Transportation Department

SIC: State Investment Council

SPO: State Personnel Office

STB: Severance Tax Bonds

STBF: Severance Tax Bonding Fund

STEM: Science, technology, engineering and math

STPF: Severance Tax Permanent Fund

TANF: Temporary Aid to Needy Families

TRD: Taxation and Revenue Department

TRANS: Tax and Revenue Anticipation Notes

UNM: University of New Mexico

WNMU: Western New Mexico University

WIPP: Waste Isolation Pilot Project


Note: See also LFC Style and Reference Manual for additional acronyms and definitions.

# 1

# PATH TO PUBLIC SERVICE

Following my retirement announcement after forty years of service in New Mexico government, a reporter for a press advocacy group emailed, "I am writing a story about New Mexico's unique legislative process (the unique unsalaried legislature, the very short alternating sessions) that results in a lot of legislation being left on the table every year. I am trying to find a way to empirically demonstrate what's lost/not passed due to this system. I'd like to pick your brain about the history of this legislative system and attempts to reform it."

That is a lot to unpack. First, the reporter thinks he knows the answer before he starts—that New Mexico's legislature is ineffective, because the members are volunteers and don't work enough. Second, there is an assumption that more legislation is better and will result in reform. What the heck is reform anyway? Third, the question for me evoked the trend in our state for progressives to dominate all branches of government and to purge fiscal conservatives.

I grew up in Washington, DC; I delivered the *Washington Post* for four years. After my route, I returned home and read the paper. In the sixties of course there were a lot of interesting things happening—the presidencies of Kennedy, Johnson and Nixon, assassinations, Vietnam, civil rights and integration and the war on poverty. The *Post* reported weekly a box score (a spreadsheet) on the progress of Great Society legislation. Rows were bills, and columns were location by chamber and by committee or floor. (See Figure 1) The cells indicated status, for example passed or hearing scheduled or no hearing scheduled. Many of the committees were chaired by Southern Democrats who were vilified as obstructionists or even segregationists.

President Johnson was highly successful in achieving enactment of landmark legislation and appropriations for civil rights, voting rights, aid to states for the interstate highway system, Medicaid for low-income and disabled Americans, expansion of Social Security payments to the elderly and disabled, Head Start, welfare payments, food stamps, aid to school districts, bilingual education, public television, consumer protection, clean air and water and more.[1] In subsequent decades, these federal programs expanded to serve many more people and provide much greater aid or benefits to clients.

New Mexico state government similarly has experienced dramatic expansion. Estimated general fund recurring revenue in December 1983 when I started was $870 million but reached $12.6 billion in FY24.

State government spending soared beginning FY19. First, this reflected explosive growth in state revenue due to an oil and gas production boom. New Mexico is now the second biggest oil producing state after Texas and has almost overtaken North Dakota with the highest oil production per capita.

Second, New Mexico after decades as a swing state sending Republicans and Democrats to Congress, seems to be solid blue. Democrats have all statewide offices and comfortable margins in both legislative chambers. Democrats capitalized on an unpopular Republican governor from 2011 to 2018. President Trump was a negative for independents and moderates in both parties, and abortion restrictions are broadly unwelcome.

Third, moderate and conservative Democrats have been mostly wiped out of the legislature. Many of these legislators represented rural New Mexico and were committee chairs by virtue of long tenure. First to go were legislators in conservative southeast and northwest New Mexico like Jerry Sandel, Don

Whitaker, Johnny Morrow and John Heaton defeated by Republicans. In 2011 Representative Andy Nunez (Hatch) changed to independent and later to Republican. Reapportionment moved some districts into large towns or cities like Rhonda King's from Torrance County to El Dorado in Santa Fe County. Then environmental groups, unions and consumer advocates took on moderates who chose not to seek reelection like John Sapien or were defeated in primaries like Senate President Pro Tem Mary Kay Papen, long-time Senate Finance Chair John Arthur Smith and veterans' advocate Harry Garcia from Grants.

The political and economic changes have allowed surging investments in public services. Public schools are funded almost entirely by the state in the interest of per-pupil equalization. General Fund appropriations for schools have grown from about $2.6 billion in FY19 to over $4 billion. School lunch is free for all regardless of income. All four-year-olds are eligible for preschool, quality childcare or Head Start. Almost half of New Mexicans receive free health care through Medicaid. University tuition is free. Childcare is virtually free.

There are some big-ticket items that are sure to be at the top of the agendas of the governor and the legislature over the next few years. Paid family medical leave is at the top of the list. Free civil legal services seem not far behind. But I also wonder whether the US and New Mexico have the same need for legislation and reform that existed in the 1960s? Does the New Mexico legislature need to meet longer? Do legislators need to be paid? How should the state manage volatility of oil prices? Should we worry about what happens if oil production turns south? How big should the permanent funds be? Why is New Mexico at the bottom of workforce participation, five percent below the US average? How much can we afford to cut taxes? How do we get third graders to read at grade level? How can we treat addiction?

In the current political environment, it's almost like a dirty word but I admit it. I am a fiscal conservative. I am of the camp that wants government to provide basic services well and cost-effectively. For towns and cities, this means pick up the trash, fix the potholes, keep the parks clean. For the state, it means ensure kids are reading and doing math at grade level, provide early education and home visiting to ensure kids are reading when they start school, provide high-quality higher education that's not expensive, build a strong transportation system, provide health care and behavioral health services to the less fortunate, avoid corporate welfare and tax breaks for people who don't need it and fight corruption.

In a word picture I contrast an emergency with brush fires in every direction with a major multi-alarm structure fire. I advise instead of taking 100 buckets to 100 fires to solve all manner of problems take 100 buckets to three fires. (See Figure 2)

Typically, there are 1,000 or more bills introduced in a legislative session. This seems like a lot, nearly unmanageable. But some are duplicate bills, and many bills are appropriation bills which will not pass individually but instead be incorporated in omnibus spending legislation. Many bills are simply inconsequential. Of the 1,000 bills perhaps 25 to 50 are major pieces of legislation with significant fiscal impacts or affecting many New Mexicans.

For the appropriators, the budgeteers, only three or four bills really matter—the feed bill to fund the legislative session, the General Appropriation Act, capital outlay or infrastructure funding and perhaps an omnibus tax measure. Aside from the essential goal of passing legislation to run the government, the appropriators hope the measures prioritize key services, lead to better outcomes in a cost-effective way and don't waste money or serve special or parochial interests.

## PURPOSE AND ORGANIZATION

The principal purpose of this book is to provide an insider's view of the development of the budget and fiscal policies by the New Mexico legislature.

A related purpose is to provide insight into New Mexico's economic, education, health and social performance; to be more blunt, why are we last? New Mexicans don't talk much about this, in fact hardly at all. This may reflect embarrassment or avoidance. The dominant modern view seems to be that we're last because we are poor. It is like, if government could spend more on a wide range of programs, we wouldn't be poor. But in the last decade in the wake of the fracking revolution, New Mexico government is not only not poor, it is rich, and spending has skyrocketed. But we're still at the bottom of most indicators except health with half of New Mexicans on Medicaid. What's up with that?

Don't expect that I will have all the answers to improve New Mexico's performance. If I did, after forty years at the capitol, we should have done better. Also, folks might think I'm arrogant or ignorant. My hope is that my experience at the capitol and examination of the historic record will inspire thinking and talking about how to make New Mexico prosper.

Chapter 2 describes where the money comes from and where it goes for state government in New Mexico. It covers sources of revenue, objects of spending, historical trends, major funds, cost drivers and revenue estimating.

Chapter 3 describes the development of budget recommendations by the New Mexico legislature and the path to passage and enactment of appropriations bills, activities generally unknown to the public and not well described anywhere. This includes a review of guidelines and principles used by staff and legislators, and key information and reports used for analysis.

Chapters 4 and 5 cover capital outlay and the ways that the legislature ensures oversight and accountability of public funds.

Chapters 6 through 12 record the history of state finances and governance from 1983 to the present. This begins with Governor Toney Anaya in 1983 and concludes with Governor Michelle Lujan Grisham through 2023. During this period, annual recurring General Fund appropriations grew from $1.2 billion to $10.9 billion. The average annual growth in recurring appropriations, 5.3 percent, well exceeded the combined average growth rates of inflation (2.9 percent) and population (1.3 percent). Real inflation-adjusted per capita income (in 2023$) increased from $2,700 in 1983 to $3,984 in 2023, a growth rate of 47.5 percent.

What was the growth in spending for? What did it accomplish? How did it happen? What were budget and tax priorities of governors and legislators? What did they fight about and how did they compromise? What spending initiatives improved service and quality of life for New Mexicans?

Chapter 13 presents key metrics for level and quality of government services and quality of life and other outcomes for New Mexicans. Despite growth in services and inflation-adjusted spending, New Mexico continues to rank at or near the bottom for many measures. New Mexicans want to know why we are last and what are the bottlenecks to improvement, the subject of the last chapter. Chapter 14 should generate the greatest interest in the manuscript, because New Mexicans are crying to be better, and money is not the problem.

To tell this story, I rely on Legislative Finance Committee reports and analysis and newspaper accounts of state government and legislative activity. But throughout, I also supplement the record based on my personal experience and observation. At risk of immodesty, this is because I am a state budget expert and had an unprecedented period of service at the heart of New Mexico state government. I have testified at hundreds of legislative hearings, sat next to the appropriation and finance chairs at final passage (third reading) of the general appropriation act in the House of Representatives and Senate since 1998, and advised legislators, governors and advocates on budget development, policy matters and legislative strategy. I liken my story to Forest Gump in the 1994 film, witness to great events for decades. Life is full of struggles—get knocked down, get up and keep trying to make a better New Mexico.

# ABOUT THE AUTHOR

Both my parents were from Cleveland, Ohio. My father's grandmother was a missionary in China for 30 years. My mother's grandfather was a cemetery superintendent. Both my grandfathers, Robert Powers Abbey and Clayton C. Townes, were lawyers and Townes was mayor of Cleveland in the 1920s.

The great depression hit my family hard. Robert P. Abbey struggled financially and died of pneumonia. My father, Robert L. Abbey, and his middle brother were sent to live with different relatives. Clayton Townes divorced and moved to Florida, and my mother moved from a mansion on Lake Erie to a garage apartment. My parents' hardship and loss certainly shaped my values and work ethic and attitude towards education and success.

World War II took its toll on my family. My father and all my uncles were in the army. I am proud of my uncle Herman Hale who was a paratrooper and a liberator of the Los Banos prison camp in Manila, Philippines. My parents married May 29, 1942 (my birthday ten years later in 1952), and my mother followed my dad to training camps. She told me it was Lake Superior in the winter and Alabama in the summer, before he went overseas on convoy duty. My mother suffered a severe sense of abandonment. Then the GIs came home and started families, and many pursued higher education, graduate school at Harvard in political science for my father.

I was born in New Orleans, Louisiana in 1952 where my father was a political science professor. Then we moved to Washington, DC where he worked for the US State Department in the leader and visitors program.

My upbringing was basic middle class. My sister says we were a dysfunctional family, but my brother and I ask, what families in the fifties weren't dysfunctional? We went to the Christian Science church, which influenced my views about health and wellness. I wanted to be a jock but was close to uncoordinated. I was a good student and motivated to excel and, as my mother said, "had my nose buried in a book all the time." Junior year in high school, I received the Brown University dictionary award for excellence in English. At a young age, I was keenly interested in politics and government, including world affairs.

I remember violent thunderstorms, wading in the gutters, the cherry blossoms, evening streets filled with kids chasing fireflies and playing kick the can, the Cleveland Indians coming to town to play the Washington Senators, old Griffith stadium, packs of kids walking to school, going to Ayrlawn park with a basketball, football and tennis racquet, a demonstration to integrate the Hiser theatre, filling my jean pockets with acorns for a fight in the woods, traveling down the creek behind North Bethesda junior high collecting crawfish, collecting pop bottles at the National Institutes for Health and trading them in at Browns' store for playing cards, the angus cattle, the hot dogs and pop bottles in a slushy tin crate at Little Three picnics (Amherst, Wesleyan and Williams), the bookmobile, the Daughters of the American Revolution's Madonna on the Trail statue next to the Bethesda library,[2] hiking along the B&O canal and Great Falls, scrambling the rocks on my eighth birthday at the Catoctin Mountain Park near Camp David (my mother made a coconut cake), a reception at the Burmese embassy (I'm still trying to taste the exciting exotic food), the Hindu wedding when the groom rode in on a white horse, the severe headaches that felt like rocks in my head lying in my mother's bed motionless (probably untreated ear infections), my mother yelling at my brother, my mother yelling at my father, Civil War reenactments, playing blue and gray soldiers with my brother, my brother and I teasing my sister and her boyfriends, duck drills under the desk, bomb shelters, visiting the Smithsonian and capitol when relatives come to town, gnats, the National Zoo, going through the fords in Rock Creek Park when it was really hot and the temperature dropped 20 degrees, peddling papers on my Columbia two- speed in quiet dawn.

I was set on going to a top college, but our family resources were limited. My sister dropped out of Ohio Wesleyan, because my dad couldn't afford it and commuted to the University of Maryland. I went to Amherst College for two years. In May 1972 Nixon invaded Cambodia (funny we say it that way, he obviously didn't do it). President John William Ward told an assembly of students in Johnson Chapel that somebody asked him to write a letter: "Write a letter? I'm going to Westover AFB in the morning to sit in and protest the war." Six hundred students including me were arrested, half the student body. Front page of *The New York Times* but the war continued, and I thought, "get me out of here."

1. Brother Doug, Father Robert and David Abbey. Circa 1957. I always wanted to be a cowboy.

My father had a visitor, Rocco Knobel, the director of South Africa National Parks. I took a freighter from Brooklyn to Cape Town, crossed the Karoo by rail to Johannesburg and flew on a light prop to Skukuza and worked at the Kruger National Park. They were at the vanguard of savannah management, conducting and researching controlled burns to maintain habitat health and diversity. Then I hitched to Durban and drove a forklift at the docks and stayed at the YMCA. Then hitching, trains and buses to Victoria Falls, Rhodesia and Lamu, Kenya. This began my destiny as a *vagomundo*. (When I crossed customs at Cape Town, I had a stack of books including Kesey's *Electric Kool-Aid Acid Test*. The agent asked if this is for your project at the Kruger NP, and I said yes because it was likely banned.) In Africa I began to see my mission of public service.

I returned home, worked construction in the summer, saved everything I made and transferred to Brown University in fall 1972. I majored in economics with an initial interest in economic development and then environmental and urban economics. I also minored in math which I was not prepared for. College was a financial struggle, but in 1974 I had a great job at Harris Lumber Co., Teamster pay, first working in the mill and then delivering to construction sites. I lived in Fox Point, a Portuguese neighborhood, rode my bike down the hill, past the capitol, through the railyards and warehouses out Atwells Avenue. Providence had an unusual ethnic mix—Italian, Irish and Jewish of course but also Armenian and French Canadian. We had 30 minutes for lunch and on Fridays would rush to a joint and line up 25 cent seven ounce 'Gansetts. One day mayoral candidate Buddy Cianci came on a campaign stop and the bell rang, and everyone had one more.

The week before senior year, I quit and drove to visit my friend Mike Waters from Denver. Eastern transplants remember their first sight of the Rockies, for me around pancake flat Goodland, Kansas. We hiked Mt. Evans, drove up the beautiful North Fork of the Platte to Saratoga, Wyoming, then Rawlins, the Red Desert[3], the Tetons, and Yellowstone. I hitchhiked back to school from Livingston, Mt. and got a ride in a van to Hershey, Pa. with a biker who'd been a marshal at the Evel Knievel motorcycle jump over the Snake River. Out in eastern Montana, past the Custer battlefield at sunset the skies darkened to the west, the clouds soared to the heavens, and "they" put on a spectacular lightning show saying, "come on back."

Senior year I took introduction to geology which was effectively a slide show of the West and started my "wanderer" reading series, Kerouac's *On the Road* and *Dharma Bums*, "Howl," Stegner's Lewis and Clark and John Wesley Powell.

As a liberal arts graduate, I didn't have much professional direction and the economic prospects weren't great, but it didn't really matter because I headed back West. My mother cried when she dropped me off on the west side of the Tappan Zee bridge.

My wandering that year was fun, interesting, exciting and lonely. I drove a grain truck on a ranch near Great Falls, Montana, worked on a section gang for Western Pacific RR in Gerlach, Nevada but ultimately ended in jobless failure with a broken-down motorcycle in Oakland.

Returning to Washington, I got a job immediately as a research assistant at Resources for the Future, an environmental think tank next to the Brookings Institution. Distinguished economists, including the University of New Mexico's (UNM's) Allen Kneese, were studying the effects of an expected coal and oil shale boom in the Southwest. Could these resources meet the nation's energy independence goals? Would there be enough water? How would it affect air quality and rural and indigenous communities. I wrote a paper that was published in the *Natural Resources Journal,* and the University of California's Los Alamos Scientific Laboratory (LASL) hired me as a staff member to continue the same work.

I flew into the little Los Alamos airport and hitchhiked to Espanola and rented a house on the west Side, *Currucu town*, from Rubio the jailer for $150 a month. Then I bought my first car, a '59 Ford, for $700. The wipers didn't really work.

I think of five years at the lab as endless days of windowless, half-motivated gloom. Not a good fit for me and arguably not a good fit for New Mexico.

For decades the national labs and air bases have been the top budget priority for our congressional delegation, and Senator Domenici (St. Pete) and Senator Bingaman were highly effective. But while the US was making great investments in ports and highways, agricultural research, schools and universities in states like Mississippi, South Carolina, Maine and Washington with key legislators on the budget and appropriation committees, we were getting fighter wings and meson facilities. There were significant efforts to promote spinoffs from the labs. But who wants to be an entrepreneur when pay and pensions and vacation time are so great?

Meanwhile, Rio Arriba County was a great place to call home. One of the largest and poorest counties in the United States, Rio Arriba then seemed more like the northern picket of Latin America. Spanish was widely spoken, and English was spoken with a sing song lilt. Many *nortenos* traced a proud heritage to Spanish settlement 400 years ago. Rio Arriba was home to five Indian pueblos and the Jicarilla Apaches in Dulce. LASL and state government were the major employers, but many families grew significant gardens of corn, beans and chile and ran cows in Forest Service allotments. Duke City Lumber was a significant employer with a big mill puffing away on Espanola's north side.

Molly Ivins wrote the county, "contains the most beautiful country, poorest people, richest history and most peculiar goings-on in the United States."[4] She called Northern New Mexico "Spanish—not Chicano, not Mexican, but Spanish by 80 percent." She reported Penitentes, hippie infestations, bomb builders, lowriders and cattle mutilations linked to UFOs.

In Fall 1978 there was a momentous election. State Senator Joe Skeen, Republican and sheepman from Picacho in Lincoln County, faced Bruce King, trying for a second term as governor with his cowboy coalition of *nortenos*, old line mining interests and many farmers and ranchers (see *Cowboy in the Roundhouse*, Bruce King). Dr. Sam Ziegler, a Republican who was said to have delivered all the babies in Rio Arriba was running against county manager, former sheriff and long-time Democratic patron Emilio Naranjo for state Senate. Emilio was a protégé of President Kennedy; Kennedy's photo graces homes all over the heavily Catholic north. Emilio or his deputies also planted pot on some *La Raza Unida* party activists, Ikie de Vargas and Moises Morales, leading to their trial. For the fiesta parade in Espanola that year hundreds of activists carried red banners and flags, marching along with the fiesta princesses, the bucking yellow jalopy truck from Las Vegas (New Mexico, of course), the high school football teams and cheerleaders and dozens of candidates for office. *New Mexican* reporter David Roybal took a photo of me and Skeen at a Republican rally at Alva Simpson's ranch near Abiquiu. I might have lingered at the beer truck too long. The caption says, "Joe Skeen makes a point with an area resident," as he jabs a finger in my chest in response to a provocative question about right to work, the big issue of that campaign.

2. Joe Skeen and David Abbey at a campaign event near Abiquiu, September 11, 1978. (*Santa Fe New Mexican* photo.)

I took Spanish at the new Northern New Mexico Community College and joined the basketball league at the Holy Cross gym. My first joint was the Mel Patch lounge, but eventually I traded up to Saints and Sinners. In 1981 I bought a ten-acre farm in Medanales, a small community on the Chama River near Abiquiu. It was a narrow strip running to the bosque with a crumbling adobe house near the county road. Grass was growing from the roof. I was inspired by the classic *Adobe: Build It Yourself*. Sometimes friends and neighbors helped—new roof, new windows and doors, wiring, plumbing, Saltillo tile, flagstone, a wardrobe and a new mudroom. My vision was to sell produce at the Santa Fe Farmers Market. The first time I voted up north at the SPMDTU hall (Sociedad por Protecion Mutual de Trabajadores Unidos) I walked in at ten 'til seven and got awkward looks from the precinct officials and realized somebody had already voted for me. They let me vote anyway.

3. My new house across from the church in Medanales.

In 1983 the New Mexico Legislative Finance Committee advertised to hire an economist. They hired Ed Howard instead (more on him in Chapter 6) but gave my resume to the Department of Finance Administration (DFA), and I was hired as a revenue estimator. With my background in natural resource economics, my key responsibility was to forecast energy prices and production and related revenue. This was a tumultuous period with OPEC dominance and deregulation of natural gas prices. In 1986 I was promoted to chief economist of DFA and effectively a leader of preparing and presenting the state revenue forecast. In 1992 DFA Secretary Kay Marr sent me to a three-week executive program at Harvard's Kennedy School of Government, an outstanding opportunity. On my return, I moved up to director of the State Board of Finance, chaired by the governor and a surrogate for the legislature when not in session. In 1995 Republicans captured the governor's office. I lasted six months but was fired, the fourth of seven "killings" of David Abbey styled after the novel about Bob Marley, *A Brief History of Seven Killings* by Marlon James. Within an hour I found a job across the street as chief investment officer for the state treasurer. I expanded my professional horizon but was on the verge of being embroiled in pay-to-play, when I was asked to apply for director of the Legislative Finance Committee in June 1997. There were only three other applicants, only one credible and I was tabbed. At first it was just get me one year before I get fired. Then two years. Then I started gaining political support and experience and adding more and more value to the legislature and public policy. At 11 years I became eligible for retirement and a lot of pressure was off. At 15 years I surpassed the tenure of the great Maralyn Budke who became chief of staff for Governor Carruthers. Of course, I was a thorn in the side of governors, but the finance chairs asked me not to hang it up. After 26 years as director, I retired in May 2023.

This brings us to our story. I may have lingered too long about me, but it is important because I believe my worldview, my education, my travels and cross-cultural experiences and my interest in people and places contributed to my success in the New Mexico legislature.

I had the training and experience to lead a professional staff in complex financial matters. I had the work ethic and drive to tirelessly seek workable solutions in the face of bitter partisan divides. I could win trust and confidence of New Mexicans with varied educational backgrounds and religious and cultural differences. I had empathy for those who needed help and services. I knew New Mexico history and geography, towns, crossroads and ruins, about language and economic and social interests. I had strong communication skills. I was able to learn from mistakes and build an exceptional, diverse staff. I could think out of the box to find technical and political solutions.

To recap, this book is a primer on state government finance and modern political history from my experience with the aim to account for New Mexico's performance.[6]

# 2
# THE FINANCIAL STRUCTURE
## OF
# NEW MEXICO STATE GOVERNMENT

## SOURCES OF REVENUE

A chapter on New Mexico government by UNM's Dr. Brian McDonald described the "Fiscal Structure of New Mexico." LFC updated this chapter in 2006 for the third edition, and I was a principal contributor.[7] This chapter presents significant new information addressing the sharp increase in energy revenue, the growing importance of the personal income tax, rapidly growing tax expenditures and gross receipts tax exemptions, the emergence of the early childhood education program, litigation to equalize public school spending, the sharp increase in Medicaid enrollment and spending for health care, more spending devoted to individual legislators' priority projects and other factors. Also, this chapter introduces many legislative fiscal reports and performance evaluations that cover valuable material not readily available to a general readership.

New Mexico statutes designate major funds for operations, enterprises, trusts for beneficiaries, debt service and capital projects. The state Treasurer and the Department of Finance and Administration maintain records for these funds in approximately 1000 accounts that may bewilder even expert observers.

Constitutional Framework. The New Mexico Constitution provides the financial framework for state and local government. Article 4 Section 30 provides, "Except interest or other payments on the public debt, money shall be paid out of the Treasury only upon appropriations by the legislature. No money shall be paid therefrom except upon warrant drawn by the proper officer." Making appropriations is the most important duty of the legislature, the branch that is closest to the people. Other important provisions include limits on debt, property tax limits, free and equal education, providing for use of state lands and creating the permanent fund and the anti-donation clause.

The Map/The Big Picture. Figure 3 provides a bird's eye view of the most significant New Mexico funds including sources of revenue and uses and transfers among funds. I suggest newcomers to the capitol keep this figure in their purse or pocket to consult from time to time when they are overwhelmed with funds, tables and flow charts. The left part highlights the two biggest funds used for state government operations. The general fund operating budget in FY20 was $7.8 billion and received the big majority of state revenue including gross receipts and income taxes, investment income from permanent funds, severance taxes and federal royalties as well as all state revenues not designated by law. General fund revenue is appropriated in the General Appropriation Act (GAA) for public and higher education, health care, public safety and many other government activities. The next biggest operating fund is the $1 billion road fund with revenue from gasoline taxes and other road user fees. Other significant operating funds are less than $500 million including risk management funds, game protection and state land management.

The middle of the figure shows two permanent funds and the treasurer's investment pool with FY20 balances of $30 billion. The land grant permanent fund (LGPF) receives royalties from oil and gas produced on state lands (typically 12.5 percent, now amounting to $1 billion per year). Eighty percent of LGPF investment income goes to the common school part of the general fund, but universities and some state agencies also benefit. The severance tax permanent fund (STPF) receives surplus severance tax bonding fund (STBF) revenue not used for debt service on bonds. Beginning 1999 to address the *Zuni* lawsuit related to funding school construction, most of the STBF revenue went to pay debt service, and the STPF barely grew, but with soaring energy revenue, annual transfers to the STPF exceeded $1 billion. Also, the legislature has authorized additional trust funds with windfall oil and gas revenue, notably the early childhood trust fund which is approaching $10 billion.

The right part of the figure shows the two main funding methods for paying debt service on bonds for infrastructure. General obligation bonds (GOBs) and severance tax bonds (STBs) are authorized by the legislature. GOBs are paid by property taxes and require voter approval every other year at the general election. STBS are paid by one of two severance taxes, mostly on oil and gas. When general fund reserves and revenue are above trend, the general fund may also be used for capital outlay.

Tax Policy Principles. The New Mexico Legislative Finance Committee lists five tax policy principles in its annual report to the legislature. Most important are: Adequacy, revenue should be adequate to fund needed government services; and Efficiency, the base should be as broad as possible to avoid excessive reliance on one tax. Ideally, New Mexico tax rates should be in the middle of the pack—like Goldilocks, not too high, not too low. If rates are too high, business activity and investment may be scared off. If rates are too low, the state may be losing revenue without a benefit to economic activity (like the motor vehicle excise tax which despite a recent increase is half the rate of some neighboring states).

Key Tax Revenue Sources and Issues. Government can tax just three things—sales, income or property. Public finance experts call this the three-legged stool.

The state constitution provides that a property tax up to 20 mills of property value (a mill equals 0.1 percent) may be imposed for government operations, and statutes allocate the millage among the state, municipalities, counties and school districts. In 1981, the beginning of the Reagan era with oil prices at a seeming high, the law dubbed "Big Mac", sponsored by Reps. Colin McMillan (R-Roswell) and John Bigbee (R-Encino), reallocated eight mills from school districts (and effectively the state) to cities and counties. Big Mac also wiped out most personal income tax revenue.

In effect New Mexico state government's three -legged stool is missing the property tax leg that taxes wealth and that provides the most revenue stability, in other words the leg that is least subject to the business cycle and energy market volatility.

The workhorse of the revenue system is the gross receipts tax (GRT) on sales, accounting for more than a third of general fund revenue as well as the major revenue source for municipalities. Unlike most state sales taxes, the GRT liability is on the seller, not the buyer. New Mexico tax experts have long valued the gross receipts tax, because it generally applies to services as well as tangible goods. This allows New Mexico revenue to keep up with the faster growing economic sectors and generates more revenue from higher income or wealthier persons. A big disadvantage of the GRT is that it is different and hard to understand; the director of the New Mexico Tax Research Institute even calls it weird. If the rate is low relative to sales tax rates in other states, then it looks sort of like a European VAT (value added tax). But in the interest of either income equity or competition with other states, there has been a steady erosion of the tax base and a steady increase in rates to make up for lost revenue. (See Figure 4) The exemption of food and certain medical services from GRT beginning 2004 now costs the general fund approximately $500 million annually. (See tax expenditure table in LFC vol. 3)

Personal income tax (PIT) accounts for almost one quarter of general fund revenue. Governor Bill Richardson may have been ahead of his time with his initiative to lower the top PIT rate from 8.1 percent to 4.9 percent. The concern was that corporate decision makers would shy away from New Mexico locations. It would cost over $100 million by FY06, lost revenue sorely needed during the Great Recession in 2009. Further, there wasn't much evidence of economic benefits. At the 2019 session, the top rate was bumped back to 5.9 percent to raise revenue and boost tax progressivity. But New Mexico may be going in the wrong direction. Some of the nation's fastest growing states don't have a PIT including Texas, South Carolina and Washington and neighboring states Arizona, Oklahoma and Utah are lowering their PIT rates.

Energy-Related Revenues. New Mexico has two significant types of revenue that in simple terms don't place a tax burden on most citizens: revenue directly from the energy industry and investment revenue from trust funds endowed by energy revenue. New Mexico can use this natural resource bounty for a combination of either lower taxes or higher government spending than would otherwise occur.

New Mexico has two significant severance taxes on oil and natural gas with a combined rate of seven percent that go about equally to the general fund and the severance tax bonding fund. Both the state and federal government also get production royalties from land they own, typically 12.5 percent. The share of oil and natural gas production on federal and state land in 2022 was about 90 percent and 40 percent, respectively.

New Mexico oil fields are over 100 years old. After reaching a peak in 1970, New Mexico oil production generally declined to a modern low in 2007 and 2008 of 60 million barrels. New Mexico ranked 4th or so in natural gas production and 8th or so in oil production.

Around 2010 oil and gas producers began to tap oil and gas in shale with hydraulic fracturing and horizontal drilling. The Permian Basin of Texas and New Mexico has the richest shale resource in the world. Production began to rise and then soar, and New Mexico is now the second biggest oil producer behind Texas and has the second highest oil production per capita behind North Dakota. (Figure 5)

The share of general fund revenue directly derived from the oil and gas industry (excluding trust and permanent funds) has increased from around 25 percent in FY11 to about 35 percent in FY24. The growth of oil and gas production and state revenue is expected to continue for five to ten years or more.[8]

Investment Income. The federal Ferguson Act of 1898 allocated four sections (a section equals 640 acres) in each township (36 sections) to New Mexico Territory to specific public purposes.[9] As fortune would have it, the state received lands that were unwanted, disproportionately in desolate tracts of southeast New Mexico, especially Lea County, that proved to be one of the world's most prolific oilfields. For decades, about half the oil produced in New Mexico came from state lands.

The Constitution in 1912 provided that the State Land Office collect royalties for use of state lands and transfer the proceeds to permanent funds for each beneficiary.

In the 1950s the legislature established a companion, the severance tax permanent fund, to receive a fraction of severance tax revenue from mineral extraction. A 1973 constitutional amendment made the STPF permanent.

Over the last 40 years additional constitutional amendments have increased allowable investment of the funds, especially stocks, changed the investment income distribution method to percent of total return instead of just dividends and interest, and most recently in 2022 provided a new permanent fund beneficiary for early childhood education and increased the distribution to 6.5 percent of assets.

Also, in 2020 Chapter 3 created a new Early Childhood Education and Care Fund to receive oil and gas emergency school tax revenue above the past five-year average that quickly grew to $5 billion. In 2023, Ch.166 directed opioid settlement revenue, expected to total about $1 billion, to yet another trust fund to be managed by the State Investment Council.

The State Investment Council reports that inflows to its investment trusts averaged about $460 million annually prior to 2018 but spiked to $8 billion in 2022 and are projected around $4 billion annually for the next decade.[10]

In sum, as energy tax and royalty revenue decline in coming decades, investment income will rise significantly.

Federal Revenue. The state receives federal revenue pursuant to grant agreements between federal and state agencies. A Supreme Court opinion in 1974 (*Sego v. Kirkpatrick*) determined that a federal grant for higher education appropriations was not subject to state appropriation, and this practice has been broadly accepted for executive agencies since. Generally, the federal revenue is reported in the General Appropriation Act for information purposes. Federal revenue in the 2024 General Appropriation Act was $11.2 billion, including $7.0 billion for HSD Medicaid, $1.2 billion for HSD income support, mostly food stamps, and $533 million for transportation.

Rarely, certain federal revenue is subject to state appropriation, notably the Temporary Aid to Needy Families block grant for which federal statutes provide for state appropriation and federal aid to the state for general revenue purposes. Also, New Mexico received $1.8 billion in 2021 for pandemic relief, and the Supreme Court ruled in 2022 (*Candelaria v. Grisham*) that the funds required legislative appropriation.

Tax Credits and Expenditures. It is important to consider not only where the revenue is coming from but where it isn't coming from. In addition to the LFC tax policy principles, LFC has six guidelines listed in every fiscal impact report for taxation-related legislation: vetted by interim committees; targeted with a clearly stated purpose; transparent with annual reporting by recipients to TRD; accountable allowing the public to determine progress to goals; effective, meets purpose; and efficient, or cost-effective. TRD prepares an annual Tax Expenditure Report summarized in LFC Volume 3. TRD categorizes tax expenditures by general citizen benefit, health care, avoid double taxation, economic development, specialized industry and environment/renewables. The six biggest tax expenditures in FY21 were food ($261 million), prescription drugs ($106 million), hospitals ($106 million), film ($69 million), capital gains ($67 million) and working families PIT credit ($63 million).

The legislature devotes considerable time during the interim and session hearing requests for tax credits, tax exemptions or tax rate reductions. A crowd of lobbyists and advocates representing corporations, small businesses, labor, consumer and environmental groups, farmers and ranchers, all manner of associations, cities and counties, and executive agencies are in regular attendance, and almost all want a break. Legislators and LFC and TRD and sometimes DFA are trying to keep the tax principles in mind, especially adequacy. Will tax changes keep revenue in balance with spending and adequate reserves for at least a few years?

Revenue Estimating and Tracking. The Budget Act, state statute section 6-4-1, provides that the Department of Finance and Administration (DFA) present a report on estimated revenue annually to the legislature. The DFA, Taxation and Revenue Department (TRD) and LFC employ professional economists who prepare and present a consensus General Fund revenue estimate several times a year. An executive/legislative consensus estimate is a best practice in contrast with, for example Pennsylvania, which has half dozen competing estimates prepared by multiple legislative committees and state agencies.

DFA Secretary Willard Lewis used to tell me, "They never fired a revenue estimator for being too low." I agree with this. Once I was fired after a bad revenue estimate, but some technical experts call for making the best estimate possible and leaving cautionary adjustments to politicians.[11]

The DFA Financial Control Division (FCD) reports actual General Fund revenue to LFC by e-mailed spreadsheet, sometimes three or four months after month-end. LFC regularly issues an essential monthly revenue tracking/variance report compiled from FCD and other agency sources. It is critical to know in real time: Are revenues running ahead or behind? If revenues are lagging, are reserves sufficient to cover the shortfall? If revenues are short, is there a taxpayer compliance problem or is the cost of a tax credit exploding? Where can we make up the difference? If revenues are running high, the finder may lay an early claim to the windfall. The early bird gets the worm. In short, don't be flatfooted on revenue. At LFC I carried on the tradition of hiring outstanding economists. Many legislators valued their independent criticism, insights and sometimes validation of executive and LFC analysis and recommendations.[12]

# USES AND EXPENDITURES

The public sometimes wants the state to prioritize spending on a few important things like public and higher education, health and public safety and cut everything else. Figure 6 shows the share of General Fund appropriations for FY20 in six categories; "other" is only nine percent. Cutting "other," which includes necessary functions like the courts and the legislature, won't get much more money for the top priorities in New Mexico.

This section provides an overview of the largest categories of state expenditures, including methods of determining funding needs, cost drivers and policy initiatives to improve services. It relies on Volumes 1, 2 and 3 of LFC's annual pre-session report to the legislature.

Demographics are a basic driver of many government programs. New Mexico population crossed one million in 1969 and two million in 2007. Like many Western states, population growth was a significant cost driver for many government services. But since 2020, population growth has been flat around 2.18 million, only nine percent growth in 15 years. Most important New Mexico's birth rate fell from 28 thousand in 2010 to 21 thousand in 2021. The decrease in birth rate is consistent with national trends but also reflects New Mexico's highly successful program to reduce the teen birth rate. In any event, declining births implies declining enrollment in early, public and higher education with perhaps the need for fewer school personnel and fewer and smaller facilities. Also, New Mexico is getting older; according to UNM's Geospatial Population program and the Bureau of Census, the population over 65 increased 44 percent from 2010 to 2020. So, New Mexico will need more health care workers and supports for the elderly.

Public Education. After Hawaii, which has only a state school district, and Vermont, New Mexico has about the highest share of school district operating costs from the general fund. Public education is the largest general fund use at about 44 percent and stable for the last decade. Public education funding is allocated by a funding formula to provide every district and school a fair share of the statewide appropriation. Public school appropriations take only a few pages of the General Appropriation Act, with the formula to distribute the state equalization guarantee appropriation established by statute.

In my experience, if one says "formula," many listeners will immediately tune out. In fact, the formula is not that complicated, and changes to the formula may have significant distributional consequences for districts, schools and students, may pose significant costs to the state, and may influence the effectiveness of instruction. For some districts and advocates the goal may be to get more money to do the same thing. For others the goal is to use the formula to incentivize better learning outcomes. Pay careful attention to the formula.

The LFC Finance Fact on schools reports, "the formula starts with enrollment, then uses multipliers for the number of students in different grades, the number of students receiving special education or bilingual education, the education and experience of teachers, the size of the district and school, the number of students at risk for developing problems and other factors." The formula calculates weighted student enrollment, or "units." Total General Fund appropriation divided by weighted student "units" equals "unit value." Unit value times number of units equals program cost. For FY24, 305 thousand students generated 681 thousand units for a General Fund cost of $4 billion and a unit value of $6,241.

New Mexico like most states has experienced litigation regarding compliance with the constitutional requirement for a "uniform education." (Article XII, Section 1). A 1999 district court decision in the *Zuni* case, brought by the Gallup-McKinley, Grants, Central and Zuni school districts, determined that the state's method of funding school buildings was inequitable, relying too much on highly variable district property tax revenue. In 2003, the legislature created the Public School Facilities Authority, established standards for school buildings, sharply boosted state capital funding by intercepting most of surplus severance tax bonding fund revenue directed to the severance tax permanent fund and introduced a school capital formula with a local school district match related to property tax valuation per student. Cumulative state funding since FY01 has reached $2.6 billion, and most of the state's 89 districts have new or rebuilt schools.

In 2003, Representative Mimi Stewart secured funding for a three-year K Plus pilot that provided five weeks additional instruction for kindergarten. The program initially served 750 children at 15 schools. By 2007 the program was expanded to a K 3 plus pilot serving approximately 100 schools with an appropriation of $7.5 million.

In 2007 Senator Smith and I attended the annual meeting of the National Conference of State Legislatures in New Orleans, the first big conference in the city after Hurricane Katrina. We heard a great presentation from Paul Vallas, Superintendent of the state-run Recovery School District and previously superintendent in Philadelphia and Chicago and before that budget director of the Illinois legislature. I asked him what's the big thing the state legislature can do for schools, and he said, "more time on task." That really resonated with me—more learning time. LFC got on board with the "plus" initiative. LFC evaluations showed extended learning improved academic proficiency, and the legislature gradually added more grades and funding and New Mexico initiated pilots for K-12 plus.

Meanwhile, in FY19 First District Judge Sarah Singleton ruled in the consolidated *Martinez v. New Mexico* and the *Yazzie v. New Mexico* cases brought by many parents and school districts that the state failed to provide adequate funding for at-risk children. The court ordered the state legislature, the Public Education Department and districts to immediately provide an education system that ensures all students have the same opportunity to college, career and civics ready. The court did not direct specific remedies but noted the benefits of extended learning, the need to boost the at-risk factor and to improve teacher quality.

The pandemic in 2020 was a huge blow to school reform efforts and worse, triggered approximately one year of lost learning.[13]

Since the *Martinez-Yazzie* ruling and the pandemic, state spending for public schools soared over 60 percent, from $2.6 billion in FY19 to $4.2 billion in

FY24. The at-risk funding formula factor more than tripled with $275 million additional funding. Virtually all four-year-olds have full day services and half the three-year-olds have half day programs. *Education Week* reported that teacher salaries in New Mexico grew an average 17 percent to $63,580, the highest growth rate in the nation and bringing New Mexico's state ranking to 22nd, sixth highest west of the Mississippi (behind Alaska, California, Hawaii, Minnesota and Oregon). In 2023 the legislature increased minimum instructional time by 15 percent for grade school but allowed up to 60 hours professional development to count as instruction. Extended learning above the minimum is optional; about $500 million of appropriations for extended learning were largely unused from FY20 to FY23.

During the pandemic, New Mexico discontinued broad use of the PARCC test, but national NAEP data shows a ten-point pandemic decline and the lowest scores ever.[14]

Early Childhood. This spending category didn't exist 40 years ago. Even half day kindergarten was unavailable, for example to my wife Lorin Erramouspe, raised in Torrance County in the late 1950s. In 1988, the state created the Youth Authority, including juvenile justice programs from the Corrections Department and in 1992 established the Children, Youth and Families Department. In 2000, with leadership from LFC (Senators Smith and Beffort), the State Department of Education (Supt. Mike Davis) and Think New Mexico (Fred Nathan), New Mexico was one of the first states to implement universal full day kindergarten.

Also, influenced by sessions at the annual meeting of the National Conference on State Legislatures, the state legislature became attentive to the growing research on the importance of brain development at an early age for wellness from adolescence into adulthood. Karin Karr-Morse, author of *Ghosts from the Nursery*, presented at an all-member forum at the state capitol in 1999, and Dr. David Olds, founder of Nurse Family Partnership, Vicki Johnson of First Born and Jack Tweedie of NCSL presented to an LFC hearing in 2004. Tweedie advised the legislature to implement home visiting programs that were targeted, intensive and use a medical model staffed with nurses or health-directed paraprofessionals. In FY05 the legislature made an initial $500 thousand appropriation to CYFD for infant home visiting.

In the last two decades the early childhood movement steadily gained momentum. Appropriations to CYFD, PED and ECECD grew rapidly, from $136 million in FY 12 to $579 million in FY23. Key developments and milestones were the universal Pre-K Now initiative pushed by Libby Doggett and Governor Richardson, annual Kids Count rankings of the Casey Foundation beginning 2012 showing New Mexico persistently at the bottom, the requirement for an annual Early Childhood Accountability Report in 2018, the creation of the Early Childhood Education and Care Department (ECECD) in 2019, the transfer of Pre-K administration from PED to ECECD, the creation of the Early Childhood Education and Care Fund in 2020, increases in income eligibility for child care, leveraging federal Medicaid funds to enhance home visiting and many LFC program evaluations of child protective services, child care, children's behavioral health, pre-K and home visiting.

Unresolved with all this activity is establishment of clear goals for early childhood programs, in particular the balance and tradeoffs between early learning and early care. The focus of CYFD and ECECD has been sharply tilted to a robust childcare system covering children to age 13. Key initiatives are increasing income eligibility to a near universal 400 percent of poverty income level ($111 thousand for a family of four), waiver of co-pays for higher income families and significant increases in childcare provider rates. Childcare provider rates increased 62 percent up to FY23, and a 2019 LFC evaluation found New Mexico provider reimbursement was in the top ten states. Meanwhile, during the pandemic ECECD shifted to telephone delivery of home visiting services, and despite funding availability, home visiting enrollment has stagnated around five thousand families, only 20 percent of the uptake target of at least 40 percent of children aged 0 to 3.

While CYFD and the new ECECD focused on child care, LFC and some advocates have focused much more on brain development and early learning. An LFC evaluation reported that one quarter of children are unable to recognize one letter on starting kindergarten and that the average child starts school one to two years behind in reading readiness.[15] A National Association for the Education of Young Children brief on the word or vocabulary gap states that, "by three years of age there is a 30-million-word gap between children from wealthiest and poorest families. ... Eliminating this inequality will require early interventions." The *Martinez Yazzie* ruling echoes this view. LFC research, policy analyses and recommendations consistently have targeted early childhood investments at the youngest ages and the most at-risk children.

In any case it appears there is sufficient funding in FY24 to effectively provide universal four-year-old pre-K (when combined with head start or high-quality childcare), half day pre-K for all three-year-olds whose families want it (a 50 percent take-up), and free childcare for most families, and higher enrollment in home visiting.

The biggest issue for the legislature and ECECD is building the provider network and workforce for pre-K and childcare, ensuring delivery of high-quality services and coordinating with schools, hospitals, doctors and community services to identify children and families needing intensive services. Provider shortfalls are acute, and enrollment is low in many high poverty neighborhoods and almost all rural New Mexico.

Higher Education. The State Higher Education Executive Officers Association reported New Mexico has the fourth highest rate of state support behind only Wyoming, Illinois and Alaska. Nevertheless, the higher education share of General Fund appropriations fell from 17 percent in FY 93 to ten percent in FY22.

Vol. 2 of the LFC Appropriation recommendation for FY24 states, "Higher education institutions play an integral role in the state's economic development by providing New Mexicans the education and training they need to compete and succeed in the labor market." The funding challenges are that first, unlike public schools there is not a constitutional mandate to provide this program, second there is not a high federal match like Medicaid that makes state investment compelling, and third, colleges and universities have significant other revenue options to complement state funding, notably tuition but also permanent fund distributions for the universities and property tax revenue for two-year institutions.

Promoting access to higher education is a paradigm for New Mexico. First, this means having institutions, branches and special schools (27) and even twigs in every nook and cranny of the state and second, keeping tuition low in the interest of affordability. LFC reports, "New Mexico students pay the least amount of tuition and fees in the region and state tuition costs at two- and four-year institutions are roughly half the national average."

Further, in 1996, the state initiated the lottery scholarship program for high school students going directly to college and maintaining good grades. In 2022 Governor Lujan Grisham pushed for a new, first in the nation opportunity scholarship offering free tuition for all New Mexicans. Other states have piloted free tuition but at relatively inexpensive community colleges. The total Higher Education Department budget for the opportunity scholarship for FY24 is $146 million, mostly General Fund and equal to 13 percent of appropriations to institutions.

LFC has advocated targeting aid to disadvantaged students and addressing total cost of attendance including support for transportation, behavioral health, food and other student support services. Also, the focus on tuition has crowded out other higher education needs, notably faculty compensation and deprived institutions of an important revenue opportunity (because the state pushes back on tuition increases).

New Mexico and the nation experienced significant enrollment declines over the last decade. Two-year colleges were down 30 percent nationally and 27 percent in New Mexico. But four-year colleges grew 17 percent nationally but declined 19 percent in New Mexico. The opportunity scholarship may slow the downward enrollment trend.

New Mexico had an input driven funding formula for institutions, called the Instruction and General formula, which depended mostly on student credit hours and facility square footage. In FY13 New Mexico adopted a base plus formula to provide incentives for certificate and degree completion, science, technology, engineering and math (STEM) degrees and disadvantaged students. Institutions start with prior year funding, perhaps with a small reallocation. New state revenue is distributed in proportion to growth in degree production, STEM degrees, research activity and other factors. The new formula has resulted in only modest reallocation of appropriations among institutions, but there is much more attention to mission and outcomes of individual institutions. A bone of contention for some legislators and institutions is significant variation in revenue per student, especially at four-year comprehensive colleges. Eastern New Mexico University and Western New Mexico University receive less funding per student than New Mexico Highlands and Northern New Mexico College, because of enrollment declines at the latter schools that have been protected by the base plus formula.

Higher education also includes appropriations to the UNM Medical School, the Department of Agriculture at NMSU and many research and public service projects which are of great interest to legislators but lacking in accountability. Witness a state auditor's appeal for greater oversight given the indictment of a prominent legislator for misusing funding for one special project at the University of New Mexico.

Health and Medicaid. The Medicaid share of General Fund appropriations grew from five percent in FY93 to 15 percent in FY24. From FY 14 to FY23 total Medicaid expenditures (including federal funds) more than doubled from $4.2 billion to $8.5 billion. The General Fund appropriation for FY24 grew 20.7 percent above the FY23 operating budget. Medicaid enrollment grew from 616 thousand to 990 thousand in October 2022; 47 percent of New Mexicans are enrolled in Medicaid. Eligibility for Medicaid is based on individual or family income with higher income allowed for children. Aside from enrollment, other Medicaid budget drivers are health care inflation, at least several percentage points higher than the general rate of inflation, provider rate increases, introduction of costly new prescription drugs, and expansion of covered services, notably for behavioral health and substance abuse treatment.

The explosive growth in Medicaid is a good thing, because so many New Mexicans get a high-quality health plan at no cost to individuals or families, and because the federal government picks up most cost, over 70 percent for most clients and 90 percent for the expansion population from the 2014 Affordable Care Act. Nevertheless, Medicaid is the biggest state budget driver and is crowding out discretionary state spending, notably for higher education.

Most Medicaid clients are covered through managed care organizations (MCOs). The state pays insurance companies a monthly rate depending on client demographics to reimburse providers for services.

Health care coverage is one thing, access to services is another. A December 2022 LFC Program Evaluation, "Medicaid Network Adequacy, Access and Utilization," reported, "The State's inadequate health care provider network continues to be a significant barrier for Medicaid enrollees to access timely care." A secret shopper survey conducted by LFC staff found Medicaid enrollees could get an appointment with a primary or behavioral health provider only 13 percent of the time. In the wake of this study and a number of hearings on provider recruitment and retention, the 2023 legislature appropriated $98 million from the General Fund to bring Medicaid rates for many providers, nursing homes and rural health care to 100 percent of Medicare rates and to take primary care, behavioral health and maternal health care rates to 120 percent of Medicare. By comparison, California in 2023 boosted many of its rates to just 85 percent of Medicare.

Through waivers to the federally approved Medicaid program, New Mexico provides home and community-based services to the developmentally disabled. This program replaced institutional care in the 1980s, but enrollment was limited to available funding. Recently, the state served about 4,000 clients at an average cost of $100 thousand, but about as many were on a waiting list for services. In 2022 partly using federal pandemic revenue, New Mexico authorized eliminating the waiting list and serving all eligible clients.

New Mexico also has a network of public health offices and state hospitals and offers state funded programs for substance abuse treatment and behavioral health. These efforts are important given a significant population of undocumented residents and limited health care access in rural New Mexico.

The Children Youth and Families Department maintains critical programs for foster children, protective services and behavioral health. However, New Mexico has consistently ranked at the bottom of the "canary in the coal mine" performance measure for repeat maltreatment of children in state custody. Funding is not the problem. The department has experienced excessive turnover of the cabinet secretary and division directors, a vacancy rate of more than 25 percent, a funded vacancy rate of eight percent and challenges hiring licensed social workers. The *Kevin S* lawsuit seeking best practice service levels for foster children may have distracted department leaders from effective day to day operations.

Public Safety and Justice. The focus of public safety funding tends to be on the Corrections Department and the Department of Public Safety (DPS) with FY24 appropriations of $336 million and $159 million, respectively. These two agencies account for five percent of General Fund appropriations.

LFC reports FBI and US census data showing declining property crime trends in the US and New Mexico since 2000 but crime rates in New Mexico higher than the nation and Albuquerque higher than New Mexico. Worse, the violent crime rate in New Mexico rose 30 percent from 2014 to 2020.

New Mexico traditionally viewed the corrections system as a growth industry and an economic development or rural job creation tool. This included a penal center in Cibola County in the wake of the collapse of the uranium industry as well as efforts to recruit private prisons to house federal prisoners in Otero and Torrance Counties. In 1996 the Johnson administration and some legislators initiated a push toward privately owned and operated state prisons with a big 1,200 bed facility in Hobbs and 600 bed facilities in Clayton and Santa Rosa. These facilities had lower capital and operating costs but were strenuously opposed by unions and other legislators. In FY20 the average cost per inmate in public facilities in New Mexico was $148/day versus $96/day in private prisons.

The male prison population peaked in 2011 at 6,175 and fell below 5,000 in 2023. New Mexico is left with a very inefficient prison system scattered around the state with prisoner transportation posing high costs and risks, with many units, public and private, half-filled and with great public opposition to closing small prisons in places like Springer. By comparison Utah has one 5,000-bed prison next to the Great Salt Lake and convenient for inmates to receive health and education services and familial visits. Arizona has a 5,000-bed facility near Phoenix.

The key activity and most of the budget of DPS is for state police, but the department also runs an important crime lab and a local law enforcement academy. In 1998 Senators Manny Aragon and RL Stockard (R-Bloomfield), a retired state police captain, spearheaded an initiative to boost force strength from 435 to 720. This target has never been realized, and DPS reached the current level of around 650 by consolidating 120 motor transportation officers, essentially truck safety inspectors, into the state police in 2015. Higher salaries have been a budget priority of the legislature, and in FY23 and FY24 salaries increased approximately 30 percent.

In recent years the legislature has sought to expand public safety investment efforts to the front end of the justice system with crime prevention strategies and diversion programs for low level offenders, including drug courts, veterans courts, pre-trial services, homeless housing services, reduction or elimination of court fees, medication assisted treatment of inmates, curtailment of the pretrial cash bail, greater attention to education and other programming for inmates and Medicaid coverage for state prisoners prior to release. This means growing appropriations to the district and magistrate courts and to local governments for programming and law enforcement training, recruitment and retention.

Other agencies. Excluding schools and higher education institutions, the General Appropriation Act makes appropriations to 119 agencies including 44 legislative and judicial offices. Many of these agencies have General Fund appropriations of less than $10 million and 19 less than $2 million. A handful are worthy of note here.

Three natural resources agencies, Environment Department, Energy Minerals and Natural Resources Department and the State Engineer, have essential duties including managing infrastructure projects for dams, parks, water supply and treatment. They are significantly involved in the state's climate change initiatives including regulatory activity and receive significant federal funds, magnifying their importance.

The Economic Development Department and the Tourism Department also have rapidly growing appropriations and expanding missions including promotion of the film industry, outdoor recreation and trails, the Local Economic Development Act (LEDA) and Job Training Incentive Program (JTIP) business incentive programs, venture capital funding, Main Street investments, a new creative industries division and skills training. The Tourism marketing budget for FY24 is up 23 percent to $20.7 million.

Transportation. The Department of Transportation (DoT) does not receive a General Fund appropriation for operations. The 17 cent per gallon gasoline tax has not changed since 1995. The tax obviously has not kept up with inflation and is further eroded by improved fuel efficiency and the growing market share of electric vehicles. In 2020 DoT reported an overall pavement condition rating of 55; a rating of 45 or less indicates a road in poor condition. Also, in FY20 only 76 percent of the non-national highway system miles was rated fair or better. Costs to maintain roads rise exponentially as pavement conditions deteriorate, for example, $1.5 million per land-mile for a road in poor condition requiring major reconstruction. Budget constraints also impair DoT's ability to implement major transportation improvement projects including adding lanes to I40 and new interchanges in the Albuquerque metro area serving industrial sites.

In 2019 the legislature boosted the motor vehicle excise tax one percent and increased distributions to the state road fund and local government road fund.

Federal revenue for state roads increased about $100 million per year beginning FFY22. Also, the legislature passed approximately $1.5 billion from 2019 to 2023 of one-time special appropriations for state and local roads. The 2023 tax bill would have phased diversion of $156 million of motor vehicle excise tax revenue from the General Fund to state and local road funds, but the measure was vetoed.

## GENERAL FUND RESERVES AND FISCAL STABILITY

The state needs a general fund reserve balance, first for liquidity to ensure funds available to pay warrants on any given day or month, second to address significant unforeseen expenditure needs such as a major tax refund or a settlement of a court judgment, and third and most important to cover a downturn in revenue.

In the 1980s, New Mexico like many states sought to maintain general fund reserves at five percent of expenditures. In the 90s due to some adverse budget experiences, ten to 20 percent became a preferred reserve target. In the 2010s, the economic downturns were unexpectedly severe (the Great Recession in 2009 and the pandemic in 2020), and state revenues were increasingly dependent on the volatile energy sector.

Figure 7 shows recurring General Fund revenue and appropriations growth from FY06 to FY24. Four years revenue growth was at least 11 percent. But five times over that 18-year period revenues declined—FY10, FY11, FY17, FY18 and FY20.

Revenue instability is challenging in a stable spending environment. It's harder when the state is implementing costly court-mandated or popular initiatives like universal pre-K or eliminating the waiting list for developmentally disabled service or raising pay for judges or state police or teachers or boosting the at-risk school funding factor. Revenue volatility makes responsible budget planning and implementation difficult. It also simply makes your head spin.

Even harder is cutting appropriations, sometimes in mid-year. Raising taxes to address a looming deficit is usually not viable, because the revenue won't come quickly enough, it is economically not viable when people are out of work, or it is a political non-starter. In 2017 at an LFC hearing in Taos, I told lawmakers that projected reserves were negative and the state was operating an illegal deficit, and the secretary of Finance and Administration was kiting checks. Senate Majority Leader Wirth recalls the night I told him I didn't know what to do and he thought, "uh oh." Lawmakers recall with distaste one of their first votes in 2016 as freshman or new committee chairs to cut teacher pay and claw back school reserves.

In the wake of the bloodshed, the state called on experts at NCSL and Moody's and the Utah legislature to advise on implementing "stress testing" to determine a prudent reserve target. Figure 8 shows a recent sensitivity analysis with upside and downside scenarios, and now both the DFA and LFC have settled on a 30 percent General Fund reserve target.

With more cautious budgeting (not spending all available revenue), longer term revenue and expenditure forecasts, growing endowments and new trust funds, one hopes the state is better prepared for the next inevitable revenue shock and downturn.

# 3

# BUDGET DEVELOPMENT
# AND MAKING APPROPRIATIONS

"Eight years is a long time to be fighting all the time. The republic is a dream. Nothing happens unless first a dream." Carl Sandburg, *Washington Monument by Night*

The Most Important Power of the Legislature. What does a legislature do? It makes legislation, or bills. The most important bill is the annual General Appropriation Act (GAA), which provides authority for most government spending by state agencies or political subdivisions of the state. The LFC produces the GAA from budget data systems maintained by DFA and LFC.

The GAA establishes the amount of spending for each agency and program, and it determines the amount of spending per client for programs, the number of clients that can be served, the amounts available to contract for government services and salaries of state, school and university employees. Fifty years ago, the GAA was produced on a typewriter and was ten- or 15-pages making appropriations for broad government categories like health and hospitals that totaled less than $100 million. My first session in 1984, recurring appropriations in the GAA for FY85 were $1.295 billion and the bill was 70 pages. Today, the GAA is over 200 pages with General Fund appropriations over $10 billion.

The most important part of the GAA is Section 4 which provides for recurring spending in the upcoming fiscal year, beginning July 1, for each agency. The GAA also provides one-time special appropriations for new programs and pilot projects (Section 5), supplemental appropriations for the current fiscal year (Section 6), appropriations for information technology projects (Section 7), budget adjustment authority, sometimes road appropriations (Section 9) and fund transfers.

This chapter describes how the GAA is made including timelines, responsibilities of agencies that help the legislature make the budget, and key legislative committees and staff assigned to support budget development. Also, there is a review of methods, procedures and reports used by the legislature and state agencies. But let's start with guidelines and principles for budget making.

Budget Principles. The most important budget guideline is to balance recurring spending and projected revenue. Sustain, cut or grow the programs or cut or raise recurring revenue. Don't spend more than you have.

A companion guideline is don't use non-recurring or one time revenue to pay for recurring or on-going spending. It is unpalatable to rent an office and hire staff for a new program and then abandon a lease and lay off staff if a revenue shortfall occurs. This is a guideline but not a cardinal rule and is routinely violated. The most common budgetary gimmick is to label new programs or new initiatives as pilot programs funded by a special appropriation from the General Fund outside the operating budget. Ordinarily, special appropriations total less than $100 million. In 2023 the Executive requested $1.9 billion for special appropriations including $100 million for law enforcement grants, $146 million for broadband projects, $32 million to subsidize medical malpractice rates, over $200 million for water projects, $112 million for childcare subsidies, $200 million for rural hospitals, $23 million for NMSU on-line learning, and $65 million for public employee health insurance. Many of the special requests are recurring and create an expectation that may not be sustainable. Further special requests are usually submitted December 1 at the end of the interim budget review process leaving little time for budget review and analysis.

The second big budget idea is "know where you are at all times." Have a good sense of the big spending demands on the horizon, how much money is available for appropriation, whether estimated revenue is tracking high or low, whether impending court decisions create new spending requirements or liabilities or bring a revenue windfall. The watch words are no surprises for legislators and be several steps ahead of the DFA economists. The key report is the General Fund financial summary which shows revenue and appropriations and General Fund reserve balances, but also essential reading is the LFC's report on cash balances of accounts greater than $1 million in the state Treasury. (See Figure 9).

Also, it is useful to consider budget forecasts for the "out-years" presented in LFC's Volume 1. The out-year forecast includes a four- or five-year consensus revenue forecast plus spending scenarios driven by enrollment growth, inflation and spending initiatives with delayed effective dates. Delaying the effective date of a spending measure is another budget gimmick allowing spending greater than available revenue. Next year it will be somebody else's problem. (Somebody else is usually LFC.)

I suggest to my staff to read the John McPhee book about Bill Bradley, *A Sense of Where You Are*. Bradley—Olympic gold medalist, Rhodes Scholar, US Senator, candidate for president when Al Gore smeared him in the 2000 South Carolina primary—had radar on the basketball court, especially from the corner. Unthinkably, in 1965 Princeton made it to the NCAA semi-finals. Bradley told a *New York Times* reporter, "You have a sense of where you are in life. You don't get carried away. You understand the environment, the context in which you're living, and you make decisions based on the centeredness. You're always working on who you are."[16]

My first year as director was shaky. Senator President Pro Tem Manny Aragon's secretary wouldn't even let me in to see him. Most folks doubted I would last a year. That was probably the year I wrote a memo to legislative leaders with the subject "Fiscal Meltdown," when the House and Senate were passing appropriation bills willy nilly expecting the governor to take the heat for fiscal discipline. I did get their attention.

Near the end of the session, there was an all-leadership junta with Speaker Sanchez, Aragon, the fiscal committee chairs and DFA Secretary David Harris and John Gasparich, DFA Budget director. In dispute was whether the spending level in the legislative version of HB2, the General Appropriation Act was affordable and whether General Fund reserves were high enough. The veteran fiscal expert Gasparich passed out a financial summary and, in a minute, I found a $10 million error to the good, higher than they thought. With no fanfare I whispered this to Representative Jerry Sandel (D-Farmington), Chair of the House Taxation and Revenue Committee. He spoke up and the DFA retreated. I am sure Sandel let folks know the back story, as if "let's keep this kid around for a while." You gotta know where you are.

An odd principle, perhaps unique to me and LFC is, "Bad data is better than no data." To prepare a fiscal impact report, to make a budget recommendation, to estimate the cost of a proposed tax change or a new insurance benefit or entitlement program, one wants to know cost per client and number of clients. A stock response of agencies is, "we don't know." If LFC reports "unknown" on a fiscal impact report, it often ends up in the "no fiscal impact pile." Failure to estimate participation in a new program or benefit expansion (called take-up rate) may lead to judgements that the initiative doesn't cost anything. So, I directed LFC analysts to use their expertise to estimate demographic and economic conditions. Agencies sometimes would "gnash their teeth" and protest that we didn't know what we are talking about. That lead to what I called "smoke them out." Okay, if you have a better estimate "fork over the data."

## KEY AGENCIES

The most important agencies for budget development are LFC and DFA. State statutes, Chapter 6, Section 3, describe the responsibilities of DFA including the requirement to submit a budget to the legislature and defining parts of the budget. DFA issues instructions to agencies which are required to submit requests to DFA and LFC by September 1 (except November 1 for higher education and December 1 for public education). The executive is required to submit a recommendation to the legislature by January 5 (for the 60-day session in odd years) or January 10 (for the 30-day session in even years).

Department of Finance and Administration. The DFA has had a history of capable leaders with significant political and fiscal experience in state government, for example Dr. Dan Lopez under Anaya, Willard Lewis under Carruthers and David Harris and James Jimenez for Richardson. The DFA is a training ground for agency fiscal administrators. In recent years, DFA's budget role has emphasized advocacy of governors' initiatives, and the budget division staff focuses on administrative activities such as processing budget adjustment requests. Consider the executive appropriation recommendation, which is mostly statutorily prescribed financial records, such as the schedule of state debt or the exempt salary plan and includes about 15 pages summarizing new initiatives. Of course, New Mexicans would expect the DFA to advocate for governors' initiatives, but one would hope to see analysis of policy options and expected outcomes along the way. Nevertheless, DFA has the bully pulpit and on behalf of the governor exerts significant influence on spending levels and key priorities in the GAA.

About LFC. The LFC was created by state statute in 1957 as a permanent interim committee with the principal duty to make appropriation recommendations to the full legislature.[17] New Mexico is one of about five states that has an interim budget arm with this duty along with Texas, Colorado, Louisiana and Arizona. By practice the LFC recommendations are adopted in December and then released in early January after the Executive issues its recommendations.

An essential provision of the LFC enabling statute section 2-5-7 requires *Cooperation*: "Each agency of the state and its political subdivisions shall upon request furnish and make available to the Legislative Finance Committee such documents, materials or information as may be requested by the members of the committee or its director or staff which are not made confidential by law." Occasionally, I had to remind executive officials of this duty. The LFC also has the power of subpoena, although it is rarely used.

LFC had a couple strong and influential directors, most of all the great Maralyn Budke.[18] She was director from 1965 to 1982 (except for two years as chief of staff for Governor Cargo), thought to be an unbeatable tenure. Ms. Budke employed a growing, professional and distinguished staff, many trained at the Univ. of New Mexico under economics professor Gerry Boyle. Ms. Budke had the ear of renowned Senate Finance Chair Aubrey Dunn, the "old apple picker" from High Rolls and HAFC Chair John Mershon from nearby Alamogordo. Ms. Budke later served as chief of staff for Governor Carruthers. Then in the 1990s, LFC brought back former analyst David Harris as director. Harris was smart and knew government but most of all relished governing as a game. Harris went on to DFA secretary and then deputy chief of staff under Richardson. Training and experience at LFC aid navigation of state government politics and budget matters.

Initially eight members, expanded to 16 members in 1991, LFC members include the chairs of House Appropriations and Finance, House Taxation and Revenue and Senate Finance and other members appointed by the speaker and the Senate Committee on Committees. The LFC appoints a director, and the legislative agency has a year-round staff of about 40 and a budget of $5.7 million for FY24. The committee meets several days per month during the interim. In the summer the committee conducts hearings around the state, in effect "kicking the tires of state government" to examine effectiveness of agency operations and policy and economic issues in the far-flung corners of the state—over the years from Aztec to Clayton to Hobbs to Antelope Wells, meetings at state hospitals, community colleges and universities, the oil fields and refineries, copper mines, power plants, the spaceport, senior centers, the national labs, Cannon and Holloman AFB, the Waste Isolation Pilot Project (WIPP), municipal water works, scenic railroads, state museums and monuments, state parks, industrial parks, border crossings, agriculture experiment stations, and several times into Chihuahua. At these field hearings the committee meets local government officials, farmers and ranchers, social service advocates, school superintendents, public health and education experts, agency heads and interested New Mexicans. LFC staff and members know New Mexico like the backs of our hands.[19]

4. Senators Fidel, Altamirano and David Abbey at LFC meeting. Circa 1998.

5. LFC members at chuck wagon breakfast, Clayton, New Mexico, July 7, 2005. L-R, Saavedra, Moore, Smith, Sandoval, Harden, Townsend, Varela, McSorley, Salazar, Wallace, Griego and Carraro.

In the fall LFC meets in Santa Fe to consider the budget request of every agency, including testimony from advocacy groups.

In 1989 a performance audit function and staff were transferred to the LFC from the State Auditor's Office. New Mexico is the only state with a legislative audit watchdog in the same office as the legislative budget office. One might wonder if that's so good, since no other state followed suit, but turns out this was smart with the work plan for the audit shop influenced by the budget analysts based on information needed and policy decisions facing the appropriators. The performance group has had strong, independent, even fearless leaders—CPA Manu Patel, social worker Charles Sallee, quantitative expert Dr. Jon Courtney and now Micaela Fischer. The performance program has evolved from a strict audit function following government accounting standards to an evaluation function with broad use of quantitative and statistical social science research methods. We joke that other states' evaluation programs under the arm of an elected state auditor or interim legislative committee are churning out reports like optimizing trash collection at state parks, while LFC is examining best practices for substance abuse treatment. The LFC evaluation staff now numbers ten, all with advanced degrees including several doctorates, and has received national recognition and impact awards from the National Conference of State Legislatures (NCSL) and the Massachusetts Institute of Technology.

In 1994 at the end of the somewhat directionless third King administration, the legislature created the Horizons Task Force to initiate a state strategic planning process. One recommendation was to link strategic planning and goal setting to the annual budget process and to implement performance -based budgeting.[20]

In 1998 LFC initiated a performance budgeting pilot for a handful of agencies, and in 1999 the legislature passed the Accountability in Government (Chapter 6, Section 3A) spearheaded by LFC audit head Manu Patel and reluctantly signed by Governor Johnson. Then Senator Manny Aragon surmised correctly that it would be hard to veto with a title like that.

# ACCOUNTABILITY IN GOVERNMENT ACT

The LFC Finance Fact on the AGA states, "The bottom line of performance-based budgeting is the effective use of taxpayer dollars. By measuring performance—quantifying what an agency does and the results—and setting goals, policymakers and the public can see whether a program is working, and worth money being spent on it."

Prior to the AGA, the General Appropriation Act was quite prescriptive with appropriations for every agency and every division in large agencies detailed in ten budget categories including personal services, benefits, travel, out of state travel, contracts and capital outlay. Some large agencies had many divisions, for example 12 at the Department of Health and Environment including a separate budget for each hospital and 20 for Corrections with a separate budget for each prison and program.

Legislators tend to focus on the material presented to them by agencies and legislative staff. Budget development and budget hearings then were about whether funding was adequate to cover costs, inflation and population growth and whether spending levels were reasonable or excessive and wasteful. LFC staff specialized in digging into expenditure records. I remember the Vice Chair of Senate Finance, Smitty Eoff (R- Gallup), lambasting the economic development and tourism secretary for spending $95 dollars each to serve six turkeys at a trade show in Houston.

The Findings and Purpose subsection of the AGA provides that agencies should have budget "flexibility"; be accountable; develop measures to assess progress in achieving goals and objectives; establish targets for outputs and outcomes; seek to eliminate duplication; and inform the public regarding benefits of public services and goods. While not specifically in statute, executive and legislative leaders agreed to consolidate ten budget categories in the GAA to four (personal services and benefits, contracts, other, and transfers) and to consolidate appropriations to larger agencies with many divisions into programs. For example, Department of Health (DoH) now has eight programs and Corrections has five programs.

Instead of many appropriation amounts, the agency mission and key performance results and targets were included in the General Appropriation Act.

Implementing the AGA was a big undertaking and posed many issues including training for agency budget personnel, defining appropriation units, establishing meaningful measures, and reworking the format of the General Appropriation Act. The DFA and LFC formed a steering committee including the judiciary represented by Chief Justice Gene Franchini who advocated a lump sum appropriation for the judicial branch.

LFC received great support from Ron Snell and the National Conference of State Legislatures along with Harry Hatry of the Urban Institute. Key appropriators from Louisiana including the Chair of House Appropriations Jerry Luke LeBlanc came to New Mexico and provided a valuable template for implementation. Keep it simple was the approach so the existing agency and division structure was mostly maintained to determine performance-based programs. (The alternative to combine many activities into "overarching programs" would have led to a quagmire.) Similarly, DFA, LFC and agencies were able to identify many suitable measures by adopting measures from other states like Louisiana, Texas and Florida and by adopting measures used and required by Federal agencies for their many grant programs to state government. Finally, LFC focused on the big agencies, generally the cabinet-level agencies.

A favorite training from the pilot period was a tape of a Louisiana House Appropriations Committee hearing on the Nutria Commission. A nutria is a non-native semiaquatic rodent described as an overgrown guinea pig. Nutria destroy (eat) Louisiana's vital wetlands, and the state established a commission to eradicate the pest. The legislature considered data showing a growing rodent population, despite a bounty offered for each tail and the commission's effort to promote consumption. Representative Diane Winston (R-New Orleans) quizzed the director about outcomes: "You can't eat them, and you can't wear them. So, what's the point of the marketing budget?"

Perhaps not surprisingly, New Mexico agencies proposed way too many measures and prioritized measures for activities like permitting. Many of the measures were improperly specified or even incomprehensible, and some of the residue remains even today. For example, for FY24 DFA has measures for "on-site technical assistance deployments related to federal grant management," "percent of agencies attending state budget division trainings," and "local government division visits to local public entities."

Some agencies also resisted adoption of outcome measures of public health and welfare like homicide or suicide rates or drug addiction. A common refrain from agencies was that they shouldn't be held accountable for conditions outside their control like the economy or poverty. For a while, it seemed that performance-based budgeting was becoming a massive, meaningless data dump on the legislature with virtually no value to the public. During the Martinez administration, DFA sought to limit performance reporting to five measures per division or agency, even the multi-billion-dollar Medicaid program.

Quarterly Reporting and LFC Report Cards. The first big breakthrough in implementation of the AGA was the publication of report cards on agency performance by LFC in 2007. The AGA provides that DFA and LFC agree on key agencies to report quarterly on performance to LFC. Generally, the key agencies are the cabinet agencies. The agency quarterly reports are due 30 days after the calendar quarter. The reports ranged from ten to 30 pages, had inconsistent reporting periods and were often late.

The LFC report card is three to four pages for each "key" agency. The report cards present ratings for the most important measures. (See Figure 10) A green rating means the data is reliable, and agency performance is on track. Red means the data is unreliable, or the measure does not "gauge the core function of the program," or the measure is not related to strategic objectives, or the agency did not report. Red does not necessarily mean failure, but agencies are at least sensitive and sometimes defensive about a red rating. The LFC report card may also include a brief narrative on major events or activities in the previous quarter, status of key agency initiatives, national benchmarks or average performance and action plans to improve performance.

From the start the report cards drew public attention and budget focus on critically important activities of state government. For example, the Children Youth and Families reported the number of children in state custody who are subject to retreat maltreatment (abuse or neglect). The *Wall Street Journal* called this measure, required by the US Administration of Children and Families, a "canary in the coal mine for a child welfare system." Can the state government protect children that the state has determined were victimized? The US benchmark is six percent or less, and CYFD reports greater than ten percent year after year. The good news is that the performance results influenced the Executive and Legislature to prioritize appropriations to Protective Services over the last decade. The bad news is that New Mexico remains near the bottom, requiring a continued focus on improving the child welfare system.

Another pair of prominent measures in the report cards is reading and math proficiency at 4th and 8th grade. Generally, New Mexico scored near the bottom of states, in the 30 percent range for reading and 20 percent for math and far below targets. However, in the five years prior to the pandemic New Mexico experience showed proficiency increases around five percent. Unfortunately, the state changed the standardized test in FY15 and FY19 and discontinued testing during the pandemic.

The report cards also served LFC as a lab for improving the quality of measures and agency reporting. For FY17, DFA, LFC and agencies reviewed the performance measures and eliminated 600 measures. Measures for CYFD, Early Childhood, Corrections, courts, the public defender, General Services and Personnel have been significantly overhauled in recent years to provide greater relevance to the budget and to report quality and outcomes of essential services.

In sum, the LFC report card is a proxy for a state of the state report. There is nothing else like it. It is a surveillance of general fiscal condition, public health, public safety, road conditions, arrests, reading proficiency and child welfare. The LFC staff present the report cards to the committee at public hearings, and other interim legislative committees use the report cards as background for policy hearings.

Using Performance Data for Budget Development. In recent years the focus of legislative performance management efforts graduated to using performance data more directly for budget development. Pew Charitable Trust in 2017 started a program called Results First with an emphasis on using cost-benefit analysis to identify effective programs and to reprioritize spending. Pew particularly worked on corrections and juvenile justice issues in many states including New Mexico. More recently Pew supported an initiative at LFC called *Legistat*. Most state performance management systems are practiced in the executive branch with an early example *compstat* for policing in New York City and Los Angeles.[21] These state performance initiatives are led by the highest levels of executive management, are data and target driven and focus on priority problems until they are resolved. Martin O'Malley conducted a government-wide *State Stat* as governor of Maryland. Dr. Andy Feldman worked with LFC in 2021 and 2022 to develop an approach to legislative budget and policy hearings that is data driven and results focused. Some of the features include deeper dives into pre-selected issues, giving agencies more airtime to present and comment, pushing agencies to commit to certain actions and having more frequent meetings with certain agencies to follow up on action items. [22]

Agency action plans are a critical element of a performance management system. An action plan details who, how, what, when to achieve a key performance goal or target. In the early years of the AGA, Representative David Parsons (R-Roswell) told the committee setting a target without an action plan doesn't mean anything. Strategic plans without action plans are vaporware. Parsons was a retired executive from the conglomerate Dial Corporation and was responsible for acquisition turnarounds. An agency like CYFD needs an action plan to close the gap between the rate of repeat child maltreatment in New Mexico, over ten percent, and the US average, five or six percent. The CYFD action plan should identify the individual in the agency responsible for achieving each goal and report milestones and progress. What are incremental and total appropriation needs to achieve the target. Are more skilled staff needed with credentials in social work? Have skill requirements been inappropriately lowered to boost staffing levels? Does the pay plan need to change? Are pay differentials needed in hard to serve areas? Are social work licensing requirements appropriate? What support is needed for families by region or county?

The LFC guidelines for report cards flag whether agencies have action plans, but the reality is pretty skimpy. CYFD, which has experienced chronic turnover of agency heads, which has been called to the carpet repeatedly by legislative committees for youth fatalities, which received sharp funding increases, does not have an action plan.

## Making the LFC Recommendation (Putting it Together)

In September 1997 as a brand-new director, I asked Representative Max Coll, Chair of LFC what he wanted to see in the LFC appropriation recommendation. He looked at me in surprise and said that's your job. This approach to budget making requires being a really good listener. What do the chair and vice chair want? What do the Speaker and President Pro Tem want? What do members want? What do the minority members really dislike? What does the governor want? What are the key priorities for influential cabinet members, especially DFA? What do influential lobbyists and advocates want, within reason?

It seems like a lot to keep track of, but experience helps. The interim hearings also help bring issues to the fore or the bottom of the pile. LFC staff, especially the deputy directors and analysts, provide critical insights for prioritization and support. The director also has to be very good at counting, especially the number of legislators needed for a majority.

My friend Philip Larragoitte, former lobbyist and legislative administrator, once asked me how the LFC staff came up with its recommendations when the divide across the political spectrum was so sharp. I said the staff was simply trying to find the middle ground between options, say do nothing or spend X dollars on a certain program. He said, "I get it. You're a bookie. You're trying to find the spending level where half think it's too much and the other half too little."

There also is a tradition at LFC, I'm sure going back to Ms. Budke, of seeking unanimous or near unanimous support for the budget rather than a party line vote. All the chairs I worked for wanted bipartisan decision-making rather than party line.

Service on the appropriation committee promotes a tendency to gravitate to the middle ground. The LFC has had some very conservative members who seemed to be against everything. But through the course of committee hearings there comes a better understanding of the needs of New Mexicans and recognition that the LFC, HAFC and SFC are not just throwing money at problems. Former Representative Don Bratton (R-Hobbs), former Senator Lee Rawson (R-Las Cruces), Senator Bill Sharer (R-Farmington) and Senator Pat Woods (R-Broadview) exemplify this. Similarly, some legislators seem to support every initiative that comes along, but at LFC there comes recognition that there are budget constraints, and there is a need to set budget priorities.

The committee leaders, chair, vice-chair and ranking members also play an important role in organizing subcommittees and sometimes an executive committee to fine tune member initiatives and broaden support for the budget plan.

The legislative leaders with some exceptions have not engaged too deeply in the appropriations process and haven't micro-managed budget choices. Speaker Raymond Sanchez just flat out didn't like the budget. It seemed like a source of problems rather than opportunities, and he counted on his lieutenants like Sandel and Coll to fix things.

A tendency for budget moderation by the appropriators also creates tension and even resentment with individual members and with the party caucuses. This is especially true when the fiscal outlook is fair to poor, which is most of New Mexico modern fiscal history, until the recent oil boom. Some individual members may think LFC spends all the money, and they have no input whatsoever. The junior appropriations bill and capital outlay are antidotes to member discontent but create another set of problems around accountability.

Chairs of the interim committees may think LFC pays insufficient attention to their interim work and recommendations. The chairs of finance and education have had especially fraught political relations, for example Senator Smith with Senator Cynthia Nava (D-Dona Ana) and to a lesser degree Representatives Kiki Saavedra (D-Albuquerque) and Luciano "Lucky" Varela (D-Santa Fe) with Representative Rick Miera (D-Albuquerque). The Legislative Education Study Committee would sometimes recommend appropriations for schools almost regardless of available revenue, and appropriators felt they were made to look like the bad guys by cutting education spending.

The LFC director plays an important role for the finance chairs and the legislature by helping to navigate these troubled waters. Of course, the director is not the decider. The elected officials are the deciders, and the director is an advisor.

In 1997, pushed by Senator Aragon, the LFC directed staff to prepare guidelines for budget development that clarify policy priorities of the legislature and direct staff on methods to prepare budget recommendations.

LFC Budget Guidelines. The purpose of the guidelines (for FY24 adopted August 2023) is "to provide analysts with directions on performance-based budgeting, the preparation of the budget narrative, the development of FY24 recommendations on recurring appropriations and priority spending and other on-time investments."

The guidelines begin with the General Fund revenue outlook, typically presented to the committee in August. The guidelines establish general spending priorities, which for FY24 as most years, were education, early childhood, public health, workforce, public safety, economic growth and transportation. Larger increases are directed to programs that can achieve significant outcomes in a cost-effective way.

The committee also asks for higher increases to address school workload, school finance litigation, workload growth and medical inflation. This may seem broad but in effect designates about a half dozen programs out of the 150 programs in the state budget to get above average increases—public school equalization, pre-k and childcare, Medicaid, developmentally disabled, behavioral health and programs in the economic development and tourism departments. These priority programs get additional discussion in the last section of the guidelines. Priorities include making up lost learning time, targeting at-risk students, improving school leadership, improving foster care, serving clients with substance abuse disorders, increasing rates for health care providers, reducing prison recidivism, increasing road maintenance funding and enhancing college student retention. Most other programs would need below average increases in order to provide the priority programs "larger increases."

Think about the simple math for a moment. The priority programs are relatively large—schools and Medicaid alone are 60 percent of General Fund appropriations. "Larger increases" for the priority programs can't be much more than a few percent above the average rate of appropriations growth without slashing most other appropriations. It is difficult to reduce appropriations for programs below the prior year. Almost every program has a special interest or agency advocate or agency directors that will push back on negative growth. So non-priority programs might get somewhere from a flat recommendation to one or two percent below the average. Without getting into any details of the budget, this general guidance already allows the budget to start shaping up.

LFC staff also present analyst work plans to the committee to begin the interim. This enhances accountability of staff to the members and allows members to direct specific studies, reviews or hearings.

Drilling Down into the Details/Line-Item Budgeting. Despite the committee's interest in legislating for results, seeking better outcomes and eliminating duplication, the budget guidelines direct analysts to get into the weeds of funding inputs, especially personal services and benefits costs and contracts.

Employee costs are the biggest operating expense of government. The State Personnel Office maintains a report called the ToOL, Table of Organizational Listing, which provides salary, benefits, and other details for every position in government by agency and division. The DFA Budget Division provides guidelines for agencies to request funding for personal services and benefits including actual salaries and benefit costs by individual and funding for vacant or unfilled positions. In the past LFC budget guidelines directed analysts to delete funding for positions that were vacant for long periods, initially in 1999 four months, then six months, then a year. This didn't really work. By the time of the agency budget hearing during the session, agencies would fill many of the vacant positions and make sure the employees whose positions were being eliminated sat in the front row during an agency budget hearing. Representative Varela, a retired state employee who represented the capitol and many state employees, would direct the funding to be restored. Generally, state agencies have been chronically overfunded for personnel. This serves the agencies because they can use the surplus to provide out-of-cycle pay raises or initiate a year-end budget adjustment request (BAR) to move the surplus to the "other" category to purchase supplies and equipment. In FY19 for example 2,584 state employees, or 17 percent, received out-of-cycle pay raises (FY23 Volume 1). In FY21, 3.9 percent of the Operating Budget for Personal Services and Employee Benefits was transferred to other budget categories (FY24, Vol. 3).

Now the LFC guidelines direct analysts to "determine an appropriate vacancy rate" to be applied to authorized positions. LFC developed the PSCALC form, personal services calculation form, to compare the cost of filled positions to the operating budget and make appropriate adjustments to reduce overfunding or increase funding to allow filling vacant authorized positions.

LFC analysis for the FY24 recommendation (Volume 3) showed an average agency vacancy rate of 20 percent and an average funded vacancy rate for FY23 of 12 percent. This reflects a mix of failure of agencies to remove unneeded authorized positions, administrative inefficiencies in hiring (an average of 69 days in FY22), increasingly tight labor markets, and inadequate salaries for all employees but especially for high-skill jobs.

For FY24, the LFC budget guidelines prioritized compensation increases, especially for hard-to-fill positions. Historically compensation increases have been funded with what's left after agency base budgets have been determined.

Insurance and post-employment benefits have been significant cost drivers for state budgets. State government has relatively rich benefit levels. The State Personnel Office (SPO) reports that in 2020 pay was 57 percent of total compensation for state employees compared to a 61 percent average for public employees in the US and 71 percent for private employees (FY23, Vol.1). The modern workforce has evolved to a much greater mobility of labor with less desire for employment stability and long-term pension benefits. Recent efforts to hold down employee healthcare insurance rates are exacerbating this problem.

The second biggest budget expenditure category is for contracts, $2.88 billion in FY24, up 16 percent from FY23. The FY24 budget guidelines directed analysts to analyze the monthly DFA Contracts report and accounting records to evaluate historical trends, avoid duplication with state employees and ensure cost-effectiveness. As far back as 1999, the budget guidelines flagged the need to review contracts because of the push to privatize government services during the Johnson administration.

A recent LFC report found $683 million of contracts in FY21 exempt from competitive procurement.[23] The report also found a rapidly growing level of purchases from multi-state or Federal price agreements, from $70 million in FY19 to $285 million in FY21. For example, in 2021 the Department of Labor contracted a $7.5 million renovation of its Albuquerque office using a price list. In 2013 the small purchase exemption was raised from $20 thousand to $60 thousand. These trends offer some savings to agencies in administrative costs and time to contract. But the LFC report says these practices, "led the state to overspending for purchases from everyday acquisitions of laptops and computers to non-competitively sourced contracts worth hundreds of millions." Analysts report these practices in Vol.2 agency narrative.

Other Revenue/Finding Money. The LFC budget guidelines also direct analysts to offset the need for general fund revenue with other state funds or federal revenue. Agencies with multiple revenue sources may understate (or budget conservatively) other state funds or federal revenue. If these revenues come in higher than expected, agencies can budget federal revenue automatically without an appropriation and typically have budget increase authority of five percent for other state funds. Agencies also have budget increase authority from cash balances.

DFA provides a monthly report to LFC from the state accounting system, SHARE, for cash balances of the one thousand-plus accounts in the state treasury. The LFC staff prepare a monthly report for every account greater than $1 million for the latest month and the same month a year ago, about 350 accounts. The report is presented to the committee every month and is the second to last table in Volume 3. The cash balance report provides a back of the envelope method to survey agency fiscal conditions.

LFC staff and members use this report frequently when agencies complain that their funding is inadequate. If the cash balance is up significantly year over year, it suggests agency revenue is coming in greater than expected, personnel turnover is high, agencies are having a hard time hiring staff, special appropriations were not initiated, or capital projects are delayed. Members use this report to dig into agency operations. For example, the Environment Department's wastewater facility construction fund has a balance that keeps growing year after year, now approaching $200 million. The department protests that a significant amount of the funds is encumbered for construction costs but acknowledges the unencumbered balance is over $50 million. Conversely, the cash balance report serves as a flag for agency overspending or even fiscal mismanagement. During the first term of Governor Lujan Grisham, the health benefits premium stabilization fund showed a growing negative balance that exceeded $100 million. This reflected a failure to raise insurance rates for both employee and employer.

In some cases, the beneficiaries of public funds act like it's their money. In 2017, when the legislature faced a recurring revenue reduction and the need to cut appropriations, the legislature took credit for school district cash balances in determining the appropriation for state equalization. The howls of protest, the vigilance to prevent a similar move continue today, even with school district average balances equal to 17 percent of operating budget. Similarly, firefighters act like the fire protection fund belongs to them. The fund derives its revenue from the insurance premium tax, which is imposed in lieu of the gross receipts tax and generates over $100 million per year. At one time most of the revenue went to the General Fund, but for mostly political reasons it was earmarked for distributions and grants to fire districts with minimal accountability. All citizens value the service and valor of firefighters, but in lean times a blank check for the best-intentioned services is challenging to appropriators.

The cash balance report is also how I find money. This was my specialty. Legislators want to find a way to fund their initiatives. I developed the ability and reputation among legislators as an expert in ways to fund "stuff." Some of the funds were like a gift that keeps on giving including the Attorney General's consumer settlement fund, the mortgage regulatory fund and the Environment Department's corrective action fund.

It's tricky, finding money. For me it was about helping people and pulling the members together to pass the budget. But it could be about power. You don't want members thinking that staff are making decisions or that staff have power. I have worked for elected officials who trust me to keep the trains running but also worked for a couple legislators who wanted to keep track of every request that came to me from legislators or lobbyists and wanted to ensure that I didn't tell or even hint what LFC was doing and that I wasn't playing favorites or making side deals.

Pulling It Together. In October LFC staff start putting together a "staff scenario" for the LFC recommendation. By then we have a General Fund revenue estimate for the following fiscal year, and we know the critical amount of "new money", next year recurring revenue minus current year operating budget. (I introduced this concept and definition in 1997, my first year as LFC director.) The director prepares a one-page scenario or strawman including current year operating budget, request for next year from agencies and a stab or guess at a recommendation for the 25 largest agencies or programs including a compensation proposal.[24] At the same time LFC analysts are preparing High Level recommendations for the individual agencies with detail by program of significant items, again with current year operating budget, agency request and staff scenario.[25] After some back and forth between analysts and the director, by the end of October the director presents the scenario to the chair and then the vice-chair. There are adjustments on every iteration, cut more, add more. Then typically the chair directs staff to start briefing members and perhaps key chairs of other interim committees, notably Education, Judiciary and Health and Human Services, and then the legislative leaders. By the November meeting, all the LFC members have reviewed the staff scenario and suggested changes, which are discussed with the chairs. Sometimes around November, the director and LFC chairs brief the majority caucuses in a very general way. This process requires iteration after iteration and then tweaking almost daily prior to the December meeting.

Although it was not sanctioned by me and the recommendations are confidential, LFC and DFA analysts fish for information and compare notes about what their counterparts are doing. The more similar the executive and legislative recommendations, the easier for the legislature to develop a budget.

I would usually get more and more high strung the closer to the December meeting. I felt the committee's action on the staff recommendation was effectively a vote on me. If there was a lot of grumbling or opposition, I didn't do the recommendation right. Probably the committee chairs felt the same way. Usually, committee adoption on the Friday or Saturday morning ending the December meeting was smooth. The deputy director and I would present the recommendation and the key spreadsheet to the committee in executive session and answer a lot of questions. Then they'd move to open session and typically vote in five minutes and the interim was over. What a relief.

However, my first year as director, the recommendation left over $200 million unspent. Senator Aragon wanted to leave plenty to address his and senators' priorities. David Harris, the DFA secretary, mocked the LFC recommendation that year as half a budget. A few years later Senator Aragon again thought the LFC staff recommendation didn't leave enough for the session, but Senator Ben

Altamirano, then LFC chair, chose to stay the course. The chairs would always say, "if you don't like it make your motions." That year Senator Aragon couldn't make the Santa Fe meeting in person, and Senator Altamirano arranged for him to be on speaker phone. He tried three or four motions that were all defeated 14-2 with Aragon joined by Senator Shannon Robinson (D-Albuquerque). It was awkward, but we had an LFC recommendation.

The Session. The governor has a press conference to present the executive recommendation on January 10 (or January 5 for a short 30-day session). The LFC has a press conference the next day in the rotunda of the annex. Usually, most members travel to Santa Fe for the press conference and usually offer broad bipartisan support for the recommendation.

Almost immediately the budget documents are distributed to staff, and analysts begin to compare recommendations, to update the General Fund high level and the agency high levels to include the Executive recommendation and to explain the significant differences. In 2011 in an alleged economy effort, the DFA discontinued printing the executive budget and distributed it electronically.

Within a couple days LFC prepares a memo highlighting the differences. Almost like clockwork, every year the LFC has a lower total General Fund recommendation. The LFC recommendation is typically higher for public schools and higher education but lower for most agencies. In cruder terms we think the Executive recommendation "porks up" agencies under the governor's direct control. Also, LFC expects to find a few large budgets that the Executive has "lowballed" in order to allow even higher recommendations for other executive agencies. Easy ways to lowball the budget include skipping a compensation increase, underfunding Medicaid (which is the only agency with statutory authority to carry forward a shortfall), and funding new initiatives as special appropriations (accounted in current year rather than next year spending). LFC is not immune from using such budget gimmicks but likely on a modest scale.

LFC staff prepare preliminary agendas for both HAFC and SFC. Both committees come a week early for the 30-day session. HAFC has a hearing for all agencies with most small agencies in subcommittee. SFC only hears the big agencies. Session committee staff also start before the session and provide clerical and organizational services to the standing committees, the chairs and members. The New Mexico legislature benefited from skillful staff leaders, often retired state government employees, notably Bill Valdes for over 30 years at HAFC and Ron Forte and Mike Burkhart for Senate Finance.

6. Bill Valdes, HAFC Chief of Staff, HAFC Chair Henry "Kiki" Saavedra and David Abbey. Circa, 2014

7. Ron Forte, Chief of Staff for Senate Pro Tem, Mike Burkhart, SFC Chief of Staff and David Abbey, circa 2017.

HAFC. With input from executive budget analysts, LFC staff prepare a "difference sheet" for presentation at every budget hearing. The difference sheet is an archaic budget tool showing differences between the executive recommendation and LFC recommendation for every agency and program and each line item for revenue or expenditures. The analysts are supposed to explain differences. In the session time crunch, the difference sheets are prepared quickly, not edited and not particularly interesting. Without public documentation of their recommendations, often either flat or at the agency requested amount, executive analysts sometimes struggle to explain their recommendations.

At the budget hearing, the LFC and DFA analysts present the highlights and differences and then the agency head presents the executive recommendation. LFC staff train extensively for budget hearings, most importantly to present information that is interesting, to not get overly technical (in the weeds) and to direct members to relevant material in LFC budget documents. In recent years former HAFC Chairwoman Patricia "Patty" Lundstrom (D-Gallup) assigned members to train and develop expertise in different aspects of budget development, and Representative Nathan Small (D-Las Cruces) continues this practice.

At the end of the hearing, the chair usually takes a motion to accept the lower recommendation, usually the LFC recommendation. LFC staff want to "win," that is for the LFC recommendation to prevail, because we believe that it is usually better reasoned, documented and fiscally sound. But at the end of the day the committee has to adopt recommendations that are politically palatable and give weight to the executive when the majority in the legislature is the same party as the executive (which has been most of the time). Occasionally, legislators push to adjust the low recommendation to add a popular Executive initiative on the spot or to ask HAFC, LFC and Executive staff to reconcile differences and come back with a consensus recommendation. For larger agencies or if the differences are significant, the chair may appoint an" ad hoc subcommittee" to prepare a new recommendation.

When Representative Henry "Kiki" Saavedra took over the HAFC in 2004, he directed me to sit up front at all hearings. This turned out to be smart. For starters I could hear the testimony and questions. (I wear hearing aids.) Second, I could work with staff to improve the quality of presentations and alert them to flag salient issues during the hearing. Third, it enhanced my knowledge of agency budgets that grew over time. Fourth, in real time or later I could figure out how to "fix" the recommendations to improve committee and agency support. Last, I developed a better working relationship with the chair.

Committee Catchup/Cleanup. After four weeks of hearings, HAFC reserves a couple days and moves to preliminary action on agency budgets. For days or weeks HAFC staff led for decades by Bill Valdes compiles a list of member "adds" or requests in addition to the base operating budget. This process is open to all House members, not just HAFC members. Priorities could include appropriation bills of other interim committees, appropriation bills of individual legislators, other local or district needs and leadership priorities. Also, the executive weighs in meeting with Valdes and the chair on their budget initiatives or initial HAFC action that falls short of the DFA recommendation. The ad hoc subcommittees, staff work groups and public and higher education subcommittees wrap up their recommendations. Then an executive committee of HAFC meets in a long, private session to review the preliminary committee action, make adjustments, if necessary, and address executive priorities and the add list. The executive committee has one member less than a quorum, a majority of the committee. In 2018 this was problematic, because an extra majority member showed up at catchup/cleanup, and then a minority member went on a long crusade against the chair and "illegal" meetings of HAFC.

The HAFC executive committee typically meets in the LFC conference room in the basement of Capitol North, the annex. There is a long table with whiteboards on two sides —the chair and Bill Valdes at one end and me and the deputy director at the other end with the deputy tallying action. After reviewing key spreadsheets, I specify the remaining amounts of recuring and non-recurring General fund left to spend, usually not much, say one percent of the budget or less. Then I present a "cut list" pre-approved by the chair. Usually, the "cuts" swap General Fund for other state funds or federal funds, in other words not really cuts. Every bit helps. The HAFC also leaves a modest amount for the Senate. The HAFC will expect the Senate to add about the same amount as HAFC.

The executive committee meeting is the veritable three ring circus. The chair tries to keep members on track working down the add list. LFC analysts are summoned to explain complex issues. Members are jumping ahead or backwards. LFC staff are writing tentative action on the board and keeping a running subtotal of recurring and non-recurring. The pace may go very fast or get bogged down into tense discussion of language or earmarks like funding for animal damage control or charter schools or whether an item is a state priority or a district priority. There aren't many votes taken. Most members aren't greedy. Dinner is brought in. At the end, the chair directs members to revisit a handful of items that weren't fully resolved. Sometimes if there is a little left, the chair may allow each member to designate a share. The chair may take an overall straw poll on the adjusted bill, typically there is broad support if not unanimous. LFC and HAFC staff stay late and check the numbers and prepare a 50-page packet of spreadsheets for a meeting of the full committee the following day.

HAFC Chair Max Coll (D-Santa Fe) used to say, "you know you're done when no one likes it, but no one knows how to make it better."

The final committee hearing on the GAA, HB2, is packed with advocates and agency personnel, but they've had their chance to talk. The committee passes spreadsheets or committee reports one by one and then votes on the overall bill. In my tenure as director, legislative staff never made a material math error at catchup/cleanup. Sometimes we'd forget to address an item or act on incomplete information. We'd start a technical correction list for Senate Finance.

It takes LFC 48 hours to prepare the HAFC substitute for the introduced version of HB2, a 225-page bill. HAFC would meet again and pass the bill, and the committee report would be adopted on the floor. The chair, Bill Valdes and I would present a summary of HB2 to the majority caucus. The next day it would appear on the temporary calendar for third reading, final passage the day after that.

Many years some members of the House majority were unhappy that the HAFC substitute didn't spend enough for schools or Medicaid or employee pay or that non-HAFC members didn't get a bite at the apple. The minority often thought the HAFC substitute spent too much or reserves were inadequate or the budget relied too much on volatile oil and gas revenue or the governor didn't get her pet initiatives like merit pay. You could count on a full three-hour debate (maximum time allowed by House rule) on HB2 on the House floor and lots of amendments and usually a close to party line vote with a handful of minority members on HAFC voting for the budget. A few times the minority caucus and Representative Joe "Moho" Mohorovic (R-Albuquerque) and recently Representative Jason Harper (R-Rio Rancho) asked LFC staff to prepare a floor substitute. That was a lot of work at a busy time, but showed LFC works for everybody.

Occupational Hazards at LFC. The LFC can mean either the committee composed of legislators, or the agency led by a director with a staff of analysts and evaluators. The LFC composed of legislators is an interim committee. During the session, legislators participate in standing committees, and the LFC doesn't meet or function. I have described how HAFC relies significantly on LFC recommendations and analysis for HAFC substitute for HB2, the General Appropriations Act.

Around the time of catchup-cleanup and final passage in the House, it starts dawning on the governor's staff and agency heads and lobbyists that the House hasn't funded much of their stuff. Lobbyists and agency heads typically only have a few priorities. Especially when state finances are flush, some of them place their self-esteem on their ability to achieve the agency request or special interest priorities. The fourth floor starts trading capital or issuing veto threats. Agency heads and lobbyists tell legislators that LFC staff didn't know what they were doing or made a mistake or had a personal agenda or whatever it takes to win. So what if the ship sinks, so what if their stuff goes down with the ship? If it does, they can blame LFC.

This might seem overly dramatic or defensive, but the pressure is rising. I use military jargon to describe what it's like for the LFC agency during the session. I am leading my troops into battle. I am on point. LFC staff need to circle the wagons. The legislature needs to use LFC spreadsheets, not DFA or agency formats, so we control the battlefield. At staff meetings, I tell them what's going on, so they don't make mistakes but, "it's a military secret, internal use only." I used to wrap up staff meetings with the admonition from Sergeant Jablonski in the eighties show "Hill Street Blues," "Let's do it to them before they do it to us;" or I'd say, "Forget it. It's Chinatown." Don't try to explain.

Senate Amendments. HAFC substitute for HB2 goes straight to the Senate Finance Committee (SFC). For the first half of the session, SFC has been hearing agencies at a moderate pace, mostly the 25 biggest agencies. In addition, SFC is hearing tax policy and capital outlay because SFC has broader duties than HAFC.

Decades ago, the House and Senate had a pretty frosty relationship. Senator Aragon knew how to get under Representative Coll's skin, and one year HAFC let Bill Valdes serve as chief negotiator with the Senate. Bill and Manny had Catholic school athletics rapport, St. Mary's in Albuquerque and St. Mike's in Santa Fe. In 1997 Senator Aragon led the Senate to go along with Governor Johnson and David Harris and adopt the Executive request for all agencies. It was called "give them all their shit." The Executive request was thought to be untenable, draconian for agencies. The House concurred with the Senate amendments. That was the end of LFC Director Anna Lamberson leading to my appointment that summer.

In 2000 late one afternoon after hearing HAFC substitute for HB 2, Senator Aragon directed me to work with LFC staff to come up with a plan to cut all the House and Executive additions to the operating budget by the following morning. With capable Deputy Director Dannette Burch, we developed a list of $80 million of spending cuts that SFC adopted along with a list of additions determined by Senator Aragon. Later at a conference committee with the House, some of the Executive adds were restored, but the Senate got to keep a disproportionate share of its adds.

A year or two later Ron Forte and Bill Valdes met on the railing on the third floor and struck a mutual non-aggression agreement between HAFC and SFC. "You don't mess with our stuff, we won't mess with your stuff." This arrangement worked pretty well, because the House does a good job funding base budgets for most agencies leaving the Senate share more for "member adds" than "fixing the base." The HAFC amendments are what we call a "good clean bill."

The chronic sore point with SFC is that they always say the House spent all the money and didn't leave them anything. I usually disagreed with that notion. I would tally for SFC staff the House adds above the LFC or executive base and show that the Senate was usually left an about equal share. But the Senate liked the messaging.

SFC is usually not in a hurry to finish Senate amendments to HB2. The longer it stays in committee, less time for the caucus or the Governor or a conference committee to mess with it.

When I started as director, an SFC executive committee would meet in Senator Aragon's office. The female LFC analysts would surround his desk. There'd be *queso*, chips and salsa, *chicharrones* and beer. Sen Stewart Ingle (R-Portales) would represent the Republicans. Senator Aragon would ask members about their priorities and then tell them an amount. At the end of one long evening session when there was a couple of million left, he asked me, "isn't there anything good we can do with the money?" I said, "at a summer hearing we heard from the university libraries, and they are really struggling and neglected." Senator Aragon said, "Okay, two million" and we were done.

By the 2000s, SFC would accept amendments to HB2 from all senators. It would take a couple of days just to compile. LFC staff would man tables in the rotunda of the annex and fill out request forms delivered by session staff or lobbyists. It seemed like opening day for hunting permits. There were up to eight hundred amendments submitted by members and a couple hundred from the executive and thirty or forty more that were unsigned that LFC staff had to track down, get signed, or determine it was a duplicate or void. SFC chief of staff Mike Burkhart called them "lost puppies." The universities specialized in getting many members to request the same thing, as if it represented stronger support for the amendment.

Senator Smith liked to meet on the amendments privately as a committee of the whole, first in the LFC conference room and later more quietly in the Legislative Education Study Committee conference room across the hall. It could take several meetings to go through all the amendments and sometimes two or three passes.

The Executive would up the pressure in the Senate to get its highest priority initiatives and threaten to veto the budget, and the Senate would be compelled to give something to avoid a special session. (In my tenure as director, the GAA was vetoed in 1999, 2000, and 2002 and partially vetoed (the legislature branch and higher education) in 2017.)

Then Senate Finance would meet in open session with one spreadsheet listing all the amendments proposed for adoption and a much larger do not adopt spreadsheet. Staff would make copies of the do pass amendments and set them on a table on the side of Room 322, and a mob would rush to get one. Then the chair would take a motion for do pass on the do pass spreadsheet and then a do pass on the bill and it was over in five minutes.

LFC also prepares the SFC amendment to the HAFC substitute. The amendment looks like the whole GAA. It strikes all sections of the HAFC substitute that changed in SFC, most of them except definitions and general conditions, and replaces them with what looks very similar except for different amounts or language.

The Senate debate on the GAA can be hard. It can be very long with no time limit on debate. Often the very liberal Democrats like McSorley or Sedillo Lopez or Soules are very negative and push amendments to increase spending for education or health care. Floor amendments rarely pass and are resisted by the SFC chair. But one year Senator Aragon got an amendment for sewers for the south valley of Albuquerque, opposed by Senators Altamirano and Fidel, chair and vice chair. Then Senator Pinto (D-Tohatchi) got one, then they passed several more and then called for a recess to go to caucus. In caucus the Democrats agreed not to pass any more amendments. Then they came out and passed a couple more amendments with extra spending $30 million above the SFC level. Then Senator Altamirano moved to send the bill back to SFC to start over.

When the GAA passed, my motto was, "it's all over but the finger pointing." A corollary was "blame the dead guy" meaning the analyst or legislator or executive official who quit, was fired or retired. Ron Forte's similar motto was, "it's time to shoot the wounded and blame the innocent."

Junior/Supplemental Appropriation Act. Who invented junior? I'm not sure anyone knows, but I'd bet Ron Forte. In the eighties Forte was planning director of the old Highway Department and House Majority Leader Toby Michael (D-Grants) ran a memorial to direct highway funding to local road projects.

Representative Michael and Forte would hold court in a tiny conference room next to HAFC, and members would line up to get their share. Junior must have been a successor.

The GAA is supposed to provide for the operations of government. Although repealed in the 1999 Accountability in Government Act, the Budget Act (NMSA 6-3-14) provided that, "the legislature shall not consider any appropriation until the budget shall have been submitted to the governor," and this practice is still mostly followed. As discussed above, Section 5 of the GAA, "special appropriations", historically included items requested by individual members and leaders. But inclusion of these items became a source of resentment from non-members of the appropriations committee and the minority party who didn't think they were getting fair consideration. Some members don't see political benefit from funding activities of state government that likely are concentrated in Santa Fe or maybe Albuquerque.

Joanne Montague, Legislative Council Service librarian, found the first supplemental general appropriation bill reported in Legislative Highlights was Chapter 366, Laws of 1993. The supplemental GAA made appropriations to all three branches of government, thereby not requiring an emergency clause and a supermajority to take effect on signing. The supplemental GAA, AKA junior, was a way to benefit all members equitably (and sometimes address requests of the executive, agencies or legislative leaders left out of the GAA). The concept of junior is that members get to decide how to address and prioritize district and constituent needs subject to guidelines adopted by HAFC and SFC that designate use for recurring or non-recurring and clarify compliance with the anti-donation clause of the constitution. Over time HAFC and SFC have enhanced vetting procedures for junior items, but it is pretty clear that junior serves highly parochial purposes. Every year some leaders and the governor and DFA say never again, but it is a popular vehicle for many legislators.

This section began with perhaps a lofty view of performance-based budgeting, which seeks to promote accountability and effectiveness of legislative appropriations. As the narrative moved further to reporting actual budget practices, obviously practice is far removed from theory. Governor and NMSU

President Garrey Carruthers would occasionally repeat the old saw that the best dissertation is a finished dissertation. Well, the best budget is an enacted budget.

On the Side/Fiscal Impact Reports (FIRs). One other key duty of the LFC tangentially related to state finances is preparing fiscal notes. LFC analysts and contractors prepare FIRs on every bill and constitutional amendment including substitutes and amendments, over a thousand bills in a 60-day session. The FIR includes a summary of the bill and detail by section, a fiscal impact table including out year costs or revenue, analysis of consequences, issues and alternatives. Agencies and institutions submit their analyses, supposedly on a short turnaround, but sometimes delayed by executive vetting.

The LFC FIR is not supposed to be a compilation of pros and cons but an independent analysis. A team of contractors, often retired public employees, supplements the analysts, and a FIR manager provides quality control.[26]

One occupational hazard of New Mexico's short session is that the FIRs appear slow in coming, especially when committees won't hear a bill without an FIR. Another is that critics may question the expertise or independence of the analyst. One year House minority leader Don Bratton (R-Hobbs) summoned me to his office and when I walked in it seemed like his whole caucus was squeezed in. One of my analysts unwisely referenced information from an advocacy group (something like "Wild Earth Guardians") in the FIR. I said we would fix it but defended our analyses compared to what we were getting from the executive branch.

The LFC FIRs might have been "a mile wide and an inch deep," but the quality got better and better.

# 4

# CAPITAL APPROPRIATIONS

# AND INFRASTRUCTURE

Infrastructure investments are critical for the state's economic prosperity, income growth and quality of life. The legislature appropriates for all manner of projects including office buildings, hospitals, roads and public transit, parks, dams, prisons, broadband, school and university facilities, wastewater treatment, sewers, tribal facilities, courthouses, libraries, firehouses, senior centers and more.

Government generally funds infrastructure by issuing bonds and repaying the debt with special revenue. Also, government may fund infrastructure from surpluses in operating funds.

## DEBT LIMITS AND GENERAL OBLIGATION DEBT

Article IX of the New Mexico constitution provides for "State, County and Municipal Indebtedness." Section 7 provides that the state may borrow up to $200 thousand to meet "casual deficits or failure in revenue." This provision has been violated as we will see but has not been used. Section 7 also provides that the state may contract debt "to suppress insurrection and provide for public defense." You never know.

Section 8 provides for a property tax to pay state general obligation bonds (GOB) up to one percent of valuation subject to voter approval at a general election. City and county debt is limited to four percent of valuation. School district debt is limited to six percent. State GOBs usually enjoy wide support, but in 2010 a $155 million issue for higher education failed narrowly and in 1990 five of six GOB questions failed.

Net taxable property valuation (one-third of market value) as of September 2022 was $87 billion, including $20 billion from oil and gas. The Board of Finance sold $233 million of GOBs in April 2023 for universities, libraries and senior centers.

In addition to GOBs, the state relies on Severance Tax Bonds (STB) and general fund surplus for infrastructure funding.

Severance Tax Bonds and General Fund. The Severance Tax Bonding Act enacted in 1961 provided that oil and gas severance tax revenue be deposited into the severance tax bonding fund (STBF) and up to 50 percent of STBF revenue be used for debt service on severance tax bonds. Surplus revenue to the STBF not needed for debt service payment goes to the severance tax permanent fund twice per year.

In most of the 1970s, the legislature passed STB appropriations for projects in individual bills with annual total STB appropriations up to $3 million. With rising oil prices in the wake of the OPEC embargo, STB appropriations increased to $37 million in 1978 and $57 million in 1980. In the 1980s, the legislature also consolidated STB appropriations in an omnibus or "Christmas tree bill."

Occasionally, if revenues were underestimated, and general fund reserves were higher than targeted (5 percent then), the legislature would use the general fund surplus for capital outlay. Capital needs had to compete with using some of the general fund surplus in HB2 for special and supplemental appropriations or with one-time personal income tax rebates.

The standard method to allocate STB capacity (and sometimes general fund surplus) was "one third/one third/one third." The governor would get one third of the capacity to fund "statewide" state agency projects and the House and Senate would each get one third for members to allocate, almost entirely for projects in their districts. There was little or no vetting of member projects. Each member got the same allocation in their chambers. Efforts to boost the allocation for majority members or for leadership were mostly rejected. This method meant that members in rural districts with many school districts and many municipalities and counties struggled to address "gotta have," critical infrastructure needs like drinking water, while urban legislators could fund the "nice things" like paving high school tennis courts.

In 1997 as a new director, my first hire was Linda Kehoe. She had a distinguished career, beginning with the 1969 constitutional convention, then chief of staff for Governor King's second term, deputy secretary of the DoH in the third King term, 20 years at LFC and then after retirement returning during legislative sessions to support LFC's capital program. Kehoe was LFC's first foray into infrastructure, and she was LFC's first capital outlay analyst. She provided expertise in developing major state projects and helping members address district needs.

At the end of the Johnson administration, the governor started using the executive share for local projects, notably a water project at Taos Ski Valley where Johnson was known to frequent and eventually owned property. Richardson picked up the practice of using the executive share for local projects. This trend had a couple significant problems. It diluted—even shortchanged—the ability to address critical state infrastructure needs like prisons and hospitals. Worse, Richardson exploited legislators' appetite for capital outlay funding by horse-trading for other executive priorities. To me this was apocryphal, the legislature giving up its power of appropriation for "pork." Even worse around this time, the Executive budget recommendation discontinued recommendations for capital outlay, despite the requirement in Chapter 6, section 3-10 that the budget submission include "all expenditures for capital projects to be undertaken or executed."

Beginning 2004 the LFC report to the legislature included discussion of agency infrastructure needs and legislative priorities, and by 2008 LFC staff prepared a statewide capital outlay appropriations framework for review by the committee. From the outset members proclaimed that the framework was not a committee spending recommendation but rather a starting point for discussions with the executive about funding agency projects. Some members, notably Representative Jeanette Wallace (R-Los Alamos) and Senator Stuart Ingle (R-Portales), zealously defended the allocation of capital capacity to legislators, especially in rural areas. With some reason, many members think a disproportionate share of funding goes north of I-40 or to Albuquerque and especially to Santa Fe.

In 2007 Ms. Kehoe and LFC also initiated quarterly status reports by agency on capital appropriations greater than $1 million. The data was derived from DFA's state accounting system and agency reports to DFA and LFC. The report, which continues today, includes amount expended to date, spending in the latest quarter, unspent balance, project phase (planning, design or construction), a note on current activity and a red, yellow or green progress rating. (Agencies with significant capital appropriations, the Big 8, are Health, Aging, Public Safety, Corrections, Higher Education, Environment, State Engineer, Energy and Minerals and General Services.) This report is widely used by legislators to determine additional funding requirements, to jawbone agency managers to get moving on a project or the need to reauthorize an appropriation from a stalled project.

In 2009 the LFC began reporting by county and agency on projects with appropriations in the $250 thousand to $1 million range. These projects are mostly sponsored by members with appropriations to DFA, PED or the State Engineer for local governments.

Underinvestment in Infrastructure. A common theme of LFC infrastructure reporting has been that agency needs far exceed available funding. For example, in 2006 estimated funding was $1.1 billion, "the greatest boon in capital funding in recent history" (Volume 1, 2007 LFC report to the legislature). But state and local funding requests totaled $2.6 billion, and DFA reported it would cost $16 billion to bring state and local infrastructure to "good" condition. The next year capital funding was a respectable $700 million, but requests rose to $3.5 billion.

For the next decade capital funding was erratic. During the great recession (2008-2010) and the 2016-2017 oil price collapse, funding for new projects dried up. Many years no General Fund surplus was available, STB capacity was minimal (for example, $35 million in 2010) and funding for some outstanding General Fund projects was transferred to the general fund ("swept") in solvency bills. For example, at a 2009 special session, 243 outstanding projects with $136 million were voided. In 2018 the legislature issued $100 million STBs to swap with funding for general fund projects, including some that were completed. Special sessions were required to fund capital in 2011, 2015 and 2016.

Initiatives for Capital Outlay Reform. The historical record consistently reports the same problems and similar solutions to improving the state's capital program.

In 2003 Governor Richardson established the Governor's Finance Council by executive order to develop procedures for evaluating projects, develop capital outlay standards and enhance central administration of projects. (Conveniently, Governor Richardson also established the Governor's Infrastructure Finance Team, GIFT, which I'm sure provided additional benefits.) In September 2003, DFA Secretary James Jimenez proposed a plan including half of all funding off the top for statewide projects, minimum project amounts, limits on reauthorizations, requirements for review by an oversight agency, and enhanced requirements for project readiness. LFC members reviewed the proposal at multiple meetings and were especially concerned about reducing funding for legislators' priorities. At the 2004 session Governor Richardson got an extra $14 million above the executive one-third share and vetoed 368 small legislative projects for $14 million.[27] Also, DFA received a $700 thousand appropriation to establish a seven-person capital outlay unit and to develop a database for all capital outlay appropriations, the Capital Projects Monitoring System.

In 2006 the Legislative Council formed a joint subcommittee of LFC members and Legislative Council members to "review capital funding options, the existing capital process, management concerns and obstacles to the progress of existing projects."[28] Key findings were agency understaffing, too many projects, lack of planning expertise, inadequate funding, cost escalation and bottlenecks in the construction market and materials cost escalation. The committee noted concerns about vetoes of legislative appropriations. The committee recommended process changes including establishing criteria for statewide projects, more time to develop the capital bill, achieving agreement among House, Senate and Executive on statewide funding level and total funding, better prioritization and better communication among members. In 2006 Governor Richardson vetoed 812 projects.

For the 2007 session DFA discontinued making a capital outlay recommendation as part of its statutorily required budget submission to the legislature.

The Joint Committee continued in 2007 and 2008 reporting similar concerns and actions. LFC Volume 1 in January 2008 reported that there were $2.1 billion of unexpended bond proceeds for 8,500 projects, and 2,960 projects authorized between 2002 and 2006 showed little or no progress.

In the wake of the Governor's Finance Council and the Joint Committee, the method of allocating funding evolved to funding statewide projects "off the top" rather than one third each, house, senate and governor. Around the middle of the session the Executive would release its statewide agency recommendations to LFC staff, and staff would prepare a side-by-side comparison to the LFC framework published in Volume 3. Because of effective communication between LFC and DFA staff, differences for statewide projects could be reasonably reconciled. Under the direction of House Taxation and Revenue Committee (HTRC), SFC and DFA leadership, a consensus statewide project list was agreed. Then remaining capital capacity would be split equally among governor, House and Senate. This method provides better prospects that statewide needs will not be shortchanged, but often there is pressure to find more capital capacity to fund member shares at a higher amount. For example, in 2023, after agreeing to a statewide project list of $600 million, members increased the three-way share by $400 million at the expense of a transfer to the Severance Tax Permanent Fund. (This is an example of how the legislature "spends its way to victory.")

Nevertheless, the problem of prioritizing "critical" needs and mounting unused appropriations continued. In 2015 Think New Mexico recommended a capital outlay reform plan that included: requiring a state infrastructure plan; creating a state infrastructure board with members including DFA, LFC, Legislative Council Service and agency officials; establishing project criteria and rankings; and cash funding rather than bond funding projects when possible.

In October 2016, the LFC, DFA, the Municipal League and the Association of Counties presented capital outlay to the interim legislative Revenue Stabilization and Tax Policy committee. Presenters agreed, without improvement, the system will frustrate stakeholders, underfund projects, and negatively impact infrastructure needs. They stated, "The current process calls for hundreds of millions of bond proceeds to sit idle unable to be expended for economic activity." The median project size of projects funded in 2016 was only $85 thousand. They called for the legislature to prioritize better, coordinate funding streams, establish a minimum project size, ensure projects are shovel ready when receiving construction funding and create a statewide infrastructure planning council.

In 2021 a transparency bill sponsored by Representative Matthew McQueen (D-Galisteo) required the Legislative Council Service to report sponsorship by legislator for individual projects.

During the 2022 interim, the LFC Capital Outlay Subcommittee recommended prioritizing 2023 funding to complete partially funded existing projects, improve vetting of local project requests and boost administrative and technical support for local projects. The LFC also supported proposed legislation to create a cabinet level infrastructure office to conduct statewide needs assessment, coordinate funding streams and assist local governments.

As of January 2023, outstanding capital outlay funds totaled $3.1 billion for 4,000 projects. There were 557 projects on the million or greater report with 126 rated red for failure to report, lack of progress or other bottlenecks and 122 projects rated yellow and behind schedule. Appropriations for these large projects totaled $2.5 billion with $1.6 billion unspent.

The 2023 legislature appropriated another $1.5 billion for approximately 1,000 new projects, the largest package to date. Funding for capital project administration increased $4.7 million, but the LFC bill to create an infrastructure coordinating office failed.

## SUPPLEMENTAL SEVERANCE BONDS AND EARMARKS

Public Schools. In 1999 11th District Court Judge Rich ruled in the *Zuni* case that the state violated the constitutional requirement for an equitable education system with its method of funding school capital outlay. Until then, most building funding came from school district general obligation bond capacity which varied greatly by district. State funding administered by the public school capital outlay council (PSCOC) was minimal, $10 million in 1997, my first year as an ex officio member of the council. In 2000, to address the *Zuni* decision, the legislature authorized an earmark of supplemental severance tax bonds for the PSCOC using an additional 25 percent of severance tax bonding fund revenue (in addition to the 50 percent share for senior STBs appropriated by the legislature).

With severe overcrowding in high schools in the Gadsden, Rio Rancho and Albuquerque school districts, that wasn't enough, so Dan Weaks and I invented "sponge bonds" to eke out even more bonding capacity for school construction. (Weaks was a former DFA official and lobbyist and public finance expert.) Because of the volatility of oil and gas revenue to the STBF, it was impractical for the state to sell more long-term STBs with a maturity of five or more years in the municipal bond market. Sponge bonds could be sold by the Board of Finance to the state treasurer with a maturity of a day or two and pose no credit risk. In effect sponge bonds "soaked up" unused STBF revenue, reduced the transfer of surplus STBF revenue not needed for debt service to the Severance Tax Permanent Fund and got around the constitutional requirement to invest unneeded STBF revenue in the STPF. There have been a lot of laughs about sponge bonds, think Sponge Bob from Sesame Street, but the innovation got New Mexico out of a fiscal pickle.

In 2003 and 2004 the legislature increased the use of STBF revenue for supplemental STBs to an additional 45 percent, or 95 percent of total STBF revenue.

Also in 2003, the legislature created the Public School Facilities Authority (PSFA) to administer the state school construction program. The PSFA set standards for school building size and programs and administered a formula for the state and school districts to share project costs. The legislature and PSFA added additional programs over the years including pre-k, teacher housing, school safety, demolition and broadband. Since FY01, the PSCOC has awarded $2.6 billion for school projects. The PSFA pioneered just-in-time funding with separate awards for school planning, design and construction. The average facility condition index (FCI) declined from 70 percent in FY01 to 50 percent and the weighted FCI, adjusted for student crowding, declined from 40 percent to 21 percent. (FCI is the cost of building repair divided by replacement cost. A rule of thumb is to replace a building when FCI is greater than 50 percent. The lower the FCI, the better school building condition.) I served as chair of the PSCOC or Chair of the Awards subcommittee for almost 20 years.

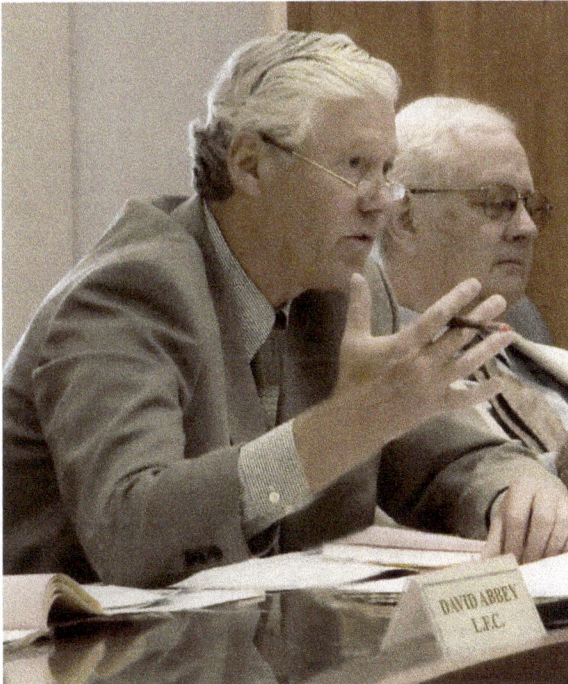

8. David Abbey, Chair of Public School Capital Outlay Council Awards Subcommittee and Bill Hume, Governor's representative on PSCOC.

9. L-R, David Abbey, student, Gallup-McKinley Assistant Superintendent Leonard Haskie and Representative Patty Lundstrom, dedication of Navajo Middle School, Navajo, New Mexico, December 20, 2007.

In 2015 the state moved to dismiss the *Zuni* case. The motion languished, but in 2021 the district court ruled the state's program remained unconstitutional. The state appealed, and a hearing is expected in 2024.

Water/Colonias/Tribal/Housing. A share of Senior STBs is earmarked to special funds as follows: water projects (established 2001) nine percent, tribal infrastructure (2005) and colonias (2010) both 4.5 percent, and housing 2.5 percent (2023). Councils were created to receive applications and make awards from these funds, and the New Mexico Finance Authority and state agencies provide administrative support. In 2023 these funds received over $300 million of senior STB proceeds.

# OUTCOMES OF CAPITAL PROGRAM

Infrastructure investments can improve public and higher education and public health, reduce road congestion and generally improve the state's economic conditions and quality of life. But the state has a unique method of allocating infrastructure funding that often rates poorly in national surveys. Executive and legislative reports and recommendations have been critical of the administration of capital funding. What does the state have to show for its investments?

Successes. Ms. Kehoe is especially proud of the state's reconstruction of the Behavioral Health Institute in Las Vegas. As a health department official, she observed undignified treatment of patients, for example "hosing down" clients in an open shower house. In three phases the state replaced all senior housing units and is set to replace the forensic unit.

I am proud of the annex to the Palace of the Governors, the State History Museum. As a kid I had the pale blue 1 1/4 cent stamp portraying the New Mexico's first capitol built in 1610. In 1996 I went to the National Conference of State Treasurers annual meeting in Boston, and historian David McCullough urged these ambitious pols to go home and find ways to enhance Americans' knowledge of history and promote civic virtue. My chance came on July 4, 2001, at the Rotary pancake breakfast on the Santa Fe Plaza. I joined three strangers at an empty table, and they introduced themselves—the venerable Tom Chavez, director of the Palace of the Governors, the Honorable Ambassador Frank Ortiz[29] and Sam Ballen, owner of the La Fonda hotel on the Santa Fe Plaza. I introduced myself as legislative budget director and in unison they said, "just the guy we want to meet." Representative Varela, history major Kiki Saavedra, Speaker Lujan, Governor Richardson, Senator Domenici, the trustees of the Museum of New Mexico Foundation and many others got on board, and we have a crown jewel on the plaza.

10. US Senator Pete Domenici, Anica Abbey, David Abbey and Lorin Abbey. Celebration of Palace of the Governors and new state history museum, circa 2005.

Senator Smith I'm sure is proud of saving the Sierra County Hospital (and many other things including the Veterans' Home in T or C); similarly, Senator Pete Campos (D-Las Vegas) saved the Guadalupe County Hospital in his hometown, Santa Rosa.

Representative Varela fought forever to create the Pecos Canyon State Park.

Representative J. Paul Taylor (D-Las Cruces) donated his house on the plaza of Old Mesilla for a state monument to celebrate our international border and culture.

Senator John Pinto would ask me every day what I was doing to four lane the dangerous 666, the "devils' highway" and now US 491.

Representative John Heaton (D-Carlsbad) got $80 million from multiple sources to prevent the heart of Carlsbad, rail, canals and highways, from falling into a sinkhole.

Representative Lundstrom and Senator Munoz worked tirelessly on the San Juan lateral to bring drinking water to many Navajo nation chapters and the city of Gallup.

Senator Nava got new high schools to relieve severe overcrowding in Anthony, Santa Teresa and Chapparal.

Senator Aragon and Speaker Sanchez got STB earmarks for wastewater treatment and protecting drinking water in the North and South Valleys of Albuquerque.

Ron Forte and Representative Lorenzo "Larry" Larranaga (R-Albuquerque) and the great highway engineers figured out how to replace the Big-I with minimal economic disruption.

Senator Roberto "Bobby" Gonzalez is proud of the new campus for UNM Taos including nursing and STEM programs.

As Senator Smith would say, the list goes "on and on." It took a village to accomplish these worthy projects, and New Mexico should be proud.

Inefficiency or Waste in Many Directions. New Mexico is on a quest for infrastructure projects that will transform the economy and improve quality of life. A handful of multi-hundred-million-dollar projects might fit that description including the Spaceport, Rail Runner, Johnson and Richardson's highway initiatives, tribal water rights settlements and water projects and deployment of broadband.

Although the verdict is arguably out, Rail Runner and the Spaceport seem unsuccessful when this book was published. Rail Runner cost $385 million to build in two phases during the Richardson administration. In 2005 LFC reported, "minimal analysis of customer demand, fee structure, economic development and return on investment was conducted prior to capital investment in rail cars or locomotives." The project used mostly state and local funds, because the state was in too much of a hurry to conduct the feasibility studies required to obtain federal funds.

Today, Rail Runner operates at about 20 percent of capacity, ridership is down 25 percent from pre-pandemic and 50 percent from the 2010 peak, farebox revenue is minimal, there are too many stops and travel times are too long.[30] Operating costs are covered mostly by federal air quality funds and local option gross receipts taxes. If ridership is minimal, the benefits for the environment and road congestion are not realized.

The spaceport was initiated in 2006 with a $100 million appropriation over three years and the authority for a spaceport gross receipts tax in three counties in southern New Mexico. The spaceport was built in 2009 and 2010 with $210 million of state and local funds. The cost included a stunning $80 million glass hangar. (It reminded me of the visionary Dulles airport designed by Eero Saarinen in 1958; you had to take a bus across the tarmac to get to a mobile staircase to board the plane.) Additional state investment since 2008 is $44 million. Virgin Galactic, the anchor tenant, hoped to offer commercial suborbital flights by 2011, but the first commercial flight occurred June 2023. Although there are other tenants with promising long-term industrial and defense related initiatives, almost half of the $11 million operating budget for the Spaceport Authority comes from the general fund. The Authority reports there were 350 spaceport-related jobs in New Mexico in FY22. Adjusting for inflation (40 percent), the original construction cost of $210 million represents a sky-high $600 thousand per job created.

Broadband funding to provide universal, reliable, high-speed internet service should reach $1 billion, including $675 million for New Mexico from the federal Bipartisan Infrastructure Act. The New Mexico Office of Broadband Access and

Equity is granting these funds to rural electric and telephone cooperatives to install underground fiber optic cable to individual homes at costs per household reaching $30 thousand or more. The Joe Monahan blog in summer 2023 urged instead reaching the New Mexico frontier with satellite service that costs about $100 per month. Frontier New Mexicans might rather have a new pickup than fiber.

More modest examples of inefficient or ineffective projects follow. They all illustrate the need for good planning and design and for the oversight agencies to conduct due diligence.

The Public School Capital Outlay Council (PSCOC) funded a much-needed replacement of the K-12 school in Des Moines School District in Union County in 2002. At that time the district had about 150 students. But the replacement school was designed for 400 students and included an expensive second story that has never been used. Today the district has less than 100 kids.

The state appropriated $5.4 million in 2007 and 2008 for an auditorium for Luna Community College in Las Vegas. A shell (an unfurnished, unequipped structure) was built for 1,200 students, but Luna's enrollment is only 400 students. Luna received $2.8 million more in 2015 and 2016, hopefully to complete the project.

Governor Richardson obtained $600 thousand to renovate the old Ribera School in San Miguel County, part of an at-risk youth camp project led by radio personality Don Imus.[31] The camp failed, and the Ribera school was sold for thirty-seven thousand dollars.

A 2008 LFC report found a seven hundred-thousand-dollar project on the Pecos River and a six hundred thousand dollar filtration plant at the state penitentiary were never used.[32] After multiple awards and appropriations of $7 million, the Cabresto Dam in Taos County still leaked, and storage capacity was inadequate for irrigation.

I asked Larry Barker, long-time investigative reporter for KOAT, to offer some of his most noteworthy examples of waste in the capital outlay system. He listed: the Mora County courthouse, still an unfinished, two-story shell; the five hundred ten thousand dollar unfinished and abandoned Watrous Community Center shell, also in Mora County; a doggie drinking fountain at a dog park in Las Cruces; the beautiful five million dollar El Camino Real museum, a compromise site halfway between Socorro and Truth or Consequences, miles from an interstate exit, maybe a dozen visitors a day when it was open and now shuttered and worthless; the eight hundred thousand dollar Lobo Rail Runner whistlestop, used three days for sporting events and closed; a fifty thousand dollar mobile heavy metal music museum in Bernalillo county; and the abandoned $2.4 million dollar visitor center with a statue of Juan de Onate at Alcalde in Rio Arriba County (to say nothing about the statue's amputated foot).[33] Barker said these weren't necessarily the biggest or most egregious and added, "the list goes on and on."

Inflation will Worsen Problems of Inadequate Planning. A joint report of LFC and Legislative Education Study Committee staff to the Public-School Capital Outlay Task Force flagged soaring inflation for school construction projects. From 2022 to 2023 the estimated cost rose from $425/sq ft to $582/sq ft, a thirty percent increase in one year. The analysts noted a similar trend in the Department of Commerce school construction producer price index. The analysts attributed soaring cost increases to materials cost increases, supply chain bottlenecks lingering from the pandemic, tight labor markets at full employment and growing public sector project demand driven by the energy boom.

The University of New Mexico received a forty-five million dollar General Obligation Bond appropriation in 2022 to replace and consolidate a dozen fine arts buildings scattered along premium real estate along Central Avenue in Albuquerque in a hundred thousand sq ft building. The project, Center for Collaborative Arts and Technology, has been in the works for years and a marquee element of the planning is for the popular film program. I was surprised UNM wasn't further along when in 2023 a request for proposals for an architect was issued for this project. Now the project has a reported cost of $82 million requiring completion with university funds.

I've said for several years we can't stuff much more in the capital pipeline. But of course, we can. It just won't all come out or in a form we like.

# 5

# OVERSIGHT AND ACCOUNTABILITY

During the Martinez administration, the governor's chief of staff asked me why they needed to respond to LFC requests for information. He added, "Why don't you have to respond to our requests?"

The short answer is that the LFC enabling statute and the State Budget Act require agencies to cooperate. There are no conditions about, "why are you asking or what do you want to use it for?" Of course, common sense and political comity suggest that the legislative branch should have answers to those questions and communicate them to the Executive branch and the public.

A longer answer goes back to the Magna Carta in 1215 which set limits on the king's power to require taxes and other payments to the crown, making them subject to "baronial consent."The Congressional Research Service reports, "John Stuart Mill, the British Utilitarian philosopher, insisted that oversight was the key feature of a meaningful representative body. The proper office of a representative assembly is to watch and control the government."[34] The CRS notes oversight improves the efficiency of government operations, detects and prevents poor administration, protects civil liberties, informs the general public and aids the legislature to develop new programs or amend statutes. Further, "The authority to oversee derives from constitutional powers of the legislature. Congress could not carry them out without knowing what the executive is doing; how programs are being administered, by whom and at what cost; and whether officials are obeying the law and complying with legislative intent."

## DEVELOPMENT OF THE LFC AUDIT PROGRAM

LFC's performance evaluation program came from the Office of the State Auditor in 1989. Manu Patel, a certified public accountant (CPA), led the program and mostly employed other CPAs. Patel established procedures for LFC studies, called audits at that time, which were conducted according to the "yellow book standards" of the Governmental Accounting Standards Board (GASB).

Representative Varela was the LFC member most attentive to the audit program with Patel. Representative Varela, a Pecos native, retired from state government in 1983 as director of DFA's Financial Control Division, effectively state controller or chief financial officer. Varela knew and loved state government and was the legislature's eyes and ears on government operations and finances. Varela practiced oversight almost daily by walking around state offices in Santa Fe and during the interim at legislative committee field hearings around the state. He often had LFC staff, especially me, in tow. Following his surveillance, a common directive to Patel and me was, "let's send the auditors to straighten this out."

During both the Johnson and Richardson administrations, some LFC audits embarrassed the executive branch and triggered significant controversy. In October 1998, a few weeks before the general election, LFC staff presented to the committee an audit of Taxation and Revenue Department's (TRD) audit and compliance program. Findings included an estimated "tax gap" or under collected revenue of $43 million, too many vacant positions, the need to beef up refund intercepts by matching databases of state payments and establishing metrics for program performance. The LFC staff also tested TRD's payment integrity by filing four false returns including Rin T. Tin and Lassie Collie using the office address at the capitol.[35] Refund payments were received at the capitol on October 5. TRD Secretary John Chavez said the LFC action was illegal and referred the matter to his Inspector General and the Department of Public

Safety. Senator Billy McKibben said the "false returns were appropriate for a department that has shown itself to be inept." Representative Max Coll told me Chavez was so angry at the hearing there was smoke coming out of his ears. The next session, Governor Johnson vetoed the $2.2 million appropriation to the LFC in the feed bill that included three additional audit staff for an additional $200 thousand. The governor said the audits constituted "harassment," and DFA Secretary Harris said the audits had become "partisan," but Senator Aragon and Representative Coll said the audits were about "accountability" and "checks and balances".[36]

In January 2005 the LFC budget recommendation for information technology (IT) listed six "failed" or "partially failed" IT projects including TRD's $60 million TRIMS tax payment processing system and HSD's $20 million SSALSA project, neither of which were completed.

In spring and summer 2006 I had conversations with the DFA Secretary Katherine Miller and Governor's chief of staff James Jimenez about perceptions that LFC evaluations were not objective, about notification of scope of work, project timing and complaints from cabinet secretaries about LFC procedures. LFC staff devoted significant effort that summer to document procedures, develop an annual audit work plan, conform to accounting standards and improve communication with legislators and executive agencies.

In September 2006 LFC initiated an evaluation of the State Personnel Office (SPO) to examine agency adherence to SPO rules for hiring and compensation. The executive questioned LFC's motivation, perhaps because Representative Varela's son, Jeff Varela, had previously served as SPO director. Separately, LFC staff received anonymous complaints regarding SPO management practices. DFA Secretary James Jimenez and SPO Director Sandy Perez advised me that Governor Richardson directed them not to comply with the LFC evaluation and information requests. Jimenez said the evaluation was unnecessary, because LFC analyst Gene Moser "practically lived at SPO," and the objective was "personal." I obtained approval of the committee leaders to prepare and issue (if necessary) a subpoena for information and on September 25 sent a letter to Governor Richardson's chief of staff James Jimenez appealing for approval to proceed with the review. I explained previous reports of the Hay group flagged a problem of pay disparity and wrote, "I assure you this is motivated by a sincere desire to improve equity and efficiency of personnel operations." On September 26 Patel and I met with Brian Condit, incoming chief of staff, and shortly SPO was authorized to proceed with the LFC review.

Key findings of the SPO evaluation issued in 2007 were violation of statutes and rules related to nepotism, failure to conduct agency quality assurance reviews for several years, decentralization of personnel functions to agencies without consistent standards, a negative employee work environment at SPO and violation of DFA travel rules, with 18 employees attending an overnight "retreat" at a Santa Fe spa.

The SPO director and the State Personnel Board chair said LFC staff did not properly validate its findings, and Governor Richardson said, "the leadership of LFC likes to sometimes embarrass the administration and the staff." But Senator Sue Beffort said SPO should be an exemplar of doing things "by the book." The editors of the *Albuquerque Journal* ("State Don't Need No Stinkin' Auditors,") said, "Richardson should remember that book contains a system of checks and balances designed to ultimately root out abuses of power."

LFC Audit Function Evolves to Evaluation. I had some prior experience in program evaluation at Resources for the Future and LANL including an evaluation of air quality management programs in the Four Corners states.[37]

The National Conference of State Legislatures has an affiliate, the National Legislative Performance Evaluation Society (NLPES). As a new director, I attended NLPES sessions and had the opportunity to learn about programs in other states. Many were led by CPAs and had a principal focus on financial and statutory compliance, but states like Florida, Mississippi and Virginia were expanding audit programs to link to budget development and policy analysis using social science research methods and quantitative analysis and hiring evaluators with training besides accounting. Directors from other states like Kirk Jonas, professor at the University of Richmond and director of Virginia's

Joint Legislative Audit and Review Committee, and John Turcotte, director of Mississippi's Performance Evaluation and Expenditure Review, provided training to LFC on broadening its methods while retaining policies and procedures of the "yellow book" government accounting standards to ensure expertise, objectivity and independence. LFC diversified its evaluation workforce with attorneys, teachers, statisticians, social workers, a school principal and journalists.

Pew Charitable Trust's State Government Budgeting program reports five components of evidence-based policy making: program assessment, budget development, implementation oversight, outcome monitoring and targeted evaluation. This describes LFC's performance evaluation program. Staff evaluate potential projects based on the following criteria: public and legislative interest (timeliness), budget impacts and service outcomes, whether the study will plow new ground or cover old news, capability and expertise of LFC staff to conduct the study, and agency receptiveness and cooperation. The studies begin with a staff planning memo on issues, methods and timeframes, an engagement letter to executive and legislative officials, an entrance conference with the agency, periodic status reports, an exit conference with the agency and an agency response. LFC found that careful project selection leads to the most interesting and impactful reports. Each year LFC Volume 1, Appropriation Recommendation includes highlights of the evaluation program for the prior year.

Not surprisingly LFC evaluations and progress reports sometimes generate significant acrimony and heartburn—from governors, legislators, agency heads and program managers and advocates. There is a perception that LFC has a "gotcha mentality," that LFC looks to make people and programs "look bad." The converse may be true, that LFC staff think the governor and agencies are preoccupied with avoiding bad press. The remainder of this chapter presents highlights of recent LFC evaluations—those that caught the press and public attention, that the agencies stonewalled, or that united the government and New Mexicans in investing in critical and effective public services.

# HIGHLIGHTS OF EVALUATIONS

Public Schools and Early Learning. LFC has conducted dozens of evaluations of public education and early learning programs that identify effective programs and methods to improve kindergarten readiness, reading and math proficiency and high school completion, and to improve school leadership and district operations. LFC reported that students who attended pre-K had a ten percent higher rate of both high school graduation and college attendance.[38] Further, "for a small group of students that participated in both K-3 plus and pre-K, the two programs combined nearly eliminate the achievement gap for low-income students." LFC also found that high quality infant home visiting programs reduce child maltreatment and improve child and maternal health.

A November 2012 LFC Performance Evaluation, "Promoting Effective Teaching in New Mexico," found that the three-tiered career ladder implemented in 2003 at significant cost did not improve student performance. To reach this finding, LFC evaluators used an innovative statistical method, value-added modeling.

In September 2021 LFC reported students lost up to 60 days instructional time during the pandemic and recommended the state make greater investments in extended learning programs and greater effort to restore in-person instruction. In September 2022 an LFC Progress Report, "Martinez-Yazzie Sufficiency Funding", detailed incremental state funding since the 2018 decision and responsibilities of the Public Education Department, the legislature and school districts to close the achievement gap.

LFC conducted eight evaluations of school districts since 2008. The "Program Evaluation of Albuquerque Public Schools" in April 2022 found that the district failed to control building and operating costs during an extended period of declining enrollment and that the district has not made learning improvements for at-risk children. A 2010 evaluation of the state's charter school program found that charter schools have relatively high administrative costs, funding formula factors provide preferential treatment, and governance at some charters allowed conflicts of interest in procurement and hiring and improper expenditures. LFC worked with the state auditor and federal law enforcement leading to a felony conviction and five-year sentence of a charter administrator for a 15-year scheme to defraud public charters of millions of dollars.

Health Care and Social Services. LFC issued dozens of reports on Medicaid, state hospitals, the developmentally disabled program, juvenile justice and other social services. A December 2022 LFC Program Evaluation, "Medicaid Network: Adequacy, Access and Utilization," reported that the Medicaid budget grew 56 percent from FY19 to FY23 to $8.8 billion. Enrollment grew 16 percent over that period, but utilization was flat or declining except for behavioral health and telemedicine. The key finding was, "Medicaid enrollees do not have adequate access to timely health care." Staff conducted a secret shopper survey and found only 13 percent of service inquiries resulted in an appointment. To promote recruitment and retention of providers, especially doctors, LFC recommended appropriating funds for rate increases to bring Medicaid rates to 100 percent of Medicare (from 80 or 90 percent) with additional increases for primary care and telemedicine. In one of the greatest examples of executive/legislative cooperation and consensus, the executive had a similar recommendation. FY24 state funding for rate increases was $88 million; with federal funds included rate increases totaled $443 million.

In 2021 and 2022 LFC issued reports on state hospitals operated by DoH, including the Behavioral Health Institute in Las Vegas with an FY23 operating budget of $184 million including $93 million of enterprise revenue. Only 80 percent of the seven facilities' beds were operational and only 50 percent were occupied. The 2021 report stated, "Lack of leadership lead to inadequate oversight affecting DoH's ability to ensure quality care and address facility construction issues, notably at the Veterans' home." Besides chronic underutilization, other key issues were accreditation risk, uncontrolled contract labor costs, staffing shortages, substandard care and patient harm. In the last quarter of 2020, 22 percent of residents at the veterans' home died.[39] Similarly, a 2015 report flagged declining occupancy, uncontrolled contract and overtime costs, high vacancy rates and failure to generate and collect enterprise revenue. Note the problem of leadership stability persists with four secretaries to date under Governor Michelle Lujan Grisham (MLG)—Kathy Kunkel, Dr. Francie Collins, Dr. David Scrase and now Patrick Allen.

Childhood and Family Services. As early as 1991, a governor's task force described the child protective services system as "crisis oriented" and proposed a service delivery model emphasizing prevention and early intervention. This work spearheaded by Alice King led to the creation of the Children, Youth and Families Department in 1992.

LFC's 2004 "Audit of Child Care" described the tradeoff between the number of participants in subsidized childcare versus investment in more costly early learning initiatives. For a 2013 follow-up, LFC's Dr. Jon Courtney said the focus initially was on childcare and the effects on healthy brain development and learning. But the staff received whistleblower reports suggesting the need to examine integrity of childcare services and payments to providers. CYFD Secretary Yoland Berumen-Deines initially denied LFC access to "case-level data" citing Federal confidentiality requirements.[40] Again, with the aid of a draft subpoena and development of a Memorandum of Understanding with CYFD "outlining the parameters of data usage," LFC and CYFD reached an agreement to proceed.

The September 2013 LFC report, "Impact of Child Care on Student Achievement," concluded that, "despite significant investments, childcare assistance for low-income children fails to improve school readiness and early literacy." Also, LFC reported, "the childcare program is at high risk for fraud, waste and abuse because of weak program integrity efforts." Specifically, LFC found provider background checks didn't include sex offenders, and these offenders were known to reside in at least three CYFD registered homes. An April 2014 progress report provided a sharper focus on repeat maltreatment of children under state supervision; the national benchmark for this measure was five percent and New Mexico was 11 percent. The report repeated the mantra to increase investment in front-end services, also known as family preservation, in-home treatment or preventative services. Secretary Deines resigned in December 2014, replaced by Tourism Secretary Monique Jacobsen.

LFC began to issue annual Early Childhood Accountability reports in 2015. These reports contributed to the creation of the Early Childhood and Care Department (ECECD) in 2019 and the Early Childhood Trust Fund in 2020 and pushed CYFD to sharpen its focus on prevention. An August 2022 LFC Results First report, "Evidence-based Options to Reduce Child Maltreatment" reported investments in front end programs grew from less than $1 million in FY 17 to $10 million in FY23. Nevertheless, protective service worker vacancies are around 40 percent, and the maltreatment rate remains stubbornly high. Horrific stories of drug exposure, abuse and death of young children in CYFD's system are all too frequent.[41] Following natural death of their mother, two young Clovis children were returned to their biological father in Carlsbad despite safety concerns. Governor Lujan Grisham's second CYFD secretary, a former supreme court justice, resigned in April 2023. The governor's deputy chief of staff served as acting secretary for a year before her recent nomination and confirmation as secretary.

A June 2023 LFC Spotlight, "Juvenile Justice Facilities," again showed benefits of investments in prevention: "Implementation of the *Cambiar* model in FY08 shifted from a punitive mode of justice to rehabilitative, evidence-based practices to reduce recidivism and improve outcomes." Referrals to juvenile justice declined from 24 thousand in FY09 to 5,600 in FY22. The caseload of juvenile probation officers and the population in facilities both declined 59 percent from FY17 to FY22, and CYFD closed two residential facilities and two treatment centers.

An October 2021 Policy Spotlight, "Stacking of Income Supports," examined the level and range of low-income supports including food stamps, childcare and tax credits to determine the effects on living standards and employment. From FY18 to FY22 general fund expenditures for these programs grew over $500 million. All benefits available allow many low-income families, particularly families with children, to receive support equivalent to a living wage. But many eligible families do not receive services, and the cliff effect of some benefit programs may discourage participation or create work disincentives. Governor Lujan Grisham vetoed tax cuts and general fund revenue reductions that grew to $900 million by FY27. But the governor signed a $100 million increase in child tax credits, including from $175 to $600 per child at the lowest income level.

Higher Education. The higher education system is hard to wrap your arms around. Like public schools, it is a sprawling system with 27 institutions and dozens more branches, twigs and satellite campuses. It includes the health sciences center, the business of university athletics and well over one hundred research and public service projects. In addition to providing dozens of degree types and credentials, the higher education system produces services from basic and applied research to dual credit for high school students.

In 2010 LFC issued the report, "Higher Education: University of New Mexico and New Mexico State University." State supported funding was third highest in the nation, and tuition was among the lowest. The higher education funding formula counted courses taken, not courses completed, much less degrees completed. Forty-three percent of graduates took six years to complete their degrees, which delayed entry into the workforce and increased costs to students and families. Prophetically, the report warned that higher education's 15 percent share of the General Fund was not sustainable due to economic conditions and budgetary pressures from Medicaid and public education. This report paved the way to budget and funding formula reforms for higher education for the next decade. Other LFC evaluations examined the funding formula in more detail, teacher preparation, the largest community colleges (Central New Mexico and NMSU-Dona Ana), financial aid and the health sciences center.

Corrections. A 2012 LFC Performance Evaluation of Corrections Department initiated collaboration among Pew, Corrections and LFC to evaluate costs and benefits of programs to prepare inmates for release and reduce recidivism. While falling crime rates contributed to falling inmate population in other states like Texas, which were closing prisons, New Mexico's population was still growing. The rate of reincarceration within 36 months of release was about 45 percent. The LFC Evaluation identified approximately 40 different programs and thirty contractors offering services to inmates to prepare for release. Corrections was spending $10 million per year to incarcerate prisoners eligible for release due to lack of a suitable release plan. Also, the department's classification tool was out of date, and the department likely classified inmates at a higher security level than needed for safety or for eventual preparedness for release.

An October 2013 LFC Results First report presented analysis of department programing, including intensive supervision, drug treatment, corrections industries and lower probation officer caseloads. The report stated the department prepared a 32-step program to improve reentry programming.

An October 2019 LFC report, "Corrections Department Capital Outlay," stated that the department could realize significant operating cost savings and improve inmate and staff safety by replacing small, hard to staff, expensive to maintain facilities with new facilities. A June 2020 LFC report, "Inmate Classification," noted progress in revising the classification system, but its effectiveness had still not been validated, and LFC estimated that deviation from scoring guidelines resulted in $28 million per year of avoidable cost.

As of FY22, prison population was down 23 percent from FY16, and the recidivism rate had fallen to 37 percent.

Government Operations. LFC has evaluated a wide range of other agency programs and issues, for example the unemployment insurance system, the state fair, the lottery and gaming oversight, crime rate trends in Albuquerque, services for the homeless, medical malpractice insurance, senior citizen centers, agriculture experiment stations, domestic violence and sexual assault, industrial recruitment and job training, substance abuse treatment, suicide prevention, reducing teen birth rates, public employee benefits and cybersecurity.

Of special note, "State Facilities and Space Utilization," in November 2022 reported that the state was spending $18 million for unused office space with whole buildings or floors unused. This reflected trends in telework, productivity of office workers and tight labor markets. The report recommended development of a state telework policy and revisiting a planned $200 million executive office building adjacent to the state capitol.

The August 2022 LFC Performance Evaluation, "Compensation and Classification Plan and Human Resources (HR) Authority," found HR authority split with rulemaking and policy at the State Personnel Office, but most staff at agencies. Hiring took an average of nine weeks; there were 1,200 job classifications, way too many; and 43 percent of workers quit prior to completing their first year of service. The report identified, "uneven or nonexistent application of employee engagement and exit surveys, studies of workforce adequacy and monitoring of ratios of managers to reporting employees," practices common in other states.

The October 2021 report, "Obtaining and Maximizing Value in State Procurement," found some progress in consolidating administrative functions at the General Services Department since a 2016 LFC report. But sole-source procurements, either emergency procurements or use of price lists, were growing rapidly, from $100 million in FY14 to $314 million in FY21. Also, agencies were overusing exemptions from competitive procurements, especially health-related contracts, for example, for actuarial services or administration of behavioral health services. Proposed legislation sponsored by LFC and Senator Tallman (D-Albuquerque) in 2023 to provide guardrails around sole-source contracts was resisted by the Executive.

So, what is the Value of LFC Evaluations? The LFC evaluations tell a story and present data about the quality of life in New Mexico, what state government is doing to make it better and what changes in government programs would improve outcomes. A story or a picture about what? About whether kids are prepared to learn when they start school, about what kids are learning, particularly can they read and do math, are they graduating college with skills needed in the workforce, about health and health care for New Mexicans (obesity, mental health, drug use and suicide), road conditions, air quality, clean drinking water availability, public safety, protection of children from abuse, etc.

State agencies typically don't answer these questions in a consistent way other than the occasional study or task force report. They want to make things look good anyway. Newspapers every day report on these conditions and what government is doing about them. The LFC budget documents provide a survey of conditions and government activities. But the LFC performance evaluations take a deeper dive not found anywhere else.

So why do the LFC evaluations seem consistently negative? Because New Mexico is at the bottom of many indicators, and we haven't improved much in decades. And even if we were at the top we would want to do better.

The LFC evaluations sometimes flag the need for greater spending to improve New Mexican's conditions. But also, the reports suggest the need to do things differently, to reprioritize, adopt practices that are proven to improve results. Leadership, or lack thereof, also figures prominently in many reports.

In the following seven chapters I review the administrations of New Mexico governors I served under or worked with at the legislature from 1983 to present: Toney Anaya, Garrey Carruthers, Bruce King, Gary Johnson, Bill Richardson, Susana Martinez and Michelle Lujan Grisham. I survey the major initiatives and activities of each administration and the internal and external events that confronted them. I also report my participation and perspective on state government affairs over this period. Did the governors achieve their campaign and inaugural objectives? Did the state improve performance or outcomes for key measures for the economy, health and social welfare during their terms? Were executive and legislative leaders visionary and effective or reactionary and embroiled in petty politics to no lasting effect?

This historical record tees up the last two chapters explaining New Mexico's longstanding ranking at the bottom of many government metrics and why we are last.

# 6

# TONEY ANAYA 1983–1986

Toney Anaya defeated Republican John Irick for New Mexico governor on November 2, 1982. He won by twenty-five thousand votes, or six percent. Anaya, 41, is from Moriarty in Torrance County, a neighbor of the Kings in Stanley. Anaya graduated Georgetown University and American University School of Law and served as attorney general from 1975 to 1978.

He told 2,500 supporters at a victory party at the Albuquerque Convention Center, "I have made no commitments about positions or appointments. I intend to choose the best, most qualified and competent people. If those who have contributed to my campaign have done so with the impression that you are going to get something personally out of this, I have a message for you. You have the wrong candidate."[42] At least half the celebrants that night probably thought "uh-oh." Do you know anyone who worked on a campaign, especially those who went to the election night party, who didn't want something, if not for themselves, for a family member or friend or neighbor or their legislator or even their pet? The *New Mexican* columnist, the irascible Fred McCaffery, wrote that week his off the cuff remark "would come back to haunt him."

Representative Vernon Kerr of Los Alamos the next morning predicted "four years of battle royal with the legislature." He said this view stemmed from Anaya's stint as legislative lobbyist during Governor Bruce King's first administration; "he had to be fired because he didn't get along with legislators."[43]

Quickly, Anaya appointed a transition team led by his nephew Steve Anaya, then 27, a Moriarty Elementary School classmate of my wife Lorin Erramouspe. Anaya also announced a contract with Peat, Marwick, Mitchell, a national management consulting firm, to compile and vet appointment applications and stated a commitment to have women make up at least one third of the appointments to high positions.

In late November out-going DFA Secretary Kay Marr started briefing groups like the Board of Educational Finance and the professional tax study committee about an impending deficit and promised details in the December 1982 revenue estimate to the LFC. (Within a couple weeks, newly elected Attorney General -elect Paul Bardacke hired Marr as Deputy AG.) The December 1 DFA General Fund report called the outlook "bleak," citing recession, federal fund cuts and volatile energy markets. On December 14, Marr reported to LFC a $165 million, or 13.5 percent revenue reduction, with FY 84 revenues estimated at $40 million less than FY83 recurring appropriations. Governor King announced a hiring freeze.

On December 21 Governor Anaya appointed Denise Fort as DFA Secretary. Fort, 31, graduated at the top of her law class at Catholic University and was a lawyer for the Public Interest Research Group. Anaya said she had a strong background in fiscal matters. He also appointed the highly competent CPA, Vickie Fisher, as secretary of the Taxation and Revenue Department. The transition and 1983 legislative session planning continued with a focus on education issues and government reorganization including a proposed constitutional amendment to move the State Department of Education and Board of Education to governor's appointment, combination of the elected State Corporation Commission with the appointed Public Service Commission and creation of a new Department of Water from the State Engineer's Office. Long-time officials like the renowned State Engineer (since 1955) Steve Reynolds and the 22-year School Superintendent Leonard Delayo were not supporters. He also wrote to all board and commission members to submit their resignation but invited them to reapply, even if their term hadn't expired. Past practice was replacement of commission members had to be for reasons like malfeasance.

Meanwhile all fiscal parties began conversations about tax increases and budget cuts to solve the fiscal crisis.

On January 1, Anaya was inaugurated governor. He called for a "New Beginning" and appealed for New Mexicans to unite. He said the "keystones of his administration would be educational opportunity, economic growth and social justice" and highlighted natural resources and environmental protection. Ominously, the *Journal* headlined the next day, "Cabinet Nominees Draw Scrutiny." Senator Ron Olguin and "Doc" Weiler, director of the Association of Commerce and Industry said the same thing: "I don't know these people."

Fortune favored Governor Anaya with the election of Raymond Sanchez as Speaker of the House replacing Gene Samberson (D-Hobbs), leader of a coalition with Republicans in 1981 and 1982. Representative Max Coll (D-Santa Fe) paved the way, switching from Republican to Democrat.

In the last few minutes of the 60-day session, the House and Senate passed a conference committee version of a tax bill, raising $112 million, by comfortable margins, 40-29 and 25-16, respectively. Increases included: personal income tax rates up 30 percent; the corporate income tax rate up 20 percent; oil and gas school tax up 0.5 percent to 3.15 percent; gross receipts tax rate up 0.5 percent to four percent; and insurance premium tax up 0.5 percent to three percent. The governor's agreement to sign a $140 million capital outlay bill seemed to advance the tax bill in the Senate. To restore General Fund reserves, FY83 (current year) appropriations were cut two percent and $55 million of road appropriations from prior years were shifted to Severance Tax Bonds (STBs) with an increase in STB maturity from five to ten years. The FY 84 budget was flat except for a two percent increase for public education for enrollment growth. There were no pay raises. The appropriators and tax experts in the legislature knew what they were doing; they knew where to find the low hanging fruit, which wasn't so hard after the 1981 Big Mac tax cut and years of inflation driven spending increases.

In FY82 net personal income taxes were only $15 million, plenty of room for an increase.

The Senate finally confirmed Alex Mercure as Economic Development and Tourism (ED&T) secretary. He triggered a Senate Rules subpoena for farmers loan records from his time as an official in the Carter administration, The legislature authorized a community college in Santa Fe, new bridge construction in Albuquerque, moved investment of the Severance Tax Permanent Fund from the Treasurer to the State Investment Council but failed to pass a lottery bill.

During the 1983 interim the governor planned for another try at education reform and a tax increase, but press commentary showed political headwinds. On April 10 David Steinberg, *Journal* columnist wrote, "Anaya is all politics. Anaya is enamored with the seat of power." He described a workaholic, self-important, ambitious governor using lawyers to run the government. Fred McCaffery of the *New Mexican* wrote that a state travel freeze should begin with the governor who in two summer months traveled to Washington, DC, Fresno, Pennsylvania, Corpus Christi, Phoenix and Puerto Rico. The *Journal* profiled executive aide Shirley Scarafiotti; her nickname was "Jaws."[44] On October 16 the *Journal* editors commented on the elevation of Bob McNeil from the Department of Health and Environment to chief of staff: "Governor Anaya jumped with both feet into the business of being the state chief asserting at the outset that he would be personally in control and personally responsible for every detail of government's functioning." Steinberg wrote in November that a tax increase would be essential to the Anaya agenda and that 1984 would be the education session. On January 1, 1984, Steinberg wrote, "Toney Anaya hit the ground running in his first year and state government is still reeling. ... Anaya's modus operandi is to make the executive branch, in particular the chief executive, the catalyst for change. By doing so, the governor is shedding consensus from lawmakers."

Mr. Abbey goes to the Roundhouse. In January 1983 in the wake of a marital separation, I moved to a farm I purchased in 1981 in Medanales, a small community 40 miles north of Santa Fe on the Rio Chama: a narrow adobe on a ten-acre strip from the *capilla* to the river, two-foot walls, a dirt roof, wood heat and one faucet. It was a beautiful place with wonderful neighbors, and, with their help, I began to rebuild a home on nights and weekends. On Easter Sunday I returned from a trip to Tucson to find the bridge over the Chama on fire. It was a state highway bridge made of creosote timbers, perhaps set on fire as a local employment project or to warn the *gabachos* to keep out. My commute grew a half hour each way, although the drive up the county road along the bosque was spectacular; you could see iconic Pedernal rising above the cottonwoods the last few miles before the El Rito highway.

In September 1983, I applied for a job as economist at LFC advertised in the *New Mexican*. A retired executive from a Midwest steel company who was volunteering with LFC on the search interviewed me. Later, no one remembered him but me, and this will make sense below. LFC hired a former State Department employee, Ed Howard, but passed my resume to DFA. I started on November 30, with an office by the east stairs on the top, fourth floor of the state capitol, widely known as the Roundhouse.[45]

It was an exciting place to work. Before the conversion of the State Library to legislative offices in 1999, there was hubbub at the Roundhouse year-round. DFA office of secretary, budget division and management analysis were crammed into the fourth floor between the secretary of state and lieutenant governor. DFA also included a team of new policy aides that replaced the old State Planning Office. They were all women, working in a boiler room next to the secretary's office including Marg Elliston, wife of former Oklahoma Senator and UNM professor Fred Harris, Susan Tixier, girlfriend of Natural Resources Secretary Brant Calkin, Duffy Rodriguez and Debbie Romero who both later served as DFA secretary and Joann Marquez of the Santa Rosa clan. DFA had an unusual management analysis division director; when he died, Dan Weaks said they didn't need to use embalming fluid at the mortuary; he was already pickled. LFC and the Legislative Education Study Committee (LESC) were on the first floor along with press offices. The wire services, major papers and all the TV stations had permanent staff on the north side of the first floor.

11. Son Clayton, Robert Abbey and David Abbey on the east side of the capitol, August,1984. Today, the Bradford pears are as tall as the capitol.

DFA was supposed to have two economists, but they both quit in the Fall in the wake of the 1982 revenue shortfall. *They never fire a revenue estimator for being too low*, as I would later learn. I had to learn quickly. In my first couple of weeks, Associated Press (AP) reporter Bill Feather asked me to explain the latest monthly General Fund Report which was a bread-and-butter story for him. He could file by mid-morning and be at the Bull Ring next door by 11.

Feather realized I barely knew the difference between the General Fund and the Road Fund, but I was a studious, quick learner and brought expertise in energy markets that proved useful to forecasting and explaining a big share of state revenue. TRD had a strong team of fiscal economists and tax experts led by Jim Nunns with Janet Peacock and Carolyn Lindberg. They too wondered why I was there, but gradually I proved my worth.

1984 Session: Failure of a Penny for Education. Governor Anaya proposed a one percent increase in the gross receipts tax (GRT) for an increase of $174 million to fund an education reform plan including an increase in the school year from 182 to 190 days. Every day, his appointees and school lobbyists wore blue ribbons with a penny taped to it. In my inexperience, I figured there would be some sort of compromise and maybe he'd get half a percent. But simple counting showed the Republicans only needed two Democrats in the Senate to defeat any increase. Senator Les Houston (D-Albuquerque) announced his opposition before the 30-day session started, and Senator Tim Jennings (D-Roswell) and Senator Harry McAdams (D-Hobbs) were unlikely. The session ended without passage of a tax increase or a budget. I learned a minor lesson about attention to detail. Senator Jimmy Rogers (R-Las Cruces) claimed recurring revenues were underestimated, because the estimate didn't include reversions of unspent appropriations to the General Fund. Some simple research validated this claim, and the revenue estimate was adjusted upward by five million. An eight-day special session in March produced a compromise between the House and Senate with modest budget growth but no tax increase. [46]

In April Secretary of Natural Resources Brant Calkin resigned, commenting that Shirley Scarafiotti blocked access to the fourth floor. The LFC and Senator "Smitty" Eoff (R- Gallup) got a lot of mileage out a tourism marketing trip to Houston. ED&T purchased hams for $195 and turkeys for $95 for the reception, and a columnist wondered why they couldn't have gone to Sadie's restaurant. [47] Governor Anaya reportedly sought the appointment of Fred Harris as UNM president, but the regents selected Tom Farer, a New Jersey law professor instead. He didn't last long. In August Denise Fort moved to the Environmental Improvement Division with Labor Secretary Dr. Dan Lopez replacing her at DFA.

Corruption reared its early head with the indictments of Chief Investment Officer Phil Troutman and Deputy Treasurer Ken Johnson for soliciting a two-thousand-dollar campaign contribution from Irving Trust which was seeking the state's custody bank contract. Officials of the state fiscal agent, First National Bank of Albuquerque, tipped off the feds. In October a *Journal* investigative reporter reported the FBI was investigating Anaya's purchase of a farm in Pennsylvania linked to real estate developer Amrep's efforts to obtain pardons for four executives.

Bill Hume, columnist for the *Journal* (who Governor Richardson hired as a policy advisor), wrote in August, "Despite going on two years of verbal bobbing and twisting, despite much high-sounding rhetoric about goals and ideals, business as usual and backroom dealings and politics-based back scratching have emerged as an irrefutable part of the Anaya administration. ... How pathetic we have degenerated to a reverse-screen rerun of the Anaya AG years. ... Shameless chasing of the national Democratic spotlight has been the hallmark of his administration."Yikes. Anaya told *Journal* reporter John Robertson," I really feel that part of the reason New Mexico is 42nd in per capita income and always at the bottom end of the scale is because we have never had effective leadership at the state level, and we haven't because the setup is guaranteed to give us a weak governor." Double yikes.

1985 Session/Confrontation and Chaos. The 1984 general election brought a shift to the Republicans in both chambers with one quarter of representatives and one third of senators newly elected. Coalitions formed in both chambers with Senator Houston leading the Senate (23-19) and Representative Ron Gentry (D - Valencia County) voting to return Representative Gene Samberson as Speaker (36-34).

New Mexico was the fourth largest gas producer in 1985, and natural gas markets were beginning deregulation with spot market prices below regulated prices delivered under contract by the two major pipelines, El Paso Natural Gas and Transwestern. In February Kerr McGee shut down its uranium mine and mill in Grants, a "death blow to the community." The Economic Development Department over the course of 1985 was working on recruiting a General

Motors Saturn plant and an aircraft factory to Albuquerque. Governor Anaya's budget recommendation continued a push for education reform, but Jay Miller, deputy director of the New Mexico Education Association, said, "We've matured as an organization. We've seen that we can't continue to say everything is okay with education and all we need are higher salaries."[48]

The *Journal* reported on February 24 the legislature had passed only three bills and devoted much of its time to "internal power struggles and to a feud with the Governor."[49] The Senate wanted to defund the LESC, and Governor Anaya vetoed the appropriation for LFC, which Bill Hume said was "usually the focal point of legislative-executive fights." Coalition members wanted a 20 percent increase for LFC to expand its audits and agency oversight. Hume quoted Governor Ed Mechem in 1962 asserting, "LFC was up to its ears in partisan politics." The legislature sent the vetoed bills back to the governor, they were vetoed again, and the *Journal*'s Steinberg said, "Mediation Needed in the State Capitol."

Several other measures were highly contentious. The US Department of Education advised that the state's method of taking credit for local revenue was inequitable between school districts with high Federal impact aid revenue for Native American students (notably, Gallup, Zuni and Central (Shiprock)) and districts with high property tax revenue from oil and gas (like Eunice, Jal and Carlsbad). Amoco pushed for severance tax relief for incremental oil production for tertiary oil production from carbon dioxide floods. Both these measures posed significant risk of lower General Fund revenue, and DFA and LFC analysts were in the thick of the fray with fiscal impact reports and analysis. The "Berry fix" from Representative Dan Berry (R- Jal) was an interim solution to impact aid. The Amoco bill failed with Representative Bob Corn (R- Roswell) and independent oil producers questioning the tax break for Big Oil.

Senate Finance Chair Jack Morgan (R-Farmington) sought legislation to create an authority and state investment in a rail project to the Star Lake coal field in northwest New Mexico. The last Saturday of the session, Senator Victor Marshall (R- Albuquerque) filibustered Morgan's bill for over two hours until the noon adjournment. The gallery was packed. Most folks had never seen a filibuster to say nothing of a freshman challenge to senior fiscal leadership of the same party.

Senator Morgan said the filibuster was "juvenile," and Representative Sandel said he was "irritated," because a compromise on funding the legislative agencies was in the works. A $1.369 billion budget for agencies and education passed earlier, but the capital outlay bill died on adjournment along with funding for legislative service agencies. Clay Buchanan, the long-time director of the Legislative Council Service, announced his retirement in June.

In the coming weeks the governor and key legislators seemed to pretend they didn't want or need a special session. Republican leaders said they were exploring funding legislative services with private contributions. But a *Journal* editorial on March 24 called for a special session to fund the legislative service agencies, and Anaya really wanted more funding for education.

For the next few months state government affairs were on the front page every day. Auditor Al Romero reported that emergency funding for flooding in Taos County went to family members of local officials and implicated governor's aide John Ramming. Names and payments were featured prominently. Leonard Delayo resigned as superintendent of education. The community assistance council granted $100 thousand to build a chopstick factory in Velarde. Day care funding was cut off. The State Investment Council wrestled with disinvestment in apartheid-controlled South Africa. Charlie Crowder was pursuing a real estate project and land trade in Santa Teresa (legislators got in on that one). Accreditation of the state hospital was at risk. The popular Republican leader Representative Bob Moran of Hobbs had a cardiac on May 5 and died. There was growing awareness of the AIDS epidemic.

Governor Anaya and legislators agreed to fund legislative agencies for $2.5 million with only a three percent increase for LFC and assurance that regular Democrats were reasonably represented on the interim legislative committees. Governor Anaya called a one-week session for May 11. The "feed bill" funding legislative agencies was passed and signed in an hour, but an $18 million supplemental school funding bill stalled. In the middle of this, Troutman and Johnson were convicted of bribery and quickly resigned. It seems odd that Troutman and Johnson remained on the payroll so long and that Governor Anaya said he was "surprised" by the verdict. A $149 million capital outlay bill passed on the last day, but the Senate did not take up supplemental school funding. Immediately

Governor Anaya and his press aide David Roybal began the conversation about a second special session on school funding.

At a second special session on June 9, the senate immediately voted to adjourn 22-19; the house deadlocked on adjournment 35-35, but Sunday morning voted to adjourn by voice vote.

Later that month Senator Francisco 'El Commanche" Gonzalez (D-Taos) resigned following a rape conviction, and Senator Bud Hebert (R-Artesia) was criticized for owning stock in oil pipelines as he pushed for tax breaks for oil production.

Meanwhile the DFA spent months on a controversial $330 million Severance Tax Bond issue that included advance refunding of approximately $180 million of outstanding STBs. The negotiated deal was advanced by EF Hutton and resulted in modest interest rate savings of one to two percent but precluded a subsequent refunding if interest rates declined from the seven percent level, which they did. Hutton and bond counsel earned fees in proportion to the extraordinary size of the deal. The *Journal* reported that Anaya 1982 campaign manager Tim Kraft was fund-raising in New York concurrently with a September 1984 bond closing in New York.[50] Deputy Treasurer Jim Steward and Auditor Al Romero raised technical issues about the deal.[51]

Oil and gas loans took their toll on the New Mexico banking industry. The state had almost one billion dollars in certificates of deposit in New Mexico banks and savings and loans. On July 19, Deputy Treasurer Jim Steward withdrew $41 million of uninsured deposits from Moncor in Lea County, and the next day the bank failed. Later that fall, Steward and the auditor reported that financial institutions were not in compliance with collateral requirements.

In August, Senate President Les Houston switched from Democrat to Republican giving the Republicans a 22-20 majority. In September Governor Anaya fired health secretary Dr. Fitzhugh Mullan, and Secretary Mercure resigned. Ramming and four others were indicted for misuse of Taos disaster funding.

In mid-September, LFC economist Ed Howard, Senator Jack Morgan and I attended a natural gas conference in San Francisco. On September 20 LFC heard presentations on the energy outlook. A Citibank expert said oil and natural gas prices could fall ten percent which would reduce general fund revenue by about $50 million. A *Journal* editorial said tax increases, especially the gross receipts tax, are a must given agency budget requests submitted on September 1.

On October 3 the *New Mexican* reported that Howard was under investigation as a Soviet spy and had escaped intensive FBI surveillance in Santa Fe and fled.

Ed Howard and the First Killing of David Abbey. He was a friend of mine. We were the same age, had young children, shared an interest in international affairs (Howard having worked for the Peace Corps in Latin America and supposedly for the State Department), worked together, traveled together a few times on state business, had a common network of friends who worked at the capitol, and favored a tan poplin suit in the summer. He was *coyote* (half Hispanic) with roots in Catron County. By accounts of his LFC directors, Howard was smart and capable and an asset to the legislature.

*Washington Post* security reporter David Wise wrote what seemed to be the definitive book about Howard: *The Spy Who Got Away: Inside Story of Edward Lee Howard who Betrayed His Country's Secrets and Escaped to Moscow.* It's clear Wise had a lot of cooperation from security sources providing fascinating details about the inner workings of the CIA's recruitment and training procedures and the activities of the Soviet division. I assume they all were eager to finger Howard and declare case closed. The frontispiece quotes a US intelligence official: "It wasn't just the human assets. It was far deeper than that. All the technical assets were rolled up. The danger was tremendous. He closed us down over there."

Meanwhile, Vitaly Yurchenko, deputy KGB chief for North America, defected to the US on July 1, 1985, and quickly fingered a guy named Robert who could only have been Howard. Howard joined the CIA in 1980 and was training in the clandestine service for posting to Moscow under State Department credentials. He was supposed to run Adolf Tolkachev, a Soviet defense researcher and prized

CIA asset. In June 1985 the Soviets caught and expelled Tolkachev's previous CIA handler.

According to Wise, in 1983 the CIA fired Howard for multiple failures of lie detector tests, supposedly related to marijuana use and maybe coke and psychedelics and petty theft. He knew enough the CIA figured he needed a soft landing, like the LFC job in New Mexico I applied for. Wise reported a disgruntled, embittered Howard who in 1984 and 1985 flirted with illicit alien contacts, made suspicious trips to Vienna and behaved erratically.

Wise reported in mid-September American assets were saying Tolkachev was caught, and Howard must have realized he was under surveillance. On September 22, he fled and embarrassed the FBI.

The big problem is that Yurchenko, the high-level official who fingered Howard, allegedly missed his girlfriend and redefected to the USSR on November 2. Wise devoted half a dozen pages to examining Yurchenko's bona fides. He acknowledged Howard couldn't have served up most of the exposures of assets he initially was blamed for. Wise said Howard insisted he did not betray the US before he fled.

The US molehunters must have figured something didn't fit. In 1993 Aldrich Ames, the CIA's head of Soviet counterintelligence, was arrested for espionage, and he said he compromised everyone he knew of. In 2001 the FBI's counter-intelligence leader Robert Hanssen was arrested; he'd been spying for the Soviets since 1979. David Wise wrote in 2015 that, "Howard was blamed for Tolkachev's unmasking and execution, although Ames too had betrayed the researcher's identity." (The same thing happened to Clayton Lonetree, a Navajo Marine guard at the US embassy caught in a "honeypot entrapment", accused of betraying identities of US assets and sentenced to 30 years at Ft. Leavenworth. But after nine years imprisonment, he was released after Ames' admissions.) Wise said some CIA officials are convinced there is a fourth mole not yet identified. The search continues.[52]

Too bad for Howard, he "fell" down the stairs and died in Moscow in 2002.

The Howard case was a blow for me. Again, Howard was a good friend and his deception, like others in my life, was painful. After a bitter custody fight, I had my young children for a two-month visitation. As a single parent living an hour from work, I was wound up tighter than a clock. In hindsight, one night on the San Francisco trip in September 1985 while heading to visit a friend north of Golden Gate Park panhandle, I was inexplicably followed from the bus stop and ran through the streets. The weekend Howard fled, a helicopter flew low over my house in Medanales. My phone was tapped. Years later at the Saints and Sinners in Espanola, a fellow told me he had investigated me for years. Important words for a career at a capitol: *Just because you're paranoid doesn't mean they're not after you.*

I wasn't the only one that was defensive or paranoid. On September 21, Governor Anaya told Democratic women in Las Cruces that the "press is quick to scrutinize the finances of Democratic campaigns and the records of Democratic administrations while not similarly scrutinizing Republicans." [53]

1985 wrapped up with one more blow to New Mexico. Treasurer Earl Hartley was convicted of a misdemeanor for using $4,300 of funds from a national treasurers' conference for personal use. Bernalillo County Treasurer James Lewis was appointed to succeed him, New Mexico's first African American statewide public official. The 1986 campaign was underway with at least six Republicans running for governor or lieutenant governor, including several senators.

The *Journal*'s top ten stories of the year revolved around the Roundhouse: #1, Ed Howard, #4 fighting between the governor and legislature, #5 Senator "Commanche" Gonzalez, # 6 John Ramming and #10 Hartley.

1986: Legislative Truce, Oil and Gas Collapse and Cash Flow Crisis. On January 5, the New Mexico Museum of Natural History, the dinosaur museum, opened to great excitement. However, Governor Anaya drew attention for intervening in selection of a vendor for the museum shop. Economic development activities included luring an aircraft factory to Albuquerque. Senators Fidel and Altamirano proposed a bill to purchase the "Maytag mansion" on a ridge north of Santa Fe for a new executive residence.

The 30-day session started with a focus again on education reform and taxes. Governor Anaya and the legislative Public School Reform Committee joined forces for $2,500 teacher raises, longer school days, stiffer graduation requirements and greater remedial efforts. The LFC wanted a bare bones budget bill with additional school spending in a supplemental, or "junior," appropriation bill dependent on tax increases. The Saudis rumbled about production increases, and DFA cut the oil price forecast $2/barrel (bbl) to $22.40/bbl. Both budget bills were moving, the House passed a bill, the Senate trimmed it, the House passed a $156 million Junior bill, Anaya threatened a veto and met with conferees and leaders on education reform. A $150 million tax increase finally passed, including a one percent increase in the GRT rate, higher personal income tax rates and replacement of the franchise tax with a corporate income tax. This was only enough to increase recurring appropriations $23 million, less than two percent.

With the 1986 session over, all eyes shifted to collapsing energy markets. On March 6, El Paso Natural Gas (EPNG) announced a 40 cent/mcf cut in prices for natural gas sold under long term contracts. EPNG reported sales of New Mexico gas to California were down 60 percent over the previous year. The AP reported "State Budget Reels," and the *Journal* reported "Oil Price Slide Imperils State Budget." At an LFC meeting on March 25 DFA Deputy Secretary Turpen acknowledged the weakness but proposed to wait a few months to see how markets shake out. Representative Sandel told Turpen to bring hard numbers to an April meeting, and Senator Morgan said, "We are in fiscal crisis. ... we blew it." Turpen and I flew to Farmington to an El Paso Natural Gas Co. public forum on natural gas. In response to Morgan, I tried to defend oil and gas price estimates as plausible instead of saying the market changed. Morgan went for my jugular. I felt like someone was strangling me with my tie from behind while I was trying to answer questions. I can still see Sandel in slow motion, elbowing Morgan, "give the kid some slack."

In April El Paso Natural Gas sold its 17-story tower in downtown El Paso. On April 16 Western Democratic Governors, including Anaya, held an oil summit in Dallas and urged President Reagan to impose an oil import fee. Oil fell to $10/bbl. Drilling rigs fell from 78 in 1985 to 16. House Majority Leader Dick Minzner (D-Albuquerque) called for a special session. DFA Secretary Lopez described language in the General Provisions section of HB2 that he said allowed the DFA to direct agencies to cut spending in accordance with available revenue. On April 30 DFA provided a revenue estimate to LFC down $77 million to $164 million with oil in a range $10 to $16/bbl and natural gas in a range $1.50 to $2/mcf.

On May 1 Governor Anaya removed long-serving museum regent, Cleta Downey, because the museums imposed a two dollar admission fee. On May 16 Governor Anaya proposed an $80 million solvency plan with two percent spending cuts, expanding use of general fund reserves and fund transfers to the general fund.

The special session drumbeat accelerated with Senator Mike Alarid (D-Albuquerque) questioning the governor's authority to make cuts, and Morgan saying the governor and Senator Houston are postponing the day lawmakers will have to grapple with the crisis. On May 29 Attorney General Bardacke told LFC a special session appeared unavoidable and promised a legal opinion on the Executive proposal. Deputy Treasurer David King said even with the Anaya plan the state might still run out of money by January. Also, LFC members discussed a statute providing a felony if the DFA Secretary or the State Treasurer issues checks that bounce. The next day DFA Secretary Dan Lopez said a special session was possible, perhaps in November. Anaya told a *Journal* reporter that Bardacke "should stick to legal advice and let our financial people give the financial advice and we'd get along better." Lopez told me recently Anaya asked him to fire me. Was it then? Could it have been the second killing, if I didn't know at the time?

On Tuesday June 3 Garrey Carruthers won the Republican nomination for governor. On Wednesday UNM bought out President Tom Farer's contract. On June 6 the Public Accountancy Board took up a request from GSD Secretary Lithgow to revoke the licenses of State Auditor Al Romero and three aides (including future LFC deputy Manu Patel) for violating professional standards.

More important, on June 6 Attorney General Bardacke presented Opinion 86-2 on the executive proposal to address the revenue shortfall. The opinion, directed to LFC, DFA and the treasurer, was signed also by deputy AG Kay Marr and five assistant attorneys general. The opinion was masterful and provided guidance for the legal framework to manage fiscal volatility for decades to come. Simply, the executive can't ignore a fiscal crisis and expect somebody else, probably a future legislature, to fix it. And the executive can't cut spending or move money around or use special revenue funds without legislative authorization. The opinion galled Governor Anaya, because former DFA Secretary Marr dumped a revenue shortfall in his lap in November 1982.

The 1986 opinion begins with the acknowledgement that there is little legal precedent on most issues and sorts out the problem between, "1) cash flow problems and 2) underfunding of appropriations caused by the projected revenue shortfall." The opinion identifies a state statute, section 6-10-42, that temporarily authorizes use of allotment accounts to cover General Fund cash requirements as long as they are restored at the end of the fiscal year; and clarifies that a violation of section 8-6-7 occurs if expenditures are made without sufficient balances in those accounts.

LFC voted 9-2 on June 6 to recommend a $109 million package of tax increases, spending cuts and fund transfers with a special session prior to June 30. Governor Anaya said the LFC plan was like his and he was lobbying for it in a "soft sort of way." He also criticized the AG opinion saying it was intended to "make life miserable for me" and change the ground rules the state has been operating under for decades. The *Journal* editorial board, changing its tune from May, called for a special session before "crisis becomes chaos." On June 17 Anaya called for a special session on June 23.

The *Journal* on Monday morning June 23 reported Senator Eddie Lopez was working to unseat Les Houston as senate president Pro Tem. At noon that day, four Republican senators, Morgan, Budagher, Vandergriff and Martin, voted to dump Houston for the venerable Senator Ike Smalley (D-Deming). They said Houston led them down the primrose path, acted like a surrogate governor, and used an iron hand to make them vote in lock step. On Tuesday the tax and spending bills passed and were signed by the governor for the ten pm news. The tax bill passed the house 55-12 and the Senate 21-20. Senator Houston denounced two of the Republican senators, and former majority leader Bill Valentine expressed bitter sentiments about violating deals.

In September, Anaya had a 12 percent approval rating. Thanksgiving eve he commuted death sentences of four inmates.

Anaya ended the year signaling as key accomplishments 1986 school reform, a pro-environment record and appointments of women. Anaya said his problem was outspoken liberalism at a time the country was trending conservative. He acknowledged that, "he spent far more time on details that ultimately had nothing to do with policymaking," and that it was "ill-advised" to characterize New Mexico as a "banana republic" in 1985.[54] To me, six secretaries of health, the conviction of top elected officials and appointees, failed special sessions, denial of the 1986 cash flow crisis, and controversy, bickering and finger pointing were his hallmarks.

# 7

# Garrey Carruthers 1987–1990

G arrey Carruthers grew up on a farm on the Animas River in Red Hill, north of Aztec. He graduated NMSU in agricultural economics, stayed for a master's degree, then earned a PhD in economics at Iowa State University and returned to NMSU as professor of ag economics. He served as Deputy Secretary of the Interior for Land and Resources from 1981 to 1984.

Carruthers is tall, handsome, very friendly, has a great sense of humor. He likes golf, Ford mustangs, politics and country music. His wife Kathy is often by his side. Carruthers still has a great following in New Mexico, especially southern and rural New Mexico after serving as chancellor of New Mexico State University from 2013 to 2018. He was elected governor with 53 percent of the vote, the first Republican elected since Dave Cargo in 1970. Republicans also won attorney general and land commissioner for the first time in half a century.

Carruthers immediately selected former LFC Director Maralyn Budke as chief of staff to universal acclaim. Budke in effect volunteered for the more than full time duty, taking an annual one-dollar salary in order to travel on the state airplane.

On inauguration day Carruthers drew praise from former governors King and Anaya and Treasurer James Lewis. In contrast to Anaya, the *Journal* reported "most appointments win high praise," notably Willard Lewis for DFA, Democrat Vickie Fisher retained as TRD Secretary and Health and Environment Secretary Larry Gordon. Gordon "delighted" environmentalists who feared Carruthers' past under Reagan and Interior Secretary Jim Watt.

Willard Lewis selected Duffy Rodriguez and me, civil servants, to serve in his management team along with appointed division directors including the capable John Gasparich as Budget Director. Lewis, a native of Jal in far southeast Lea County, a UNM grad and CPA, and official in the Department of Interior during the Nixon administration, became my first great mentor.

To begin the session, the Senate, tied 21R-21D, elected Republican Senator Les Houston and Democrat Senator Manny Aragon to be co-presidents of the Senate. The Supreme Court quickly rejected that arrangement, and then the Senate reelected Senator Ike Smalley (D-Deming) as president. For the state of the state address, Governor Carruthers emphasized the themes of his campaign— economic development, streamlined state government and improved education. (Sound familiar?) Carruthers used phrases like "positive attitude," "upbeat" and "can-do."[55] Remarkably, in his budget recommendation Carruthers, billed as a conservative candidate, recommended $115 million of tax increases plus retention of $59 million of additional personal income tax revenues resulting from the federal Tax Reform Act of 1986 (which expanded federal taxable income and in turn state taxable income, because the state definition of taxable income piggybacks (mimics) the federal definitions). Carruthers also advocated merit pay for teachers and cost-savings from delaying smaller class sizes except kindergarten.

I learned a lesson about sticking around that session. I covered Senate Finance for DFA. One evening, at the end of a long agenda with only a memorial by Senator Benavidez (D-Albuquerque) to return the US to the gold standard remaining, I split for the Bull Ring for a nightcap. A few minutes later, SFC staff walked in and told me SFC just passed Senator Lopez' bill to rebate the $60 million federal personal income tax pickup back to New Mexico taxpayers.

Senator Aragon's favorite story from that session related to budget negotiations with DFA, Willard Lewis and Tom Hoover, and Senator Houston and other Republicans regarding the size of the budget. They asked Manny if they could get him anything and he said, "How about a beer?" The Republican took a bathroom break to discuss strategy, and Manny said, "1776. They're patriots, they're bound to go for it." And they did settle on an appropriation level of approximately $1.776 billion.

In March the legislature passed a $99 million tax package and retained the federal pickup, the third tax increase in 13 months. The budget grew five percent. The legislature also passed a bill to create a tax stabilization reserve and limit the increase in the executive budget recommendation to an amount adjusted for inflation. The legislature passed four bills consolidating energy, natural resources and highway department functions. The legislature also passed HB 360 sponsored by Representative Barbara Casey (D-Chaves) and Representative Charley Winters (R-San Juan) that converted the severance tax on natural gas from a unit tax of 16.3 cents/mcf to 3.75 percent of value, phased in over three years. With average natural gas prices down almost 50 percent, the unit tax represented an onerous 15 to 20 percent of the value leading to premature abandonment and lower drilling activity. But in the near term the bill reduced severance tax bonding capacity. For years this bill was a sore spot for Representative Ben Lujan (D-Santa Fe). He would ask me to calculate the lost severance tax revenue and lost funding for capital outlay projects and imply the DFA and the oil and gas industry pulled a fast one on the legislature.

With Budke at the helm of government operations, Carruthers implemented management by objectives (MBO) in the larger agencies. MBO was pioneered in a 1954 book by Peter Drucker for business applications. It entails setting goals for the CEO and key managers and objectives for their staff. It includes quantification and measurement of results and periodic performance reviews. In the Carruthers application, departments held planning sessions with staff to determine mission statements, goals and objectives and appropriate measures. With a 21st-century lens, performance-based budgeting looks like a descendant of MBO.

Carruthers and Budke also required agency heads to submit weekly activity reports. In turn, Lewis required these reports from his management team. This is a best practice for any government manager. My weekly activity report to LFC members and legislative leaders garnered a growing following, with bootlegged copies required reading among lobbyists and fourth-floor staff.

A June 28 *Journal* retrospective of Carruthers first six months described a low-key agenda with the honeymoon not over yet and a confident Carruthers getting good marks. But Senator Aragon said, "he has yet to make an impression," and "he basically doesn't make waves."

On June 30 there was a two-day special session to appropriate $11 million of STBs for land acquisition for the Federal superconducting super collider contingent on selection of New Mexico as the project site. In the fall New Mexico was not one of eight state finalists, and the project was never constructed anyway.

Other significant events in New Mexico in 1987 included the location of TMC, a Greyhound bus manufacturing plant in Roswell, a dramatic escape from the state penitentiary in Santa Fe with a hijacked helicopter landing in the yard, and the Supreme Court ruling in favor of Texas for under delivery of Pecos River water. There was more turmoil at the state hospital with the beating of the hospital director by an employee. The director had terminated ten percent of the hospital's 900 employees. The AG ruled collective bargaining with state employees was not permitted under state law. Natural gas pipelines abrogated contracts with producers, because deregulated spot market prices were far below contract prices leading to protracted litigation. Mike Gallagher, a *Journal* investigative reporter, started a series critical of Corrections procurement practices.

Governor Carruthers met with legislative leaders in November to discuss the 1988 legislative agenda and indicated there was a sense of "optimism." In the year-end wrap-up the *Journal's* John Robertson said the governor has been, "gregarious, enthusiastic and unfailingly optimistic."

In January 1988 LFC without precedent failed to reach consensus and submit a budget recommendation. Senator Houston tried unsuccessfully to return as Senator President; the *Journal* called him a "tireless political plotter." The *Journal*'s John Robertson said the Senate's coalition politics were "perplexing." Governor Carruthers proposed a 3.1 percent spending increase, no tax increase, a moratorium on severance tax bond projects, merit pay for public employees and a constitutional amendment to limit state expenditure like Colorado's TABER amendment. I staffed Senator Victor Marshall (R-Albuquerque) on the constitutional amendment, and former TRD Secretary and lobbyist Franklin Jones took it upon himself to provide what seemed like endless, nitpicky language improvements. Jones appropriately said we'd better get it right, because it might pass and become a subject of regret.

At the 1988 30-day session, the legislature passed a budget with a 4.3 percent increase, including a big increase to open new prisons and contract for a women's' prison in Grants, 1.6 percent raises for school employees, four percent raises for higher ed employees, a one-time merit bonus payment of $739 for state employees and funding for smaller class sizes. A Senate amendment to the budget introduced the concept of "sanding", reducing amounts across the board by 1.5 percent to fund pay raises. Other measures created a new Youth Authority, authorized interstate banking and welfare reform and permanently repealed higher income personal income tax rebates which were suspended in 1986. But the capital bill had drafting errors and died on adjournment. Carruthers immediately called a special session for capital outlay at noon the same day. A $126 million package with General Fund, STB and general obligation bond projects passed the next afternoon.

The *Journal*'s post-session wrap-up declared, "Peace returned to the capital with adjournment of the legislature." Again, the governor and most Democrats got much of what they wanted. Carruthers said few legislative sessions had been more productive; a few Democrats again said Carruthers didn't ask for much.[56]

The *Journal* described how budget development works in March. The budget "changes only in small increments," and the governor's budget isn't that different than the legislature's final version. "Most of the fighting involves no more than a fraction—maybe five percent of the total. ... That's because the legislature, the governor, Republicans and Democrats agree on most of the programs supported by state dollars."[57]

In March LFC Chair Max Coll and Vice Chair Ben Altamirano asked the Supreme Court to nullify 16 line-item vetoes in HB2 claiming that the governor sought to usurp the legislative power of appropriation and to use the funds in a different way than intended by the legislature. Carruthers hired former governor Jack Campbell and his son Mike to represent him. On April 20 the Supreme Court ruled that 11 of 12 line-item vetoes were valid. Although at the time perhaps viewed as a defeat for the legislature, *Coll v. Carruthers* better defined the implementation of the line-item veto and language conditions in the General Appropriation Act that have served the legislature and executive well for decades. The veto is the power to destroy, not to create. If language in a contingent appropriation is vetoed, the appropriation is void, the money goes away. The legislature can attach reasonable conditions to appropriations but may not micromanage executive functions. Over the years the Executive has complained that language in HB 2 is unreasonable, and sometimes ignores vetoed contingencies. They tend to get away with it, because legislators rarely want to sue the governor. But generally, such disputes are not common.

Other 1988 events of interest included the replacement of economic development secretary Nick Jenkins with combative Santa Fe businessman John Dendahl and the retirement of popular Health and Environment Secretary Larry Gordon, replaced by his deputy Carla Muth, a nurse and protégé of Maralyn Budke. Mental health issues garnered growing public attention abetted by Senator Domenici and the strife at the Las Vegas state hospital. Muth fired the administrator at Las Vegas though advocates held him in regard. The teachers' unions mounted a persistent drumbeat for a special session to boost teacher pay. In November Carruthers expressed interest in Representative Dick Minzner's bill to allow school districts to impose a two or four mill property tax with provisions to recapture some revenue from the richest districts and to guarantee a minimum yield for poorer districts. Carruthers and Minzner claimed that not only would the measure boost funding for schools but promote local control and accountability.

In December, the *Journal* had a five-part series on the state's economic development failures and inefficient expenditures; "New Mexico's attempts at economic development suffer from a combination of hype, duplication, factionalism and in many cases plain know how."[58] Some examples were a $600 thousand federal grant to a failed mobile home manufacturer in Lordsburg, a flexible flashlight company in Valencia County, empty industrial parks, failure to audit job creation from training awards, lack of accountability for tax incentives and industrial revenue bonds, 1984 grants to an Israeli firm that got training funds leading to a federal investigation, and failure to retain high tech startups.

The *Journal* columnist Larry Calloway profiled Governor Carruthers methods: "the governor hands the reins to the Clydesdales in his cabinet so he can go SELL." He works the Dodgers and golf into his pitch to a group of Japanese trade specialists. Then green chile. Then he is passing around pictures of his old Mustangs. "From that point on Carruthers has their undivided attention, and it seemed, good will."[59]

In January 1989, the highly regarded Michael Francke, former district judge and corrections secretary under Anaya was stabbed to death outside his office in Salem, Oregon, where he again served as corrections secretary.

The Democrats gained half a dozen seats in the Senate and had solid majorities in both chambers for the 1989 session. Freshman senators included future state leaders like Walter Bradley (Lieutenant Governor), Marty Chavez (Mayor of Albuquerque), John Arthur Smith (LFC and SFC Chair), Mary Jane Garcia (Majority Whip) and the colorful lawyer and rugby coach Shannon Robinson. HB 1, the feed bill had a 44 percent increase in appropriations to the legislative branch compared to the 1987 60-day session, and Carruthers grumbled about it. The Senate failed to confirm Health and Environment Secretary Carla Muth and the Senate Republicans filibustered for nine hours that day led by Albuquerque Senator Bill Davis. The *Journal* headlined, "Carruthers, Dems on a Brink of a Feud." The Senate majority proposed a rule change to limit debate triggering a 12-hour filibuster and then the Senate came to a standstill for three days. On

March 3 Governor Carruthers vetoed HB2, citing a recurring deficit, special interest funding and underfunding corrections, the first time a New Mexico governor ever vetoed the entire budget. (The GAA also was vetoed three times in Governor Johnson's second term, 1999, 2000 and 2002.) But in the final three days, the legislature and the Governor got in a compromising way. On March 19 Carruthers signed a $1.72 billion budget with a 7.5 percent increase and five percent raises for teachers and 15 percent raises for nurses. There were no line-item vetoes for the first time in modern memory. A $71 million capital bill passed with $57 million from the General Fund. The AP's Ed Moreno figured Carruthers got "two thirds" of his requests, but the Democrats were happy too. Speaker Sanchez said, "we are proud of what we accomplished," and Senator Aragon said, "I think we did all we could do." Carruthers vetoed a landfill bill but promised to impose a one-year moratorium on new landfills and consider an improved bill in 1990. The legislature initiated a $24.5 million remodeling of the capitol building, which eventually grew to $32 million.


Also, in March the Navajo Tribal Council removed Peter McDonald as tribal president and appointed Leonard Haskie as interim. Haskie went on to serve as assistant superintendent for facilities for Gallup McKinley School District; we were great friends and allies. Haskie was born in Los Angeles. At age two his parents died in a car accident, and social workers took him by train to Gallup where his grandparents met him and traveled 90 miles by horse-drawn wagon to their home in the Chuska Mountains, near Sanostee. He went to a BIA school in Phoenix and ran away twice. Despite this hardship, he graduated with bachelor's and master's degrees in civil engineering from Northern Arizona University and Brigham Young University. He was a medicine man, had a sly sense of humor, couldn't hear most of the time and fought tirelessly for state funding to build schools all over the reservation. I am exceptionally proud of working with him, Senator Leonard Tsosie (D-Whitehorse) and Legislative Council Service Director Paula Tacket to fund Tse-Ye-Gai High School at Pueblo Pintado. Previously kids from the checkerboard traveled up to 60 miles one way to either Crownpoint, Bloomfield or Cuba. They didn't travel; the dropout rate was thought to be 90 percent.

12. L-R, Senator Leonard Tsosie, Navajo Nation President Joe Shirley, PSCOC Chair Paula Tackett, Gallup Assistant Superintendent Leonard Haskie and me at dedication of Tse Ye Geh HS, Pueblo Pintado, circa 2006.

In April DFA Secretary Willard Lewis received UNM's Distinguished Public Service Award. In July Carruthers became chair of the Education Commission of the States. Also, a *Journal* investigative reporter detailed conflicts of interest, mismanagement and maybe a coverup involving a road project in Mescalero. Highway problems worsened, at best mismanagement leading to a five-part Mike Gallagher highway probe a year later. Governor Carruthers appointed a mental health advisory task force, and critics thought it was all talk and no action. The new Health and Environment secretary advocated a waiver from Medicaid rules to serve 300 clients, then called "mentally retarded." (Today, this waiver program serves over seven thousand New Mexicans with the state cost share only 25 percent.) DFA contracted with the Hay group for $350 thousand to implement the Act on Compensation Equity (ACE) for state employees. Representative Varela was a ramrod. Larry Calloway told the story of how the roadrunner got its name: "The trash of departing chiefs can be instructive. Cargo left nothing but a carved woodpecker which King mistakenly called a woodpecker in an interview with me."[60] A 1989 year-end wrap up noted, "The success of a relatively scandal free administration is due to the single thesis Carruthers adopted in1987. 'If you surround yourself with good people and delegate the proper amount of authority and responsibility, good things can happen.'"[61]

In a New Year's Eve op-ed, Carruthers laid out his 1990 legislative agenda topped by education reform. He promoted the "Re: Learning" initiative with teachers as coaches and students as workers, with less emphasis on rote learning and lectures. He advocated a 200-day school year and an eight-hour school day with greater responsibility for local school boards. Separately, he advocated for Representative Minzner's local option school levy, and representing DFA, I helped Minzner. I got a real lesson on that from Representative Varela. I learned at a young age not to lie, and generally I adhered to that. Representative Varela asked me if I was working on the bill, and knowing the rabid opposition from Representative Sam Vigil (D-Las Vegas) and LESC's Placido Garcia, I said no. What was I thinking? He wouldn't have asked if he didn't know. Varela was like the wizard of oz behind the curtain, he who knows all. He didn't call me out and I was lucky to get busted early in my state government career. Later, a couple times cabinet secretaries wrongly accused me of lying. They were adamant about it and insisted I lied. It just goes to show the need for some forgiveness and benefit of the doubt in the fog of legislative wars.

Sam Vigil was President of Luna Community College and Chair of House Education. The main reason he was on LFC was to make sure we didn't do anything policy-related for education like full day Kindergarten. A few times I drove Sam with Representatives Coll and Varela to LFC meetings. They could get pretty cranky but knew a lot of history and Sam was a scholar of Don Quixote. Sam told the story of former Senator Junio Lopez (R-Las Vegas). The Republican leaders told him they would signal how to vote by various hand signals. Junio said when I hold my hand with the middle finger up you know what that means.

Tax talk really heated up. On January 6, 1990, Carruthers outlined his budget request, a seven percent increase with no tax increase, no pay raises and funding for education reform. Carruthers said, "frankly, if a tax increase is to occur in this state, it probably will occur only if I ask the legislature to do it. I will only ask for it if it is a good program and it will pass."[62] The legislators effectively put the onus on Carruthers to ask for a tax increase. HAFC even tabled action on HB2 pending a proposal from the governor. On January 31, Carruthers came with a $75 million tax plan including a quarter percent increase in the GRT. Calloway said the governor resented being left by himself on the tax proposal. The House passed the budget assuming more revenue, but then the Senate pushed a statewide property tax requiring voter approval. In the waning days the Senate defeated a GRT bill with a tie vote and Lieutenant Gov Jack Stahl voting no. Initially, the bill failed 19-23 but Senator Mary Jane Garcia (D-Las Cruces) and Senator Johnny Morrow (D-Capulin) changed from no to yes forcing Stahl to decide. Oh, the fun and games. Then, a conference committee passed a $1.8 billion General Appropriation Act assuming no tax increase, no pay raises and a 7.4 percent overall spending increase including a 17 percent increase to expand health and human services programs and only four percent for public education and little for Carruthers' education reforms. Minzner's local option for schools failed with strong opposition from rural school districts, despite support of Albuquerque Schools, the State Board of Education and teachers' unions and favorable commentary from the *Journal*'s Bill Hume. Workers' comp reform also failed. The landfill bill passed along with a new retiree health care benefit.

In February the Resolution Trust Company took over Albuquerque Bank, New Mexico's largest savings and loan, and by the end of the year the savings and loan industry was virtually gone.

On March 7 Carruthers signed HB2 but line-item vetoed $38 million including most social service increases. He said he would consider restoring up to $17 million of social service funding if there was a special session. He noted that his recommendation for the social services programs was only $5 million, adding, "I've come a long way on this myself." He also vetoed $12.6 million of the $49 million capital outlay bill. He knew what many legislators really wanted and announced a leadership meeting that day.

After three bipartisan leadership meetings, Governor Carruthers on March 9 announced a special session on March 16. They needed a couple of senate votes to get the GRT and compromise among teacher pay, state employee pay, education reform and social service programs.

The House and Senate met in the auditoriums of the PERA and Land Office buildings due to the renovation of the capitol. Senator Fernando Macias (D- Las Cruces) said the governor's leadership helped him get to yes on the tax bill. After five days, the legislature passed a $45 million GRT increase and a $4 million motor vehicle tax increase and authorized five percent raises for schools, $15 million for the state employee ACE plan, $17 million for social service programs and $4.7 million for Carruther's education initiatives, including report cards for school districts and pilot programs like a longer school year. Senator Mickey Vernon (R-Albuquerque) said Carruthers "really shafted the Republicans," but Speaker Sanchez said, "the governor has grown in my estimation. He's shown a great deal of courage in his legislative package this year."[63]

Kids Come to Medanales. In late January my life really changed. I got a call at the Bull Ring, perhaps rare to get a call there, but not rare to be there. "Come get your kids in Los Alamos; their Mom is taking a break for a while." Pretty much forever. No more Bull Ring and Saints and Sinners, no more pub crawls. I picked up the kids and drove to Abiquiu, ten miles past Medanales on the Chama Highway and enrolled them in Abiquiu Elementary, Clayton in third and Anica in kinder. (I called her Betsy then, her middle name and my mom's name.) Abiquiu was a new school with about 150 kids. (The old school was in the old parochial school on the plaza across from Miss O'Keefe's house. It became a public school in 1957 when the New Mexico Supreme Court disallowed parochial education for public education.) There were some good teachers. Clayton (and Anica later) had Vonnie Owen, the wife of Ghost Ranch's Aubrey Owen, in third and Clayton had Miguel Gonzales, the rancher from Canjilon, in 4th and 6th. Anica had special education services including some home visits. All the kids and parents knew each other, from Chili to Los Silvestres, just below the dam. The kids were on the basketball team, and we enjoyed the games all over Rio Arriba, from Mountainview to Dixon. Little league and gymnastics were in Espanola. I had great after school support from Marcie Coronado, the postmistress and weaver, from AnnaMae and Tim Roybal and from the LaFormes next door with two girls a similar age. Weekends were home improvements—a new pitched roof, a mud room, Saltillo tile on the floors—chopping wood for the week, irrigating the pasture and a pretty regular Sunday excursion or hike with a pack of kids and dogs in the bosque. I was stretched to the limit, like the day I got a call to look for Clayton, because the bus driver threw him off the bus near the El Rito highway.

13. Betsy's three. My front yard was a riding arena. With neighbors Ginny, Jouelle and Celeste LaForme and Clayton Abbey. October 28, 1986.

Following the 1990 special session, the AP's venerable Bill Feather retired. Carruthers announced a worker's comp task force, and a September special session yielded a pathbreaking reform bill. On Friday of Fiesta weekend, the first weekend of September, the new DFA payroll system failed.

In October, candidates for governor, Democrat Bruce King and Republican Frank Bond, disagreed about the investment strategy for the Permanent Fund.[64] The constitution provided that only interest and dividends from investments of the permanent fund be distributed to beneficiaries. Stocks had a higher expected return than bonds, but the current income distribution was lower because capital gains were retained in the corpus of the fund. Members of the Investment Council, notably Land Commissioner Bill Humphries and New Mexico Tech VP for Finance Denny Peterson, were pushing for an increase in the stock share of the portfolio to 20 percent, the constitutional limit, up from eight percent. King aides and Representative Varela advocated for a lower stock share in order to boost current income to the General Fund. Say that again? By today's standards an investment portfolio should have 60 percent or more in stocks. In the coming decades the legislature passed a constitutional amendment to boost the equity share and change the distribution method to a total return basis. It just goes to show how innovative financial and political leadership can create great long-term benefits for New Mexico, despite the clamor to spend more today.

Five of six state General Obligation bond authorizations failed at the November general election including a high-tech research center at UNM, public school computers and classrooms and the Museum of Natural History in Albuquerque. Before the election, Maralyn Budke wrote a letter to the *Journal* opposing the bond issues, because they included too many special interest items, notably $3.7 million for the stadium at UNM.

In the 1990 wrap-up John Robertson of the *Journal* said, "discussions of the Carruthers record often gravitate to style versus substance." Carruthers touted the unemployment rate falling by half.

I rate Governor Carruthers the highest in modern history. Don't undersell the value of positive energy and leadership. We all know from our personal work experiences the challenges of a hostile work environment. We want to work in a place where folks are rowing together in a common direction. His top priorities of education and economic development were consistent with a market-oriented worldview. He didn't get too distracted with the small stuff. He was a great compromiser which was welcome in the wake of the Anaya administration and when state finances were just turning around. After the Prussian chancellor Bismarck, Willard Lewis used to say, "Politics is the art of the possible."

It's hard to reconcile my view with the refrain that Carruthers really didn't do anything. Studying the Carruthers record brings to mind the growing hegemony of the progressives in New Mexico. Carruthers represents the old school of taking 100 buckets to three fires. In the progressive era there is a desire to help many people in what almost seems like an endless or bottomless list of needs.

The Third Killing of David Abbey. I never planned a career as a civil servant for state government. I was an aide to Republican officials, and some folks actually thought I was a Republican. In October I went to a Frank Bond rally at a ranch in the heart of the King homeland, near Stanley. Sometime in December a colleague ratted me out to Kay Marr, DFA Secretary designate for Governor-Elect Bruce King. I probably was loose-lipped and should have known better. She phoned me in my office one afternoon and reamed me a new one for half an hour. I left for home shaken. Things look different when you are a single parent with a big mortgage and a home 40 miles from work in a company town. Yet, all I could do was put my head down and do my job. I am pretty sure in the Spring, Senator Eddie Lopez told Governor King to tell Secretary Marr to leave me alone.

# 8

# BRUCE KING 1991–1994

Bruce King grew up in Stanley in Torrance County. His big family is active in politics and government. He served in the Army in occupied Japan, two terms in the Santa Fe County Commission and was elected to the House in 1958. He was a legislative appointee to the State Board of Finance and served three terms as speaker. He was elected to a two-year term as governor in 1970 and a four-year term in 1978. In 1990 he was elected to a third term (second four-year term) beating Frank Bond by 20 thousand votes. He said the 1990 campaign was "fun and never got mean." He promised to make education a "top priority" and focus on the needs of families and children.

King liked people. See him as the networker in chief, shuffling through the Roundhouse, back-slapping, saying "mighty fine," calling folks together to problem solve and compromise.[65]

Out of the gate King's appointments drew high marks, including James Lewis, chief of staff, Kay Marr, back as DFA secretary, Dick Minzner, Rodey lawyer and HTRC chair as TRD secretary, and Dick Heim, Medicaid director under Carter as HSD secretary. Anita Lockwood stayed as energy secretary. Carruthers said, "he's heading in the right direction." He picked his son Bill King as legislative liaison, and wife Alice King was at his right hand. In a year-end roundup, Bill King said, "I'm a messenger. I listen to people for an hour, condense it to five minutes for my Dad. He still makes the final decision."[66] John McKean, the governor's spokesman, said Alice is the most influential adviser.

The day after the session started, the Persian Gulf War started (and ended before the session was over). America watched the green paths of missiles raining on blacked-out Baghdad. For a second year the governor was in the PERA building, and the House and Senate met at PERA and the Land Office. Networking among agencies, lobbyists, constituents and lawmakers was spotty.

Projected revenue growth for FY1992 was only three percent but was further reduced one percent in a mid-session review by the revenue estimators. Senator Aragon said the governor should be more optimistic. LFC Director David Harris said, "it's blood and guts out there."[67]

House Majority Leader Mike Olguin (D-Socorro) and House Education Chair Sam Vigil pushed again for a statewide property tax. Senator Aragon had a $110 million tax plan. But King quietly sent a "no new taxes" message to the legislature. The Senate on the last morning was bogged down in parliamentary maneuvers and filibusters, and Representative Fred Peralta (D-Taos) said, "it's absolute chaos over there."[68] The House property tax died on the Senate floor without a vote. But the executive and legislative fiscal experts cobbled together $40 million of revenue with a 0.125 percent reduction in the distribution of gross receipts tax revenue to municipalities, transfer of a share of motor vehicle excise tax revenue from the Road Fund to the General Fund, another delay in permanent fund stock purchases and eliminating a deduction for interest on out of-state municipal bonds. The GAA increased spending by 4.2 percent with four percent for schools, six percent for health and human services and small pay raises. The legislature also passed a controversial school funding formula sponsored by Representative Kiki Saavedra providing an "urban density factor" for $9 million. Carruthers' education initiatives were discontinued.

Other key measures included a new infrastructure finance authority advocated by Senator Eddie Lopez which was vetoed (a *Journal* editorial called it the "Frankenstein authority"), and new departments of tourism and the environment. Representative Paul Harrington (R-T or C) sponsored a committee bill to repeal the one percent for the arts set- aside for capital outlay appropriations. Hundreds of arts advocates showed up in protest, and even Harrington voted against his bill. Unfinished business for the next session would include the lottery and legalized gaming, opening WIPP and business tax incentives.

During the 1991 interim, projected budget shortfalls for schools and Medicaid received significant attention and concern from LFC hinting that agencies understated their needs. The school shortfall was covered by examining the Federal impact aid revenue pipeline and accruing more than budgeted. The Medicaid "shortfall" seems almost laughable by today's standards, $2.2 million over the $179 million general fund appropriation. HSD Secretary Heim proposed cutting Medicaid in schools, which didn't fly.

US District Court Judge Parker ruled that the state's services for disabled citizens violated their constitutional rights and ordered implementation of community programs. The Health Department led by Mike Burkhart (later SFC chief of staff) chose to close the Los Lunas and Ft. Stanton training centers housing 500 clients. Some parents and guardians opposed the closures and presented a petition with six thousand signatures. At the time approximately 350 clients were served in the waiver program and 677 individuals were on a waiting list for services.

Federal supervision of the Corrections Department under the Duran consent decree ended after ten years.

In July Governor King appointed DFA Secretary Marr, Bill King, Representative Barbara Perea Casey, Senator Carlos Cisneros and Lynn Medlin, state school board president from Tatum to a school funding formula equity task force. The *Journal* had a five-part series on the funding formula—adequacy, mechanics, role of local revenues, the density factor, small school and district size adjustments and other special components, cost of living issues, rural versus urban equity, teacher performance and retention. LESC analyst Brian McOlash said, "it doesn't matter what you do with the formula as long as you have enough money." NEA's Charles Bowyer said, "we don't have enough money."[69] Some of the options were counting enrollment at the end of the year to incentivize student retention, narrowing the gap between micro-districts with highest funding per student and mid-sized districts with lowest funding per student, channeling funding to at-risk students and eliminating some size adjustments which appear duplicative. I took minutes for the task force meetings in the governor's conference room. In late November Secretary Marr said it would be hard to add or expand formula factors without new money, otherwise some districts would take a cut. The report was due December 1, but the task force faded from sight.

Secretary Marr and DFA General Counsel Carolyn Wolf reined in the new Retiree Health Care Authority. The director claimed that it was not a state agency and not subject to laws and rules governing state agencies like the procurement code and vouchering through DFA. This was an important precedent but displeased key legislators.

Also, in November Secretary Marr told LFC that DFA found $24 million of "unspent, unencumbered and unreported" balances in agency accounts. Nevertheless, the December revenue estimate was down $34 million with new money of $75 million, or 3.4 percent.

Political corruption reared its head in a big way in 1989 with savings and loan fraud and political contributions touching Congress, including Arizona Senators McCain and DeConcini. On February 7, 1991, seven Arizona state legislators were indicted for kickbacks related to legalized gaming; they had the House Judiciary chair on video taking $55 thousand in a brown paper bag.[70] At the 1991 session the New Mexico House adopted an ethics rule, but a Senate effort led by Marty Chavez failed. Attorney General Tom Udall went after Senator Aragon for not reporting as a campaign contribution a Philip Morris sponsored trip with tobacco lobbyists to the Super Bowl in Orlando. In September Aragon made headlines for a budget amendment that favored certain school bus contractors in Albuquerque who paid Aragon to represent them. LFC had a hearing on the topic, but Representative Saavedra said, "the news media has it wrong." In

December Representative Ron Olguin (D-Albuquerque), former senator and Bernalillo County manager, was indicted for taking $15 thousand to support a $100 thousand appropriation for community corrections. A *Journal* editorial on September 7 stated, "Blurring lines between client and constituent is what makes New Mexico politics a game to be avoided by the average citizen." In November the Legislature Council sponsored an all-legislature panel on ethics. Under a citizen legislature, this conversation reasonably led to discussion about paying legislators and restrictions on eligibility to serve. For example, a January 1991 Court of Appeals decision provided that public school employes could serve in the legislature; but an April attorney general opinion concluded that university employees couldn't serve in the legislature; then it was clarified that the university exclusion didn't apply to employees of two-year colleges.

The 30-day session in 1992 was low key with minimal revenue growth, little appetite for new taxes in an election year, and a debate about censuring or expelling Representative Olguin. The Senate added $20 million to the House version of the GAA, and the conference committee added $3 million more. They swept $54 million from other state funds in the Treasury to the General Fund including the road fund and risk management funds. LFC staff call this "spend your way to victory." The legislature created a new Children, Youth and Families Department and established the New Mexico Finance Authority.

The US attorney threatened to "move against" tribal video game rooms, and Mescalero sued the state and the governor for not negotiating in good faith on a gaming compact.

King was an early supporter of Bill Clinton with friendship dating to King's second term and the National Governors Association. Clinton came to New Mexico in 1991, and they had breakfast with key New Mexico politicos at *El Comedor* in Moriarty. In 1992 King and half a dozen western Democratic governors went on the stump for Clinton.

At year end Governor King said his "philosophy is to work out consensus as much as you can." He told columnist Calloway, "If I had a Christmas wish, it'd be please

not elect any more retired state employees from Santa Fe to the state legislature."
King added, state employees call Representative Varela every morning and he
comes to his (King's) office with their problems every afternoon. [71]

Professional Development. Secretary Marr invited me to apply to a three-week
program for state and local government officials at Harvard's Kennedy School of
Government. My cousin, an alumna and Bush official, may have helped me get
in, and I received a partial scholarship. This rejuvenated my career and attitude
toward government and public service. Further, the instruction in public policy
making became the backbone of my fiscal leadership in New Mexico. The
Kennedy School uses the case study method and has two simple paradigms for
problem solving. First, be clear about the problem definition and define and
analyze options to address the problem. Too often new initiatives lack a clear
purpose and direction and expected outcomes. Second, analyze and recommend
initiatives based on Capacity, the capability of government to find funding and
qualified personnel to address a problem, Values, the worth or importance of
trying to fix a problem, and Support, the level of advocacy from citizens, interest
groups and officials for the initiative. CVS.

The professors, the networking with peers, and the instruction were outstanding,
and to be on the banks of the Charles River in Cambridge was fun and exciting.
Later, as LFC director, I sent about a dozen LFC employees to the program who
went on to distinguished service as state officials.

My kids spent a month with my parents in Tucson which was good for all.

In August 1993, Governor King and Secretary Marr appointed me director of
the State Board of Finance. It was a great fit and step up for me. After ten years at
DFA, I had broad knowledge about state budgets and finance and governmental
laws and organization. The Board of Finance has the duties of the legislature
when it is not in session and executes key financial actions including issuing
state bonds, administering emergency funds, approving fund transfers, state
investments and capital projects. Members include the governor, lieutenant

governor and state treasurer. I learned to staff a board: prepare an agenda, move items forward and recommend changes, and brief all members in person prior to the meeting. I continued to "double-hat" as DFA chief economist—one more responsibility for which I was overextended.

King and Marr saved my bacon. I had a small staff—an office administrator with a disability preventing use of a keyboard, Julie Trapp, the daughter of the editor of the *Rio Grande Sun* and a radical, Danny Tinoco, a clerk whose mail runs took a very long time, and Dennis, who I once carpooled with to LANL and later became Denise. My approach was to work hard and push the staff, probably too much. Their approach was to complain about me to higher-ups. Marr reassigned them to other duties, and I got a fresh start learning to be a manager.

I was stretched thinner with Anica at Abiquiu Elementary and Clayton in 7th at McCurdy School in Espanola. I was the morning carpool driver with Clayton and three girls from Medanales, and in the evening I was looking for Clayton at basketball or Little League practice. I ran the show with a boot camp style and wasn't successful. I sold the farm, abandoned some dreams and bought a house in Santa Fe a mile from the capitol. It was a convenient location to walk or bike to work for the next 30 years.

1993 Session. On Christmas Eve a drunk driver killed a mother and three daughters and severely injured husband Paul Cravens. (His brother Kent was elected to the Senate in 2000.) A clamor for reform of laws for liquor sales and DWI and programs for alcohol treatment ensued.

A new border crossing opened at Santa Teresa, offering vast long-term opportunity with the onset of NAFTA. Also, in 1993 Intel initiated a huge expansion of its semiconductor plant in Rio Rancho, and Leprino foods opened a mozzarella cheese processing plant in Roswell, which kickstarted the dairy industry. Former DFA secretary, Dr. Dan Lopez was appointed president of New Mexico Tech.

Bill Hume kicked off 1993 with a column on Democrat hegemony. "If New Mexico's track record of Democratic mansion and Democratic legislature is any harbinger, don't expect too much. There is no unity of purpose to lead New Mexico anywhere among the Democrats. Instead, there is a concentration of power, which allows a few in the legislature to bend the process to their personal agendas. New Mexico's leadership is more reactive than proactive, listening to special interests and clogging the limited legislative time with dogfights on what should be non-issues—such as the perennial proposal to legalize video gambling. Special interests such as the liquor and tobacco industry have exemplary track records with those in charge."[72] Yikes again.

The *Journal* profiled departing Senator Johnny Morrow (D-Capulin) who lost the Democratic primary to a retired teacher from Tucumcari who lost the general election to Quay County rancher Pat Lyons. Morrow said, "When I started in the 70s, the voters sent you there with an understanding that everything wasn't available from the government. You didn't have the advocacy groups you have today. They started coming in during the eighties with all their special problems. People started acting like the government was responsible for them from the cradle to the grave."[73]

A land swap between King ranches and BLM drew scrutiny, even though it had been in the works for a decade. King traded 20 thousand acres on the York ranch south of the *Malpais*, next to Acoma appraised at $90 per acre for 740 BLM acres west of Santa Fe appraised at $2,300 per acre. The Baca family, including Phil Baca, former LFC director, had a grazing lease on the Santa Fe acreage and stirred it up.

Beginning the session, King opened the tax floodgate with a recommendation to boost the severance tax on natural gas and cigarette taxes. There was pressure from the Medicaid budget with estimated needs in the range $25 million to $30 million because of health care inflation and enrollment growth. Representative Miera and school advocates complained that the executive and LFC budget recommendations shorted public education which would only receive 40 percent of spending growth. On February 18, DFA reported to HAFC that revenues were coming in strong and added $18 million to the FY93 forecast and $25 million to FY94. King's spokesman told the *Journal* that Corrections, Health and CYFD were short in the House version of the budget. According to King, in the last week of the session Speaker Sanchez and President Pro Tem Aragon came to his office to push for a gasoline tax arguing that a third of the tax would be paid by truckers and other out of state interests. King had misgivings and wrote, "Bill King just about came unglued. He said, Daddy, you'll lose this election if we support this gas tax. We can get the money in other ways."[74]

The final revenue package included a six-cent gasoline tax increase with five cents going to the general fund, ostensibly to support school transportation, an increase in the natural gas severance tax up to four percent, and higher alcohol taxes.

The budget grew 9.3 percent with 8.6 percent for schools and raises in the range four to six percent. School superintendent Alan Morgan and NEA leader Charles Bowyer, both said it was the best education session in over a decade. Corinne Wolfe of the Human Services Coalition said they got just about everything they wanted.

The legislature also passed tougher DWI laws, ethics reform and a constitutional amendment to provide exceptions to the anti-donation clause for economic development, and a real estate transfer tax which was vetoed along with almost 100 other bills and 50 items in HB2.

Over the coming months, DFA provided revenue estimates to the legislature that were significantly higher each time because of a stronger economy, higher natural gas prices and higher personal income tax payments: in May, FY93 up $65 to $80 million; and in June, FY94 up a range of $71 million to $121 million.

King called for a special session to repeal the $47 million gas tax increase but said he would consult with legislative leaders. A *Journal* editorial quickly called for a special session. The legislative leaders not only didn't bite but pushed back questioning whether the revenue estimates were reliable and evoking the memory of Big Mac that triggered a quick shortfall that took a decade to unwind.

In June, the *Journal* reported growing dissatisfaction with King including native Americans, principally due to gaming compacts, environmentalists wanting a stronger stance on WIPP, gays who wanted stronger support on a human rights bill, liberals who expected more for social programs, Lieutenant Governor Casey Luna who complained about not having enough responsibility and of course rural and business interests unhappy about the gasoline tax. Speaker Sanchez said, "It's unusual to have so many groups publicly disagree with him."[75]

Legislators were cranky in the wake of vetoes. In September LFC had a hearing on the State Fair, with sharp questioning led by Senator Robinson (with the fair in his district) complaining about alcohol sales disrupting the neighborhoods. Senator Altamirano and King exchanged testy letters, and the *Journal* headlined, "King and legislators ready to rumble."

In the Fall legislative leaders begin working on a long-term fiscal planning project foreshadowing the Horizons Task Force. A draft legislative report said, "Some will say repeal of the gas tax increase is the beginning and end of the political debate in 1994; legislators look beyond this worn-out partisan brain-dead politics to building a bridge to a better future."[76] In October DFA reported FY 95 revenue growth would be in the range of $250 million to $330 million. The interim Health and Human Services committee presented to Senator Aragon a wide-ranging list of needs including childcare, child abuse prevention, and domestic violence shelters that Aragon said were more important than cutting the gasoline tax. David Harris announced his resignation to serve as CFO for Albuquerque mayor-elect Marty Chavez but quickly reversed course saying legislators asked him to stay. The "continuing rift" between King and legislative leaders made the front page of the *Journal* in December.

1994, Capital Outlay Bonanza. For FY95 the Executive recommended a ten percent spending increase and LFC recommended 7.4 percent. But with huge surpluses, capital outlay was on everyone's mind. The Executive recommended $229 million for projects, and the legislature proposed $338 million, headlined on January 19 by the *Journal*, "Legislature Smells Pork" and inside "Lawmakers Hungry for Pork." Mid-session Senator Aragon moved 45 vetoed bills from 1993 to the president's table. Calloway called the bills hostages with a threat of veto overrides and asked King what he might give Aragon to release the hostages. King said, "I've got a lot of things to bargain with. Friendship, loyalty, good government and if that doesn't work then they might want a message or they might have something, and I might not sign it. Or I might have to put together a coalition between the house and myself." He added, "I just resent Senator Aragon messing around. I talked to him, and I thought we'd agreed he wouldn't do it that way."[77] On February 3 DFA added $35 million in FY94 and $25 million in FY 95 to the revenue estimates.

The legislature passed HB2 with an eight percent increase and $47 million of tax cuts including lower personal income tax rates, suspending two cents of the gas tax for three years and a prescription drug tax credit. The capital outlay bill totaled $487 million with $17.5 million for prisons, $15 million for sewers in Albuquerque's North and South Valley, $12 million for the Hispanic cultural center, $6 million for a balloon park, $11 million for a new state library, $8 million for a library at Western New Mexico University and science centers at New Mexico Tech and NMSU. King said, "I see a situation developing that's going to need attention as we go down the line. One of these days we're going to have to quit."[78]

King beat Lieutenant Governor Casey Luna and former land commissioner Jim Baca handily in the primary. Gary Johnson, an Albuquerque businessman, beat John Dendahl and Representative Richard Cheney (R-Farmington). Then, former Lieutenant Governor Roberto Mondragon signed on to the Green party ticket, which was never more than a spoiler.

In July, Moody's upgraded the rating on general obligation bonds a notch, from Aa to Aa1, a feather in the cap of King, Secretary Marr, the legislature, the economy, and the whole state.

Patsy Madrid, King's running mate for lieutenant governor, said at a Las Vegas rally in October that, "Gary Johnson will surround himself with nothing but *anglos*," and added, "newcomers to the state don't appreciate your values. They don't appreciate Hispanics."[79]

Just before the November election King was closing and 12 percent were undecided. But the undecideds broke entirely for Johnson who defeated King 49 to 40 with ten for Mondragon.

Quickly, Johnson tabbed Lou Gallegos, former state director for US Representative Manuel Lujan, to head his transition team along with former Summa Medical executive, Cisco Urrea, to head the finance transition. (Later, I served with Gallegos on the Public School Capital Outlay Council, he knew everyone and everywhere in New Mexico.) Then Johnson picked LFC director David Harris as DFA secretary along with James Jimenez as deputy and a handful of other LFC staff. Representative Coll angrily accused Johnson of stealing the legislature's financial brains.[80] But Senator Altamirano said I am sure we can find somebody else and a *Journal* editorial applauded Johnson's good, bi-partisan picks.

The *Journal's* retrospective on King noted he'd been governor for half of the previous 24 years. King said he was especially proud of the school equalization funding formula, the Severance Tax Permanent Fund, the state's new rainy-day reserve, a hard rock mining law (sponsored by Representative Gary King (D-Stanley)) and the establishment of the Children, Youth and Families Department: "King's brand of governing was tranquil and middle of the road, liberal leaning on social issues and more conservative on finance. His administration was mostly scandal free. But King may be remembered more for his personality as for his government deeds." Senator Aragon said, "King wasn't a risk taker or one that would try to speed up change, but overall, King served the state very well. He was a steady leader." Senator Tom Rutherford (D-Albuquerque) said, "It takes a strong leader to keep people from constantly trying to pull things one way or another. I think he wanted to keep us on an even course."[81] Calloway said giving in to Aragon on the gas tax was his "undoing."

The great King Democratic coalition of farmers and ranchers, Hispanics, native Americans, and labor was over.

# 9

# GARY JOHNSON 1995–2002

Gary Johnson graduated Sandia High School in Albuquerque and the University of New Mexico in 1975. He started a construction services company in 1975, obtained significant contracts from Intel and grew the company to 1,000 employees. He was an avid triathlete with the ambition to climb Mt. Everest. His run for governor in 1994 was his first venture into politics. Johnson contributed $450 thousand to his campaign and received $250 thousand from tribal gaming interests.

On New Year's Eve, exempt governor appointees, 295 in number, were notified to submit resignations with just a few exceptions, including DFA Comptroller Anthony Armijo and me. The *New Mexican* called it a purge, and the *Journal* named all the fired employees on January 10.

Johnson turned 42 on inauguration day, January 1, 1995. In his address he highlighted fighting crime and streamlining government. He said his recommendation would address, "education, crime, economic development and government efficiency" but deferred specifics to his budget proposal.

The First Three Sessions/Increasing Acrimony between Executive and Legislature. Johnson inherited a growing economy, notably in manufacturing led by Intel along with Motorola, Philips NV and General Motors. New Mexico ranked 6th in population growth. Nevertheless, in February DFA lowered the revenue estimates by $27 million for FY95 and $36 million for FY96. Also, LFC economist Anna Lamberson found a $10 million error in the calculation of severance tax bonding capacity. This was my spreadsheet error; I failed to include two years outstanding debt in the calculation. LFC acted like there was something nefarious in the error, but Harris in effect said to the legislature, don't worry about it, no reason to change the administration's capital outlay proposals. But legislators feared that if capacity was short the Board of Finance would prioritize funding executive projects before legislative projects. It was awkward for me and the beginning of me getting crosswise with Harris.[82]

Also in February, Johnson signed gaming compacts with 12 tribes and pueblos, drawing a quick challenge to his authority to bypass the legislature.

The legislature passed the budget in two bills requiring executive action before the session ended and posing a theoretical veto override threat.[83] Johnson vetoed $36 million of appropriations including appropriations for children's cancer treatment and for medical exams for sex abuse victims. An override of a vetoed appropriation for school supplies failed by one vote in the house with one Democrat voting no. The legislature also passed a state lottery with proceeds earmarked to school construction and financial aid, $96 million for capital projects and authorization of two new prisons with over 1,500 beds in Hobbs and Santa Rosa.

Ominously, Johnson vetoed 200 bills out of 424 passed, including 36 percent of Republican bills. Johnson said he vetoed bills that committed funding the state couldn't afford, created unfunded mandates to agencies and local governments, intruded into the private sector, or usurped executive power. This triggered bipartisan bafflement and ire and a search for explanations ranging from inexperience of key governor's staff to misinformation to indifference.

The *Journal*'s John Robertson summed Johnson's first few months: "He doesn't care much about politics and wants to do what he thinks is right, to wit, 'individual freedom, individual rights, less government.'" Johnson said, "I'm surprised about how much I'm second-guessed." Robertson noted criticism from legislators that Johnson skipped a Republican retreat to participate in a triathlon in California and wrote, "As he did during the campaign, Johnson sometimes struggles with explanations of his positions."[84]

Dr. Anna Lamberson was appointed director of LFC in June. Lamberson had a PhD in economics from the University of Utah and worked for me briefly at DFA and at the Environment Department. Rumblings of a revenue shortfall began at $40 million in July, grew to $40 million to $80 million by August and morphed into wide discussions about a special session. In September DFA implemented a 2.5 percent reduction in monthly one-twelfth allotments to state agencies, and the district attorneys challenged the executive authority to withhold appropriations.

Also in summer 1995, Johnson proposed a new private prison that stayed on the front burner for the next couple years. Johnson took Texas as a model and advocated smaller cell sizes and no air conditioning to reduce cost and make incarceration even more uncomfortable. In addition to design issues, financing method and location (Hobbs, Santa Rosa or both) were debated.

On September 7 Johnson discontinued the long tradition of authorizing four hours administrative leave for state employees the Friday afternoon before the Santa Fe Fiesta celebrations. But Johnson gained publicity and good will with an "Open Door After Four" program each Thursday afternoon. First come, first served, sign up for a five-minute slot with a hard stop.[85]

In November the Supreme Court ruled that Governor Johnson couldn't enter gaming compacts without legislative authority, and in December the court ruled the executive didn't have the authority to reduce appropriations without legislative authority. The Supreme Court also was reviewing Johnson's authority to replace two regents at New Mexico Tech, one of whom was Diane Denish, future Lieutenant Governor. *Journal* columnist Bill Hume said the Supreme Court put the leash on Johnson; Johnson blamed his court losses on Democrat judges and "chicken bone voodoo."[86] DFA Deputy Secretary James Jimenez resigned to take the finance director post at Rio Rancho, and David Harris was one of four finalists for the City Manager job in Rio Rancho. Hume noted the loss of Johnson's "dynamic duo."

On December 31, 1995, in the *Journal*'s year-end roundhouse wrap-up, Johnson said, "I have no expectations to get anything out of the legislature. The bottom line is we have two different philosophies. ... We've not had a governor who has stood up and wanted to have an agenda as governor." DFA Secretary Harris said, "He doesn't pick up the phone and call anyone. The only person he calls is his stockbroker." The *Journal* reported it's hard to find a happy medium between a leaner government and expanding services, and "Johnson has ended up in court a lot." The *Journal* noted Harris, Lou Gallegos, policy advisor Kelly Ward and wife Dee Johnson were his close and reliable confidantes, and Johnson competed in two marathons and 20 other events in 1995.[87]

RIP Eddie Lopez. A sad day January 19,1996. Senator Majority Leader Eddie Lopez died of a heart attack. He was colorful, described as "low-key and taciturn," a fiscal expert and master tactician. Senator Lopez initiated the important interim committee on Revenue Stabilization and Tax Policy that developed legislative expertise and rarely recommended tax increases. (A DFA official called the committee the "per diem express" with meetings in Ruidoso and other garden spots and adjournment by lunchtime with an early afternoon tee time.) Speaker Sanchez said he had been a "Mama Lucy" when he served in the House, and the rest of them were waiting for him in heaven.[88] Aragon, Sandel and Smith were among his many comrades, and his lobbyist friends included the notable Sammy Fields who represented El Paso Natural Gas Co. The press noted his frequent sessions at the capitol watering hole, the Bull Ring, to which I'll add Evangelo's when the booths had a Tahitian motif.

Larry Calloway covered the funeral, "Old Santa Fe's Sense of Place."[89] After a Senate session of eulogies, the whole capitol walked down the Old Santa Fe Trail, 1,500 strong and packed the cathedral. The mass had a southwest flavor, not just because of the santos and mariachis but because of things that "go a long way back in this ancestral country." Eddie's daughter Melinda gave Senator Aragon Eddie's watch as the official timepiece of the Senate. Aragon said Eddie was a "saint and a sinner and a visionary and futuristic thinker. ... Eddie knew the best way to predict the future was to create it." His cousin Col. Joe Black related that Eddie's ancestral home was razed for construction of the new capitol and that their grandfather and great grandfather built the cathedral. (Black was forced into retirement at the military affairs department, but Lopez said he was "pure as the driven snow.")

I felt like an insider (like dozens of others I'm sure) when Eddie greeted me, "Hey, cowboy."

The headlines tell the story of the 1996 session: "State's Budget Recipe: Borrow and Cut", "Theater in the Roundhouse" and "State's Rosy Forecasts for the Session Turned into a Thorny Problem." The legislature passed $2.9 billion general fund appropriations for FY97, up $98 million or three percent, sanded FY95 appropriations up to 2.5 percent with smaller reductions for schools and corrections to restore General Fund reserves, and added modest amounts to agencies favored by Johnson like tourism and economic development. The governor and legislature disputed whether he'd agreed to sign the budget. The budget writers left very few appropriation amounts "hanging" out and therefore vetoable. The governor did sign the budget and 88 other bills but vetoed 57 bills and $3.4 million of the budget. The vetoed bills included capital outlay and a General Fund solvency measure that looked to be leverage for a special session that Johnson called for March 20. Harris said, "the governor achieved the objective of addressing the revenue shortfall, but in doing that he made it harder to achieve a good working relationship."

A special session was ostensibly needed to "fix" a "just discovered" loophole that would allow gasoline distributors to launder sales through tribal entities and eliminate some gasoline tax revenue for the Road Fund. Many wondered if the special was another run at allowing tribal gaming, which failed at the regular session. At this point legislative leaders and governor's staff basically weren't talking, because they disputed the details of agreements made in private discussions. The special session adjourned March 23 with no gasoline tax fix after passing the capital bill for $58 million and the solvency measures tweaked to the executive's liking.

In April 1996, the General Services Department issued a request for proposals for prison construction and in June announced plans for Brown and Root to construct prisons to be operated by Wackenhut pursuant to long term leasing agreements funded with annual appropriations by the legislature. DFA initially estimated costs at $40 per inmate per day and total savings at $40 million per year, but later Harris acknowledged the cost figure was too low. Nevertheless, the Governor fired the Corrections Secretary and Deputy Secretary for not supporting the lower cost numbers. Calloway on August 13 described a letter war between Governor Johnson and Senator Aragon with the letters drafted by the DFA Secretary and the LFC Director. The governor's legislative liaison Dan Hill said, "If you disagree with Aragon, he doesn't confirm your appointments; he doesn't fund your programs; he threatens to cut your budget; he visits with the bond market; he goes to the press and rages."[90] On November 21 Representative Max Coll and Representative Jerry Lee Alwin (R-Albuquerque) sued to halt the prison plan. A *Journal* editorial on November 24 called the Executive plan a "Rube Goldberg financing scheme" and appealed to the legislature and executive to cooperate to fix the prison mess.

HSD Secretary Dorothy Dannenfelser resigned in July saying that she'd been left out of planning for welfare reform and implementation of Medicaid managed care. In October HSD reported the $200 million Medicaid budget was $50 million short.

LFC developed projections that budget drivers like Medicaid might require sharp spending cuts and asked agencies to analyze 16 percent budget reductions, and Lou Gallegos directed agencies not to respond to the LFC request. An October 10 *Journal* editorial appealed to Representative Coll and the Governor to tone it down. The *Journal's* Bill Hume said, "Hard Feelings will Poison the 1997 legislative session." Calloway on November 24 said the governor was generally inaccessible to the press.

In the November election the Republican picked up a few seats in the House and Senate, undoubtedly putting a veto override out of reach. Pojoaque Pueblo Governor Jake Viarrial called Representative Coll a racist amidst a sharp campaign by Republican Greg Bemis in Santa Fe.

In 1997 the House passed two budget bills similar to the LFC recommendation with a combined four percent increase for FY98, and the Senate Finance Committee added $52 million more, and a range of bills raising taxes on cigarettes, gasoline and more were moving. But on March 12, Senator Aragon on the floor moved to strike the SFC amendments and further amend HB2 by cutting $156 million, including all raises and a Medicaid bump, and adding $52 million additional spending requested by the executive. Aragon said, "I give up. I'm tired of criticism that there are ways to fund everything with existing resources."[91] Capital wall leaners called Aragon's strategy, "the give them all their shit" budget. A conference committee made a few fixes to save general fund, and the bill passed on Saturday, March 14. On Thursday, March 20 a tribal gaming compact bill failed 35 to 35, but on Friday it was called back up. Representative Debbie Rodella (D-Abiquiu) changed from no to yes, and it passed the House 35-34 and then quickly passed the Senate 27-15. Prison financing failed.

On May 25, LFC director Anna Lamberson announced her resignation, although she said her letter was dated January 25 in response to a request from Senator Aragon. Aragon said it's time for the House and Senate to have separate fiscal staff.

Board of Finance and State Treasurer. In January 1995, Tom "Hot Rod" Hundley, appointed chief investment officer by new state treasurer Michael Montoya, bought and sold $35 million of US agency securities for a loss of $670 thousand. Hundley was former director of the New Mexico Mortgage Finance Authority. The transaction was reviewed at the monthly meeting of the Board of Finance with attention to legality, the use of Raymond James on both sides of the transaction and pricing. Board members asked the treasurer for a moratorium on trading activity, pending modernization of the board's investment policy for the treasurer.

The State Board of Finance (SBoF) powers and duties are the general supervision of the fiscal affairs of the state and the safekeeping and depositing of public money (state statute section 6-1-1 (e)). The state treasurer has the power to invest public money with the advice and consent of the SBoF. The governor is president of the SBoF, the treasurer is a member, and the DFA secretary is the executive officer.

I was the Director. With advice from the board's financial advisor, Barbara Fava of Public Financial Management (PFM), the board developed a new policy approved at the April meeting that ratified the three key investment objectives, safety, liquidity and return in that priority order, updated the eligible broker list, required three bids on each transaction, and required a monthly report from the treasurer to the board on balances by asset type, yield and trading activity.

In the Spring the treasurer and DFA received a proposal from Cisco Urrea for lending $100 million of state securities to a firm to be determined for an expected return of five to seven percent above the underlying rate on the US securities. (Urrea, a former member of the State Investment Council, headed Johnson's DFA transition team.) Urrea described this as a new product with collateral for the loaned securities in a letter of credit. Though the proposal looked too good to be true, proponents saw the solution to the state's financial needs. DFA sought an opinion from the attorney general regarding legal authority, financial analysis from PFM and contacted the Securities Exchange Commission which provided advice regarding the proliferation of "prime bank certificate of deposit scams" which were mushrooming. Marty Daly, AG's Counsel to SBoF, determined there wasn't authority for the transaction.[92]

In early June 1995 the Governor, Secretary Harris, Deputy Secretary Jimenez and I went to New York for standard presentations to bond ratings agencies. As reported by the *Journal*'s John Robertson, after a long day we were feeling adventurous, and the governor wanted exercise, so we walked 40 blocks from a Greenwich Village restaurant to our mid-town hotel with a late stop at the Empire State Building.[93]

The Fourth Killing. About June 18 Secretary Harris summoned me to his office and fired me. He didn't offer a reason. I can guess that he blamed me for bad revenue estimates, I was too independent, bond salesmen viewed me as an obstructionist and wanted my head, or he just didn't like me. I was devastated, because I loved the job and needed a job. I had just learned that Treasurer Montoya terminated Hundley for making an unauthorized bond transaction. So, I walked across the street to the NEA building and met with the treasurer and had a tentative job offer as investment officer in about half an hour.

The treasury job was challenging, interesting and sometimes fun executing high dollar transactions. I was mostly self-taught, but I had a lot of free advisors including bond salesmen and the Education Retirement Board's investment officer Frank Foy. With the support of the treasurer, the office contracted with Bloomberg for $30 thousand for their financial news and securities trading platform which allowed real time market pricing and execution and lessened the reliance on market information from salesmen. Major initiatives were: 1) to boost income by shifting investments from the daily repurchase agreement pool, over half of assets, to the US treasury and agency bond market; and 2) to develop a cash flow forecasting model for the state treasury.[94]

I also served as analyst and advisor to the treasurer for his duties on dozens of state boards and commissions, including the Board of Finance, the Investment Council, the state's two pension funds and the Mortgage Finance Authority. The State Treasurer, the state's chief elected financial officer, has high visibility which in many cases has been a stepping stone to higher office, for example Clinton Anderson elected state treasurer in 1932 served as Secretary of Agriculture and 28 years as congressman and US Senator. Texas' Kay Bailey Hutchinson was elected treasurer in 1991 and senator in 1993 serving three terms.

The risk for an ambitious treasurer is being around a lot of money. Financial salesmen and advisors would approach Treasurer Montoya, and he'd send them to me to examine their proposals. The state continued to receive securities lending proposals, sometimes fronted by relatives of lawmakers. In August 1996, I asked a regulator of the Securities Exchange Commission to review one of these proposals. Also, regional securities firms generally couldn't compete with money center banks on pricing, so they pushed me and the treasurer to purchase non-competitive new Treasury issues. Guy Riordan, a politically connected stockbroker, was relentless. With growing insistence from the treasurer, I purchased several securities through his firms, the last for $5 million on June 2, 1997; the treasurer wanted $10 million. (More on Riordan in the next chapter.) It was becoming clear that I couldn't continue in this job.

The risk and pressure were not just hypothetical. In June 1996 the Clovis finance director wired $4 million to the Bank of New York on representations of a Clovis financial advisor and a Briton and Ugandan that the overseas investment was riskless and would yield six percent per month. In June 1997 the investment loss was disclosed, and the finance director was fired. The funds were then tracked to a bank in the Canary Islands and used to support a rebel movement in Uganda. The Clovis director pleaded guilty to embezzlement and later committed suicide.

In late May 1997, I received a call from LFC's outgoing Anna Lamberson indicating that Representative Coll wanted me to apply for the position of LFC director. Although advertised, there were only three other applicants—the capable insider Dan Weaks, lobbyist and former key aide to Governor Anaya, Lawrence Trujillo, a DFA budget analyst, and some unknown individual.

I was at the monthly Board of Finance meeting, and Lamberson walked in and whispered to me, "you're it." I went down to a closed-door interview before the committee; they were eating Lotaburgers. Joyce Pankey, the committee secretary asked what I wanted, and I was horrified to be eating in front of lawmakers or the public for that matter. Pankey said, "you'll learn to eat when they eat." I told the committee my goal was to restore LFC to its glory days when "powerful" was routinely an adjective preceding LFC in news accounts. They moved to open session and appointed me.

Legislative Finance Committee. It was probably Representative Coll who told me my first assignment was to call Senator Aragon who was vacationing in Costa Rica and tell him the LFC selected me, which I did that night. I'm sure he was stunned, and I thought what have I got myself into? My mother would say, "I went from the fat to the fire."

Calloway in the *Journal* reported on my appointment: "Abbey's a sophisticated financial analyst who carries no political baggage and has the bearing of a conservative bond advisor. Although he never took credit, he's the architect of the new State Short Term Cash Management Act which sets up an ingenious way for the state general fund to earn $8 million a year from tax and revenue anticipation notes (TRANS)."

Senator Joe Fidel (D-Grants) sponsored the TRANS bill; he was a great ally and so was Charlie Young, former bill drafter and lobbyist, key aide to Fidel and father of future Representative Justine Fox Young. The erudite Charlie took me to lunch at the Pink Adobe and sang the Gilbert and Sullivan song, "monarch of the sea" to the effect that everyone would be right behind me.

Interviewing staff, hiring and analyst assignments were the first orders of business. My first hire was Linda Kehoe, former King chief of staff and deputy secretary of health and Senate Finance analyst, as LFC's first capital outlay analyst. Then LFC auditor and CPA Danette Burch as deputy director. Dannette was the foremost expert on producing the General Appropriation Act, had broad knowledge of agency operations and all-around expertise. Other hires in the first few years brought expertise and legislative support to LFC including Gene Moser, Bill Dunbar from HSD (and classmate of Senator Aragon at St. Mary's HS), Mark Valdes, Mark Valenzuela, CPA George McGeorge, Senator Robinson's rugby player Lawrence Trujillo and economist Arley Williams. I contracted with UPI journalist Helen Gaussoin as LFC's first editor, retired King hands Ron Forte and Mike Burkhart as session staff, retired EMNRD secretary Anita Lockwood as a management advisor and UNM Health Science's Pam Galbraith as a health and Medicaid expert.

In July 1997, two LFC hearings drew attention. First, the DFA Local Government Division and law enforcement were called to explain the Clovis investment loss and DFA's ability to oversee local government investments. Second, the SHTD was called to report on an "innovative financing plan" to widen NM 44 from Bernalillo to Farmington at a cost up to $250 million at seven or eight percent interest without an appropriation. Highway Secretary Pete Rahn announced the plan with no legislative input, sent his deputy to the hearing and the department got a "bipartisan blasting." Representative Sandel asked, "What is the analysis for spending that additional money by a conservative administration?" Senator Billy McKibben (R-Hobbs) said, "The fact that it's going to take that much money for this scheme and the way you're doing it is unbelievable."[95]

In September legislative leaders and SHTD Secretary Pete Rahn met with Federal Highway Administrator Sandra Jeff at Speaker Sanchez's law offices in

Albuquerque to review highway needs and funding and resolve the 44 dispute. If the US Treasury/Wall Street invention, "Garvee bonds," was good for the highway to Farmington, legislators asked, what about the rest of the state? The outcome was a plan and sort of agreement to fund about a dozen more projects committing federal funds for new construction and shorting highway maintenance decades into the future. This was "borrow and spend's" first big toehold in New Mexico. It also set in motion the irregular and unprecedented procurement of the Hwy. 44 project with design, build, finance and warrant in one consolidated RFP and contract. The $295 million project received only one bid, from Koch Industries with its owners deep into right wing politics.[96] The 20-year term of the highway bonds was extraordinary, almost certainly longer than the life of new asphalt pavement.

Reducing the state workforce was an administration priority and SHTD also was at the fore of that effort. SHTD announced a reduction in force (RIF) of 71 employees in tandem with privatization of highway striping and signage. The department allowed the striping contractor to use state equipment. The RIF required approval of the Personnel Board, and after months of hullabaloo, less than a dozen highway workers were laid off.

Also, in July 1997 a bipartisan group of legislators (including Representative Murray Ryan (R-Siver City) and Senator Mary Jane Garcia (D-Dona Ana)) sued the HSD for implementing a welfare reform plan without statutory authority. HSD Secretary Duke Rodriguez was colorful and inflammatory. He won fame with an exhortatory demonstration to staff atop a conference room table that capitol wags likened to a rug dance. He argued that the new federal Temporary Aid to Needy Families (TANF) initiative required a new state program. The US Health and Human Services Department summoned Rodriguez and legislative staff to a meeting in Washington, DC and clarified that no federal funds were in jeopardy and there was time to develop a consensus program. The Supreme Court sided with the legislators in September and Rodriguez resigned in October, partly stemming from a *Journal* investigation into personal business matters. (He was replaced by longtime UNM hospital administrator Bill Johnson who in a December Supreme Court opinion was found in contempt of court for pursuing the executive initiative.) Bill Hume said, "the opinion memorializes in stark detail Johnson's unlawful conduct in welfare reform. It further bolsters the body of case law restricting New Mexico's governor, a strait jacket that will be one of Johnson's legacies."[97] Secretary Bill Johnson later collaborated with legislators to develop a consensus TANF bill for the 1998 legislature.

Meanwhile Department of Corrections issued an RFP and contracted with the Wackenhut Corporation for construction and operation of two prisons pursuant to a pass-through financing with Lea County. Pursuant to the Duran consent decree, Corrections finally closed Penitentiary of New Mexico "Old Main" in November and sent some prisoners out of state temporarily. (The LFC, including women legislators and staff, toured the general population unit earlier that fall.) Wackenhut hired Senator Aragon as an operations consultant.

On November 20 Victor Marshall, attorney for Representative Max Coll, requested a subpoena to the Wackenhut CEO pursuant to the 1996 lawsuit challenging the prison financing scheme. The subpoena addressed information about political contributions and business arrangements between Wackenhut and Manny Aragon related to concrete work at the Santa Rosa prison. LFC was meeting and on Friday morning Senators Aragon and Senator Robinson walked in about 930 and glared at Coll and then Aragon walked out. Robinson said to Senator Altamirano and others, "Let's go boys." Only Senator Ingle (R-Portales) was left on the Senate side, Friday hearings were cancelled, and the committee adjourned. Senator Aragon said Coll disrespected him and the legislative institution, and Robinson said, "we're really sick of Max right now."[98] That was one of the lowest days of my legislative tenure. Representative Varela found me, and we went to Tommy's downtown for lunch. Again, I wondered what I got myself into.

On an up note, I had lunch with Paul Minogue, former LFC analyst, Deputy Secretary at DoH and new DFA Budget Director. He advised me that it was guaranteed that our bosses would be fighting, but our job was to help them figure out solutions and a way forward.

Governor Johnson announced that he would not submit Rob Perry, Acting Corrections Secretary, for confirmation and that triggered another round of criticism of Johnson circumventing constitutional duties of the legislature.

In January 1998 at a joint session on the judiciary, Chief Justice Gene Franchini said, "the public doesn't care who wins or loses the conflicts between branches. Every time there is a conflict, we all lose."[99] (Sort of like the 2023 pickle in the US House of Representatives fighting about the budget, Ukraine, border security and the speakership.)

At the December 1997 LFC meeting, Senator Fidel was the only Senate Democrat that attended. He denied that the other Democratic Senators were boycotting. LFC adopted a budget recommendation for FY99 that included $60 million of tax reductions and reduced agency appropriations $49 million, partly by not funding 650 FTE that were vacant at least four months. The LFC recommendation left a whopping $243 million of recurring revenue unspent for the full legislature to prioritize. DFA Secretary Harris criticized the LFC recommendation as a "partial budget," but I was happy that we had a recommendation at all, and the practice of a legislative set-aside continues today.

A Calloway column on January 15, 1998, noted the LFC budget document was the lightest since 1992, down from five pounds three ounces in two volumes to three pounds eleven ounces in one volume. Calloway asked why and reported, "Abbey, obviously a man of science answered 'good,' that means we saved six hundred pounds of paper. In about three seconds Abbey had multiplied the savings of one and a half pounds per book times, four hundred the number of books printed this year. Abbey asked the staff to shrink the document to make it more readable and accessible. Pages were streamlined and compressed to eliminate white space and sections reserved for comments were deleted if there wasn't anything to say."

The big budget issue for the 1998 session was whether to count revenue from tribal gaming, the legislature of course thought yes. Twice the governor vetoed funding for interim legislative committees from the feed bill along with a third bill with $1.4 million for a pilot project for legislative staffing. Johnson also vetoed a 12 cent per pack cigarette tax increase earmarked for the UNM cancer center enraging Senator Billy McKibben (R-Hobbs), sometimes called "chainsaw" because of his buzz haircut. A *Journal* editorial on March 8 said Johnson stood up for Joe Camel. McKibben appealed for a veto override, and Lou Gallegos and

Republican party chair John Dendahl criticized McKibben as "five links short of a full chain." McKibben shot back, "Dendahl reminds me of a eunuch in a brothel. He knows exciting things are going on but never having been elected he can't participate. He's relegated to peeking through a keyhole and making value judgments about others."[100]

The legislature passed the 1998 General Appropriation Act with FY99 appropriations of $3.05 billion, but the governor vetoed $57 million. A supplemental appropriation bill, including budget adjustment authority and additional appropriations for agencies, died on adjournment (HB448), and Johnson called a special session for May 1. Johnson said it could be done in a day, but the special session feed bill budgeted ten days.

At the special session, the legislature overrode a veto of a bill providing services for DD clients, the first veto override since 1970 with Republican Representatives Townsend, Carpenter and Alwin voting yes. The cigarette tax increase override stalled, but the legislature passed the supplemental appropriation bill with BAR authority. Finally, a bill passed that Johnson signed to ban drive up windows for liquor sales.

I survived my first session as legislative director with some things looking up. The *Journal* had a photo of me behind Senator Altamirano voting for HB2. I helped Senator Aragon find emergency funding for jury trials from the Board of Finance, resisted by Harris. I helped the speaker on an op ed touting the legislature's fiscal leadership and helped Senator Aragon on oversight hearings related to Los Alamos National Laboratory. I also provided technical expertise and authority in some of the fights related to layoffs, costs of privatization, and revenue estimates. LFC and DFA budget staff were collaborating on a pilot project to implement performance-based budgeting. But I was still hanging on by a thread.

14. David Abbey with Senator Ben Altamirano voting on HB2, February 18, 1998. (*Journal* photo.)

Almost out of nowhere Johnson's public standing improved in the 1998 election season. A *Journal* profile described a reappraisal.[101] UNM political science professor Gil St. Clair said he initially thought Johnson was naïve but credited him with perseverance in key goals such as reducing the size of government, holding the line on tax increases, and exiting the Duran consent decree. The big issues on which he was sued successfully or criticized by the legislature for his unilateral executive action—tribal gaming, prison construction, highway projects, welfare reform—were achieved with legislative support in 1998. A September poll showed Johnson with a 61 percent approval rating.

State finances were on the upswing too.[102] The revenue estimates were too low by $50 million to $100 million. The attorney general reported settlement of litigation with tobacco companies would bring in $1.2 billion over 25 years. The Starr report and Clinton lying on TV also probably helped the Republicans.

Governor Johnson was reelected to a second term on November 3, 1998, 54 percent to 46 percent. His opponent, Senator Marty Chavez, said it was a good, hard fought, clean campaign.

Representative Murray Ryan (R-Silver City) retired in 1998 after 30 years. Ryan, a West Point graduate, worked in the family liquor business, was truly an independent and an ally of Senator Smith. Murray Ryan Jr. was a doctor in Espanola and informed legislators of the opiate crisis in its early days. Senator Smith told of opening his grandfather's bar in Deming as a young teen to take deliveries and maybe serve an early customer. One time Murray came in and shouted, "liquor inspector," and John hightailed it from behind the bar. Representative Tommy Foy (D-Bayard) retired after 28 years. He was a Notre Dame grad, a Bataan vet and POW. His kids included a district attorney, an appeals court judge and a highway official. Phil Larragoitte says he was most renowned for serving libations for the Roundhouse lawyers on St. Patrick's Day. Visualize the twinkling eyes of Ryan and Foy. Representative Richard "General" Knowles (R-Roswell) also retired after eight terms. He was a collaborative LFC member; the legislature-initiated scholarships to the New Mexico Military Institute in his name.[103] His son was a district judge in Albuquerque.

Representative "Dub" Williams (R-Glencoe) retired in January 1999 beginning his 8th term. He was a Louisiana native, retired teacher, football coach and rancher. He was soft spoken, kind and friendly. I'd talk to him after a long day walking back to our offices in the annex. One night he told me about coming home after the war in the Pacific. He was almost 18, and he flew a kite from the fantail as his naval vessel passed under the Golden Gate Bridge. His daughter-in-law was a district judge in Carrizozo.

## SECOND TERM

In December 1998, DFA reduced the General Fund revenue estimate by $60 million, a hard way to start.

Both the LFC and Executive budget recommendations at the 1999 session for FY00 were in the five to six percent range with the executive pushing for personal income tax cuts. While the House was working on HB2, the Senate initiated its own version of the General Appropriation Act creating some confusion. The LFC recommendation assumed significant savings by eliminating positions vacant for at least four months. The LFC also assumed savings from privatization, for example, the license plate (tag) plant at the state prison. TRD claimed savings of $400 thousand but struggled to document the savings and explain the contract award to a Nova Scotia company. The LFC recommendation included a $1.6 million transfer from the Road Fund to the Cultural Affairs' Office of Archeological Studies to ensure that the highway department didn't skimp on requisite roadside archeology or privatize the duties.[104] On January 21 Johnson vetoed salaries of LFC in HB1 for $2.2 million, complaining of LFC "harassment." Larry Calloway of the *Journal* said, "the governor's vindictive veto accidentally performs a service," by reminding legislators the LFC is necessary.[105] On February 26 the legislature passed an appropriation bill for LFC salaries $70 thousand lower than the vetoed bill and with three FTE removed.

On March 6, busloads of citizens, oil and gas employees and local elected officials rallied at the Roundhouse and packed the House gallery appealing for tax relief to aid the struggling oil and gas industry. Senator Carroll Leavell (R-Jal) said West Texas sour was at a record low of $5.65/bbl; Hobbs school enrollment was down ten percent. On March 11 Johnson vetoed SB2, and the legislature sent up SB 378 with modest changes that passed the House 39-26 and the Senate 29-13. But Johnson quickly vetoed that too and said the legislature would be coming back, that it was the worst ever budget: "It's bad news. It's terrible. It's incomplete. It's an abomination. It's abominable."[106] He said meetings with the legislature are fruitless, "they don't listen to anything I have to say." Johnson also vetoed the $87 million capital outlay bill.

The big issue for Johnson was $3,100 per pupil vouchers for public education phased in over 12 years. He went on a nine-day campaign swing and called the session for May 5. He also called for $30 million more for agencies and broad budget adjustment authority. He said the session could be done in a day, but the special session feed bill budgeted ten days. Vouchers were, always have been a nonstarter in New Mexico. Conservative rural areas generally don't support vouchers, because they generally don't have private school or even charter school options. The session lasted five days, and the legislature passed a 21-member voucher task force, a $3.3 billion budget, up five percent with $23 million more agency funding, limited BAR authority and a $90 million capital bill.

At the LFC meeting in May, the committee voted in a bipartisan way to subpoena all state contracts unless provided by June 30. The *Journal* editorialized, "So it's come to this?" The DFA provided the contracts and initiated a monthly report which continues to the present. June editorials criticized HSD's child support enforcement division and the warranty for Hwy. 44. Calloway in July criticized LFC for a nitpicky audit of PERA based on an anonymous complaint.

In July Phelp Dodge shut its smelter in Playas for a loss of 400 jobs, a blow to southwest New Mexico.

In early September riots broke at Wackenhut's Santa Rosa and Hobbs prisons, an inmate was killed and then a guard, Ralph Garcia from Tucumcari. Finger pointing erupted with Corrections Secretary Perry saying staffing was inadequate, State Police saying they weren't notified timely, and Wackenhut saying the state's classification system was sending violent inmates and gang members to the medium security (Level 3) facilities that should be in maximum security levels. A September 9 mass junta including a federal judge, legislative leaders (both chambers, both parties), Corrections and Public Safety secretaries and other agency officials, and Wackenhut executives met for a broad review of incident timelines, security, classification, emergency procedures, prison design, liability and funding. There was an agreement to form an Independent Board of Inquiry (IBI). The *Journal*'s Mike Gallagher declared, "the inmate uprisings at both prisons have rocked the state and called Johnson's policies into question."[107]

In October Johnson triggered an uproar with a call for a national debate about drug policy. Clinton drug czar, Barry McCaffery, traveled to New Mexico to explain the federal initiatives. A *Journal* editorial said, "With Johnson there's no meat to temper the hot sauce of his ideas."[108] Department of Public Safety Secretary Darren White, sometimes called the Singing Sergeant because of his days in an anti-drug rock band sponsored by Albuquerque PD, resigned in protest. Separately, RLD superintendent Robin Otten fired Anita Lockwood, the well-regarded director of Construction Industries.

Eleventh District Judge Joseph Rich from Gallup ruled that the state's method of funding school buildings was unconstitutional, and the Public School Capital Outlay Council began the search for an earmarked revenue source to achieve "adequacy."

Senator Aragon and Representative Saavedra initiated meetings to identify additional funding for the new Metropolitan Court building in Albuquerque with a focus on land acquisition and construction of a $20 million parking facility.

In December, the *Journal* had a four-part series on the Highway 44 project.[109] A Koch Industries proposal became the basis of the Department of Transportation's RFP with Koch saying the proposal was solicited by SHTD and SHTD saying it was unsolicited. Five DoT officials went to Wichita to discuss the project with Koch asphalt division representatives who touted a "Euro design" method. Recall that Koch was the only bidder for the unique design/build/ finance/ warrant project. The 20-year road warranty was the first (and apparently last) of its kind with a few states looking at three-year warranties. Construction costs were only $180 million of the $420 million project total. The 44 project was rated lower than other roads on the State Infrastructure Plan and jumped to the top with limited public input. The *Journal* also profiled the Koch family's activities to promote the Republican and Libertarian parties and the Cato Institute. At the initiative of legislative leaders, SHTD dumped private financing in favor of much cheaper tax-exempt financing offered by the New Mexico Finance Authority. Secretary Rahn claimed savings of $89 million which were not verified.

In December LFC moved from the fourth floor of the Roundhouse to the basement of the old state library, a remodeled annex connected to the basement of the capital by a tunnel and breezeway.

2000, Feed bill Veto and Two Budget Vetoes. Governor Johnson vetoed the legislative feed bill. A *Journal* editorial on January 30 criticized "non-stop bickering" between Johnson and Aragon and Sanchez, noting that a business day event at the capitol turned into an episode of the three stooges.

Gross budget differences were small with the Executive recommending a 3.9 percent General Fund increase and LFC at five percent. But with a week to go in the 30-day, Governor Johnson vetoed the GAA in two hours and noted agencies are $30 million short, but Johnson also wanted $15 million of personal income tax cuts. The Senate followed with SB2, the replacement GAA, adding $6 million to agencies with an overall General Fund increase of 3.9 percent and reserves at 4.7 percent. Mild-mannered SFC Chair Altamirano in his floor speech on the budget said, "We have hit the governor's target spending. Governor Johnson doesn't seem to realize that. Instead, he seems intent on creating a moving target, so we are guaranteed to miss."[110] Altamirano criticized mismanagement at Motor Vehicle Division, the most-inept tax department in the country, rising costs of privatization, inconsistent positions and ignoring budget savings.

On Wednesday, February 16, Senator Aragon moved to reject the nomination of Robin Otten as HSD Secretary, and Johnson withdrew the nomination and double-hatted Lou Gallegos as acting HSD Secretary with Otten as deputy. On Thursday, the final morning, Senator Joe Carraro (R-Albuquerque) filibustered the capital bill, complaining it didn't include his priorities. and it failed along with a fix for state park operations.

Legislators appealed to Johnson to sign the budget and avoid the cost of a special session, but on March 8, the last day of the signing period, Johnson vetoed the GAA for the second time. But he signed full day kindergarten and $60 million short-term bonds for school buildings.

On Sunday after the session, February 20, a *Journal* editorial headlined, "Voters Need to Fix Broken Government." Blame was all around with the Senate staging override votes on opening day and making Johnson wait for his speech: "The arrogance of Senator President Pro Tem Manny Aragon is amply matched by the uncooperative contempt of Governor Gary Johnson." On the same page Calloway had a similar theme, "New Mexico's Roundhouse Needs a Whole New Script." But a Bill Hume column also on the same page pointed the way to a breakthrough. Hume reported oil prices are $30/bbl thanks to OPEC, but the revenue forecast was based on $21/bbl. On February 27 Calloway described the budget dispute as much ado about nothing with only $3 million difference in recurring appropriations and $10 million in General Fund reserves. You could bet that the Roundhouse would spend its way to victory.

On March 8 the Governor, legislators of both parties (Sanchez, Ben Lujan, Hobbs, Ingle, Coll, Altamirano, Sandel) and DFA and other officials and staff (Lou Gallegos, Harris, Budget Director Kormanik, Duffy Rodriguez, Billy Sparks and Tom Clifford) and legislative staff (at various times the Speaker's Annie Murray, Aragon's Frank Martinez, Paula Tackett, Bill Valdes, LESC's Pauline Rindone, and Janet Peacock ) began a series of mass juntas every few days to resolve the budget differences. Duffy Rodriguez started off with a one-hour budget presentation. Someone on the legislative side taped one meeting triggering complaints. At a March 13 meeting Kormanik stated a common theme of the Executive: "the governor is ascertaining a pattern of agency underfunding leading to supplemental funding and allegations of mismanagement." I'd been telling members revenue estimates were going up, and Clifford agreed $40 million was reasonable. Harris said at one point he had the impression they were not talking to the right people. (Harris practiced what legislative staff called "chaos theory", planting rumors, stirring up controversy and even animosity and then leading the way to a solution.[111]) Lou Gallegos said he didn't want a 15-minute harangue. Day after day going through lists of agency needs. Corrections couldn't produce an expenditure forecast. Legislative leaders proposed adding $18 million, and by late March, $27 million. The caucuses met. Public school funding up $90 million was OK, but budget adjustment authority (BARs) remained a bone of contention, with the Executive wanting flexibility up front before the fiscal year started and Coll saying the legislature has been generous with supplemental BAR authority.

On March 26 Bill Hume had a remarkable report on one of the last meetings, "Governor, Legislative Leaders Playing Different Ball Game." The legislature was criticized for holding private meetings, so Aragon invited the press without notice to the executive. Hume wrote "chess for the legislators, checkers for Johnson," and, "Johnson acknowledges a surprising lack of knowledge of the details of budget differences." For example, legislators flagged potential savings by funding inmate medical care based on population rather than beds, a difference of 200 inmates, and Johnson indicated he hadn't heard about it. But winding up Johnson acknowledged substantial progress.

The session started March 28 and lasted eight days. The budget was $3.5 billion, up 5.8 percent or $192 million and included 6.25 percent raises for teachers and adding two days to the 180-day school calendar. Vetoes were only $8 million including an expansion of Medicaid eligibility for adults from 37 percent to 75 percent of the poverty level and $2 million for infant home visiting. Capital outlay passed for $212 million.

Special sessions sap the body politic. It becomes too much for many legislators who are employed or live in a hotel in Santa Fe, sometimes with their spouses. Before and during the session(s), the governor, cabinet secretaries and aides, budget officials and many others are preoccupied with legislative affairs from attending hearings to reviewing fiscal impact reports. The day-to-day operations of government take a back seat to say nothing of implementing long-term initiatives. The focus of the capital is getting money, not achieving results.

In my view, Johnson wasn't much interested in running government to begin with. Consider the remainder of 2000 mostly uneventful from a governmental standpoint.

Medicaid cost overruns continued. The Santa Teresa port of entry and industrial park boomed. In April, the land acquisition for the $60 million Metropolitan Court project came under scrutiny, in particular the parking garage owned by Raymond Gallegos of Gaim-Ko.[112] The purchase price, including 35 percent of parking garage receipts for 25 years, was figured at two- or three-times appraised value. In May the Cerro Grande fire consumed portions of Los Alamos and LANL. DFA Secretary Harris retired in August, replaced by Harold Field, an executive of Johnson's Big J. Johnson said he would play a greater role in budget and legislative affairs. Harris said, "collaboration with the Legislature is a real art form. It takes a lot of patience, it takes a lot of listening skill, and it takes a lot of time. It is intensive. If truly that is his objective, I would laud the governor for making that kind of commitment, because I think it would be rewarding for him."[113]

In September El Paso Natural Gas Co. merged with Coastal and moved its headquarters to Colorado Springs.

At the general election Gore nipped Bush in New Mexico by 366 votes. Speaker Raymond Sanchez and Rep Jerry Sandel, each with 30 years' experience, were defeated, but the Democrats gained two seats in the House. A $26 million general obligation bond issue for state buildings, including the new history museum, failed 57-43.

2001, Senate Coalition and Tax Cut Veto. The DFA projection of new money for FY02 was an extraordinary $400 million, and the Executive and LFC General Fund recommendations were seven percent and nine percent, respectively. Natural gas prices soared from $2/mcf to $8/mcf. Johnson's big priority was a two-year reduction of personal income tax rates for $72 million.

Corrections Secretary Rob Perry gave legislative leaders and LFC members and staff monogramed jackets from corrections industries that cost $400 each, and after bad press Perry reimbursed the cost of jackets that weren't returned. I still have mine. On February 28, Governor Johnson broke his back jogging on an ice patch.

There were 25 freshman legislators at the 2001 session. The Senate voted 21-20 to replace Senator Aragon as President Pro Tem with Richard Romero, a retired assistant superintendent of Albuquerque Public Schools. All 18 republicans and

Senators McSorley (D-Albuquerque) and Tsosie (D-Whitehorse) voted for Romero. A *Journal* editorial March 8 applauded Senator Altamirano and the Senate Finance Committee for crafting the budget in a collaborative way rather than under the control of Senator Aragon. HB2 passed with a $400 million, or 11.5 percent increase. In a series of juntas Johnson appealed to legislative leaders to pare back spending and pass a bigger tax cut, but Coll, Altamirano and Lujan said there wasn't a will to make cuts and said, "you do it." Johnson said Ok but you're not going to like it.

The legislature passed a tax cut billed at $54 million including a reduction in the top PIT rate from 8.2 percent to 7.7 percent for $27 million and low-income rebates for $10 million.

On Friday March 16 Johnson vetoed $90 million from the budget including $50 million of pay raises which the legislature passed Saturday morning. Johnson vetoed the tax bill (and 131 other bills) saying it wasn't enough and a $260 million capital outlay bill as hostage for a bigger tax bill to be considered around a special session in September for reapportionment. With Raymond Sanchez gone and Aragon off Finance, Bill Hume for the *Journal* said on March 25 the public could only blame Johnson for gridlock. Commenting on the vetoed capital bill on March 31, LFC's Linda Kehoe said it was the best capital bill in 31 years and the legislature prioritized funding off the top for state agency projects. I said, "The way this often plays in the press is that this whole thing is pork laden. It is much better."

Representative Varela was appointed chair of LFC on May 4 instead of HAFC Chair Max Coll. Speaker Lujan said Varela's knowledge of government operations could enhance oversight.

All summer there was a drumbeat of stories about the consequences of the failure of capital outlay—from not matching $400 thousand from Colorado for the Cumbres and Toltec Scenic Railroad to not matching $15 million of federal appropriations for the new history museum to nixing $17 million to acquire Eagle Nest Lake for a fishing-oriented state park.

New Mexico Highlands President Selimo Rael, who double hatted as VP for Finance, was out after reporting a $1.5 million FY01 deficit and a much bigger FY02 shortfall.

In August I was driving to Santa Fe after an LFC meeting in Farmington and the news came that Governor Johnson was advocating decriminalization of drugs. I was ecstatic. Regardless of the merits, I knew that his libertarian initiative would fracture his conservative base. The chickens would come home to roost the next May at a special session.

The September revenue estimate turned down sharply and tax cut talk was over, (voucher talk too). The events on September 11 changed America's world view.

The September special session on reapportionment lasted 18 days. The governor vetoed house, senate and congressional bills, and the courts drew the map.

Treasurer Scrutinized. On August 30 State Auditor Domingo Martinez wrote to Board of Finance Director Curt Porter directing the board to conduct special audit procedures to ensure state treasurer compliance with the BoF investment policy and to determine competitive pricing for bond transactions.[114] At the September 14 Board of Finance meeting, the Treasurer criticized the auditor, LFC and me and represented that it was unfortunate that the state and the Democratic party didn't recognize his good work.[115] Board members generally complimented the efforts of the treasurer.

The same day the BoF's custody bank advised that the Treasurer purchased a $400 million AIM Treasury Portfolio mutual fund which was not an approved investment. The transaction fee was an extraordinary 0.6 percent, later reduced to 0.18 percent after public scrutiny. Treasurer Montoya claimed alternative investments for surplus cash were not available in the wake of market disruption after 911.

On September 28 LFC Chair Altamirano wrote to BoF Executive Officer David Harris and Treasurer Montoya reiterating LFC concerns about treasurer's investment practices that were reported in LFC's FY00 budget analysis and appealing for improved controls. At a testy November 9 LFC meeting, the treasurer didn't appear, and Senator Altamirano and Representatives. Coll and Varela criticized deputy treasurer Robert Vigil for being arrogant and uncooperative. Assistant AG Al Lama advised LFC that mutual funds were not an eligible investment.

Internal, unreleased LFC analysis documented mispricing of bond transactions.[116] Senator Altamirano, Representative Coll and I discussed these concerns with the attorney general, but nothing came of it. Too bad. Board of Finance Director Jan Goodwin advised the board of finance by letter on February 11, 2002, that treasurer's investment practices in 2001 cost the state in excess of $30 million. Were the pirates emboldened by inaction? Did they see greater opportunity with the state's permanent and pension funds in the next administration? Events in 2005 and then 2008 validated the concerns of the auditor and LFC.

On December 9, the Journal's Bill Hume summed up the political year in New Mexico: "The truth on tax cuts after all, is that Johnson missed his best opportunity by not taking what the legislature offered last regular session. The state was flush with cash and the Democrats had expressed a willingness to consider more tax relief depending on how financials developed. Johnson vetoed the half-loaf tax credit and punitively vetoed the entire capital package."

2002/Veto Override. On January 13 Bill Richardson announced a run for governor. He said he, "will treat the legislature as partners, not adversaries."

The state budget preoccupied the capitol for most of Johnson's final year in office. This was odd considering that FY03 new money was a mere $8 million, called the worst fiscal condition since 1983. Medicaid was the root of the budget battle with enrollment up sharply for kids up to 235 percent of the federal poverty level ($41 thousand for a family of four) and managed care rate increases projected at 13 percent. Johnson requested $50 million less than the

HSD request of $381 million. A week before the session ended, the legislature passed a budget with $27 million of tobacco settlement revenue supplementing the General Fund for Medicaid allowing more General Fund for agencies. It was quickly vetoed as "unfixable," Johnson said the use of tobacco revenue was "smoke and mirrors." Speaker Ben Lujan noted that Medicaid cuts would cost the state economy a three to one match of Federal funds for Medicaid. On February 12 the legislature sent up a second bill with General Fund appropriations up 0.6 percent, $10 million less spending including a $3 million reduction in Medicaid and eliminating a one percent raise for teachers. Johnson said it was worse than the first one and threatened to veto two capital bills with $319 million.

Senator Altamirano and Reps. Coll, Saavedra and Varela scheduled a meeting with the editorial board of the *Albuquerque Journal*. Unwisely, I offered to drive. I had an old Mercedes two-door coupe, the seats were crumbling, and it looked like the passengers were lowriders. Thereafter, Representative Saavedra called me "Columbo" after the rumpled Peter Falk character.

A *Journal* editorial on February 17 urged Johnson to use line-item vetoes to trim the GAA and capital and avoid the cost and waste of time of a special session. The *Journal* noted, "in a manner eerily reminiscent of earlier constitutional slowdowns, Johnson says he can veto the budget and unilaterally authorize state spending at last year's level." At a luncheon of the Association of Commerce and Industry, Johnson said, "If pigs could fly, maybe I could sign that budget." A photo showed Johnson twirling a toy pig with flapping wings.[117] The crowd laughed, but President Pro Tem Richard Romero said Johnson's remarks were "immature" and "irresponsible." Speaker Lujan joined in appealing for the governor to line item the budget rather than a wholesale veto.

On March 6 Johnson vetoed the budget but signed capital outlay without any line-item vetoes. This seemed odd with capital including $79 million of General Fund appropriations for 23 statewide projects and Johnson later complaining that General Fund reserves were too low at eight percent.

On March 26, Lujan and Romero appointed twelve legislators to a committee to develop another budget compromise: Reps. Burpo, Coll, Larranaga, Marquardt, Saavedra and Varela and Senators Altamirano, Beffort, Carraro, Rawson, Smith and Tsosie. In early April the "bipartisan legislative committee" presented a discussion proposal to the caucuses, and on April 19 legislative leaders presented the plan to the governor although details weren't public. During this period Speaker Lujan called me every day to get a progress report on support for the bipartisan plan, especially among Republicans. The leaders met again on April 29, and Johnson said they weren't far apart, just a couple of "dealbreakers." There was dispute whether reserves were 7.1 percent (governor) or 7.7 percent (legislature), but there was an expectation that May revenue estimates might trend upward and aid resolution. Also, Johnson wanted more BAR authority. On May 9 legislators presented another proposal that Speaker Lujan said doubled BAR authority and boosted reserves to eight percent. House minority leader Ted Hobbs said the proposal "works", and Senator Ingle predicted the governor would be OK. But Johnson pushed for more BAR authority and advocated delaying a special session until after the June 4 primary, but legislators said public school budgets required a quick resolution. Speaker Lujan and Senator Romero said they were prepared to call an extraordinary session of the legislature which required signatures of three-fifths members of House and Senate, a milestone previously never reached, rarer than a veto override. They said the signatures were in hand, while Johnson continued to say we're really close.

On May 18 a petition declaring an emergency and requesting an extraordinary session was delivered with 47 representatives, five more than needed including five Republicans, and 30 senators, four more than needed with seven Republicans. Minority Leader Ted Hobbs (R-Albuquerque) told the governor a veto override was not sustainable. On May 22 Johnson said he would veto the bipartisan plan and scheduled the session for May 25. Senator Romero said, "I think people are frustrated, exasperated and willing to bring closure."[118]

A *Journal* editorial on Thursday, May 23 headlined, "Johnson Makes History with Fiscal Recalcitrance.": "Governor Gary Johnson has long proudly stated that he doesn't do politics. But politics—the art of give and take compromise—was the only game in town for settling the impasse over a state budget. ... Johnson didn't play—and he appears to have maneuvered himself out of the process. ...

Johnson seemed to relish the potential for a constitutional crisis of attempting to run state government without legislative fiscal instructions. ... The situation is all the more surreal in that Johnson balked over a million here, a few million there in a budget totaling about $4 billion. Legislators complain that Johnson's budget demands kept shifting. ... Taxpayers will find out Friday whether enough Republicans will put the imperatives of responsible state government ahead of lame-duck rigidity by overriding the veto and letting all the vital state-funded functions once again move forward." Senator Lee Rawson (R-Las Cruces) urged the governor to veto the budget quickly so the legislature could override it quickly and go home.

On Friday, May 24 in two hours, the legislature passed the bipartisan budget, the governor vetoed it, and the House and Senate overrode 62-7 and 36-4, respectively. Republican leaders Hobbs and Ingle supported the override, Senators Aragon and Robinson voted no. The budget included $15 million to purchase Eagle Nest Lake from CS Cattle Co. of Cimarron for a state park.

Johnson lamented he was "steamrolled", but a May 25 *Journal* editorial stated, "perhaps the near unanimity on the veto override will start a post-Johnson return to civility between the parties in the legislature."

Posters of the May 23 and May 25 *Journal* editorial and a Trevor cartoon of a flying pig still adorn the walls of the Roundhouse.

Richardson was campaigning in Dona Ana County in August and joined the majority members of LFC for breakfast at the old Hilton. Steve Terrell of the *New Mexican* reported that Representative Varela and Representative Coll threw cold water on the campaign proposals of both Representative John Sanchez and Richardson to cut taxes. But at the gubernatorial debate on Sunday night, Richardson laid down the gauntlet. Democratic legislators he said, "had been whining and carping about his proposed income tax cut. You're either with us or against us." Dan Weaks told me that New Mexico legislators were like good old boys sittin' on a porch shootin' the breeze and drinking moonshine and Richardson comes up with an AK-47 and sprays them all into submission.

Richardson crushed Representative Sanchez 56-38; for the southern US Congressional District Republican Steve Pearce beat Senator John Arthur Smith handily; Senator Pat Lyons (R-Cuervo) was elected land commissioner; and former State Auditor Robert Vigil was elected state treasurer.

# 10

# Bill Richardson 2003–2010

Bill Richardson grew up largely in Mexico City, went to prep school in Massachusetts and graduated with bachelors and masters in international affairs from Tufts University. He was tall and handsome, typically long-haired and smiling broadly, and a great baseball player. He worked for the State Department and the US Senate and moved to New Mexico in 1978 to work for the Democratic Party. He barely lost to Representative Manuel Lujan in 1980 and was elected to New Mexico's new northern district in 1982 with the theme and ubiquitous bumper stickers, "Fighter for the North." After 14 years in Congress, he was appointed by President Clinton to United Nations (UN) ambassador and then US secretary of energy.

Richardson was 56 on his inauguration. He spoke of boosting teacher pay, ending partisan bickering, cutting taxes and running a tight fiscal ship, and said, "give me the tools and I will put New Mexico on a path to progress." His inaugural committee spent $420 thousand with 3,500 attending several balls. Country star Randy Travis entertained.

His appointments were top caliber and politically and demographically balanced (although a handful of minor appointees quickly resigned drawing criticism for sloppy vetting). Campaign aides were key appointees, including Rick Homans, Economic Development, David Contarino as chief of staff, and Billy Sparks as press chief. James Jimenez was back as DFA secretary and David Harris as deputy chief of staff (and New Mexico Finance Authority director by April). Rhonda Faught, the first female highway district engineer, was appointed the first female transportation secretary. Board of Finance Director Jan Godwin went to TRD and the capable and long-suffering Pam Hyde to HSD. *Journal* columnist Bill Hume joined the Governor's staff, and Representative Varela's son Jeff was personnel director. Michelle Lujan Grisham was retained at aging affairs, soon to be cabinet level. Gary Bland, chief investment officer at Boeing, was appointed State Investment Officer for an eye-popping salary of $225 thousand. LFC Deputy Director Dannette Burch went to DFA as deputy secretary along with LFC analysts Mark Valdes to Board of Finance director, Ruby Ann Esquibel to HSD special assistant, Lawrence Trujillo to Corrections deputy and Wanda Carillo to deputy secretary at GSD. (Shortly after the election, insider Jamie Koch asked me to meet at Inn of Loretto and I was relieved to discover Jimenez leaving as I arrived, knowing an appointment for me was unlikely.)

Richardson was always on the go. A week after the election he met with Intel executives in Silicon Valley. He met with North Koreans in January. In February the Chihuahua governor and El Paso mayor accompanied him to a NAFTA-themed mission to Chicago. The President of Spain came to Santa Fe in July, including a meeting with Richardson and pueblo governors, and in November 2003 Mexico President Fox addressed a packed crowd at the Roundhouse.

In his first session, his budget made lemonade out of lemons, almost LFC style, perhaps with our help. A bit of smoke and mirrors too. Mid-session, before even passing the budget, Richardson muscled through a big tax cut billed at $900 million over five years. The top rate for PIT fell from 8.2 percent to 4.9 percent along with a capital gains deduction up to $1,000. New money was only $146 million, but several bills added $100 million with diversion of tobacco settlement revenue to the General Fund, an increase in the cigarette tax from 21 cents to 91 cents per pack, elimination of the insurance premium tax deduction for managed care (effectively, legally taxing federal Medicaid expenditures at a cost only of the 25 percent Medicaid match) and an expanded TRD taxpayer audit program. Two constitutional amendments were billed as school reform with a boost in the Permanent Fund distribution rate from 4.7 percent to 5.8 percent (phasing back to 5 percent after ten years) and creation of a cabinet level Public Education Department. The amendments required voter approval at a September 23 special election.

General Fund appropriations were up 5.5 percent with public education and Medicaid the top priorities and most other agencies at two percent. Minimum teacher salaries went to $30/40/50 thousand for Level 1, 2 and 3 teachers, respectively. The appropriation for the governor's office rose 73 percent. The tobacco settlement permanent fund was incorporated into the general fund for window-dressing the reserve level. The capital bill was $141 million for 1,823 projects; only $110 thousand was vetoed, but the message called for a "rational planning process" to review capital requests of legislators. Collective bargaining for public employees also passed.

In the wake of the session, New Mexico had a billboard in Times Square and an ad in the *Wall St. Journal* touting the tax cuts. A *Journal* editorial on March 25 headlined, "Session Yields Progress, Richardson in Charge." Richardson was tabbed to chair the Democratic convention in Boston, and the *Journal* reported, "It's very clear Richardson is positioning himself as a major player in the national political arena with a possible eye on the White House in 2008."[119]

Early Signs of Trouble. The 2003 LFC budget recommendation for the state treasurer for FY04 flagged that Wachovia Securities and Southwest Securities, regional securities firms, were improbably the brokers for 91 percent of bond transactions in 2002, even though Board of Finance policy required competitive bids. Guy Riordan, a stockbroker, handled the bond transactions for Wachovia and previously worked for Southwest. Riordan had been in the news in fall 2002 for selling 160 acres with recreation access to the Sandia mountains to Sandia Pueblo for many times his purchase price. Riordan was also a boxing promoter and owned a hunting preserve and shooting range near La Joya. Governor Richardson appointed Riordan chair of the state game commission in January.

A March LFC forecast projected the state could face a shortfall of $200 million in FY04 rising to $450 million by F08.[120] Representative Coll and some other legislators questioned the authority of the governor to allocate $64 million of federal aid to New Mexico (Coll said it was totally unconstitutional), but legislative leaders wanted to find consensus with the governor.[121]

During the 2003 session Richardson drew some flak for requiring appointees to pre-submit an undated letter of resignation. This seemed to blow over, but in April Richardson sought to replace six members of the Judicial Standards Commission. 12th District Judge Frank Wilson of Alamogordo petitioned the Supreme Court to prevent their replacement.[122] The Supreme Court in July ruled 3-2 that Richardson had authority to replace members with Justices Patricio Serna, Edward Chavez and Petra Maes in the majority. But Chief Justice Pamela Minzner and future Chief Justice Richard Bosson dissented. Bosson wrote: "Wholesale replacement of Commission members will subject future Commissions to the unfettered control of one political office. Once ratified, however improvidently by this Court, that power may be exercised for good or ill by future governors."[123] Richardson sought to influence Bosson and communicated his displeasure for some time to come.

In June the state sought an operator for a racetrack and casino license in Hobbs. Three of four applicants were powerful allies or donors to Richardson.[124] Santa Fe gallery owner Jerry Peters contributed $102 thousand to the campaign along with use of his Lear jet. Paul Blanchard, president of Albuquerque Downs and partner in Zia Partners along with Ruidoso track owner RD Hubbard, was chair of Richardson's transition team and was appointed to the Board of Finance. Ken Newton, former owner of Santa Fe Downs, donated $12 thousand to two Richardson galas. (The Hubbard group, the winner of the Hobbs license, sold the track in 2007 for $200 million, four to five times the cost of building the track.)[125]

In the fall Richardson barnstormed New Mexico to support the two school reform constitutional amendments on a special election ballot September 23. Senator Domenici and Governor Carruthers joined Richardson in support, and unions spent $1.2 million to advocate passage. With only about $30 million of new money, the boost in the Land Grant distribution worth $68 million in FY04 seemed critical. But Land Commissioner Pat Lyons, Senator Ramsay Gorham (R-Albuquerque), state Republican chair, and former Senate Finance chair Aubrey Dunn notably opposed the amendment. Richardson and Lyons feuded about Lyons' hiring James Varela, Representative Varela's son, who had been fired by CYFD for emailing sexually inappropriate material. On Wednesday after the election, in a shocker the permanent fund amendment was down by 23 votes. Calloway reported NMSU history professor Ray Sadler saying, "Education is God, motherhood and apple pie but Richardson made it a referendum on his governorship. …The way he treats his staff and his imperious arrogant attitude toward appointees came back to haunt him in September for his sins in January and February."[126] Calloway also noted Amendment 2 was "decisively rejected outside Santa Fe and Albuquerque" and speculated if the three-member canvassing board headed by Richardson were to "certify some funny-looking turnaround on Amendment 2 in a way that arouses the suspicions of the newly discovered non-urban voters, Richardson will suffer a loss of credibility affecting his future career." On October 4 the Canvassing Board certified Constitutional Amendment 2 passed by 195 votes. It was a miracle.

In the wake of the 2003 regular session, Richardson appointed a 23-member blue ribbon tax commission headed by expert and former representative Jerry Sandel. They labored all summer and came up with 71 recommendations that included a net revenue increase of $152 million, partly for state roads. Richardson called a special session for tax reform, but as the October 27 session approached, tax opponents picked the agenda apart. House minority whip Joe Thompson (R-Albuquerque) said, "the session is going to be like the bus on "Speed." You have to maintain a speed of 50 miles or hour or the whole thing blows up."[127] Richardson submitted a sharply scaled back proposal including low-income tax rebates. The legislature recessed Friday, October 31 without any action. Richardson pivoted to a mostly roads proposal. The legislature authorized $1.585 billion of road projects to be financed by bonds issued by the New Mexico Finance Authority and adjourned November 5. The road plan, known as Governor Richardson's Investment Partnership (GRIP) included four lanes on US highway 491 (formerly 666), I-40 improvements and a new I-40 interchange at Coors Blvd. in Albuquerque. The bill raised road revenue with a 38 percent increase in the weight distance tax, a three-cent increase in the special fuels (diesel) tax, and higher vehicle registration fees. The governor vetoed a provision requiring the highway bonds be issued in increments of $350 million with legislative specification of project funding.

The Fifth Killing/Collateral Damage. After my divorce, in 2002 I started dating Lorin Erramouspe, a dance teacher from Albuquerque who brought kids to the capitol to perform in the rotunda and advocate for legislation naming the state butterfly, the Sandia hair streak. Lorin worked on the Richardson campaign and was named director of the Arts Division of the Department of Cultural Affairs. Lieutenant Governor Diane Denish was a strong supporter and her husband, Herb Denish, was chair of the Arts Commission.

In 2003 I started going to Lorin's dad Louie's ranch to help with branding calves in May and gathering, weaning and shipping in the fall—at first a few days a year and later for longer periods. The L-Bar was a Basque family ranch with Louie at Pintada Canyon on the Mesa de Leon Road between Milagro and Vaughn. I started out on the old nag "Peaches" and pulling the herd in a feed truck which signifies my skill level as a cowboy, but I got to be pretty handy in the pens, at least as the pusher in the alley bringing up the rear. We had Lorin's cousin Joseph from the headquarters at Corona, sometimes her sister Lisa Rodriguez from Gallup and her son Austin Wallace, family friend Brian Bunce from Clovis, stepsister Shalei Erramouspe, a Clovis school teacher and a Miss Rodeo New Mexico and her husband Jason Bennett from Dora, the hired hand at the ranch, mostly Bob Martin from Wink, Tx and neighbors for day work as needed. They were great cowboys and cowgirls. Those were the best days of the year, but Governor Richardson was increasingly rough with Lorin. He'd ask her, "How's your shitty-ass boyfriend?" In November, the Cultural Affairs secretary, former Representative Ruben Smith, was fired and in December his successor fired Lorin. She was scarred for life.

15. L-R, Jason Bennett, David Abbey, Louie Erramouspe, and Brian Bunce, after branding at the L-Bar, June 3, 2017. (Lisa Rodriguez photograph)

2004/Repeal Tax on Food. The 2004 Highlights report of the Legislative Council Service said "contentiousness and acrimony awaited at every turn" of the 2004 legislative session. Richardson vetoed the $2.8 million appropriation to LFC for personnel complaining $147 thousand for two additional audit staff was "unacceptable." Quickly, House majority leader Danice Picraux (D-Albuquerque) moved to override which passed 66-0. Speaker Lujan said the legislature counted on its "hard working staff" for checks and balances with the executive. Senator Altamirano said he wanted his staff back. But Senate president Pro Tem Richard Romero, running for Congress in Albuquerque, tried to smooth things over, and there was no vote in the Senate. The *Journal* editorialized on February 1, "The Year of the Legislature Doesn't Last Long." Later, full funding for LFC was included in the 2005 General Appropriation Act.

On February 5, Richardson called two meetings with health care lobbyists to demand support for revenue initiatives. A *Journal* editorial on February 7 said, "Richardson was rude, profane and threatening." Senator Tim Jennings, whose wife Patti was at one meeting, said, "if this was a family meeting, he would be arrested for domestic violence."[128] Jennings demanded an apology on the Senate floor which Richardson rejected. Aging Secretary Lujan Grisham announced plans to audit nursing homes. Win Quigley of the *Journal* on February 9 reported, "Lobbyists, Lawmakers Say Tensions High." JD Bullington of the Association of Commerce and Industry and Dan Weaks of the New Mexico Hospital Association both said it was harder than any year they remembered. They said, "the groundwork for those bills was not well laid."

Yet at the end, the budget and capital passed along with a food tax cut, there was no special session for a change and the legislative Highlights described 2004 as "one of the most productive sessions in recent years." Chapter 116 eliminated the gross receipts tax on food and certain health care services and provided a phased out hold harmless distribution to municipalities. The cost of tax relief was offset by repealing a half-cent credit (reduction) on the state gross receipts tax for transactions in municipalities. Never mind that food purchases with food stamps were already tax exempt or that tax experts like UNM's Brian McDonald argued against the big hole in the GRT tax base or that the cost of hold harmless was greatly underestimated. The legislature also passed a high wage jobs tax credit which proved expensive and allowed retroactive credit claims requiring a fix in 2013. To address soaring Medicaid costs, Chapter 4 imposed a nursing home bed tax to raise $22 million (repealed in 2006) and a one percent increase in the insurance premium tax for $20 million. FY05 General Fund appropriations were $4.38 billion, up $252 million or six percent, including an increase of $67 million or 16.5 percent for Medicaid. A special appropriation for $8 million funded contracts for GSD's Save Smart efficiency initiative, contingent on achieving "2x" projected savings.

Adoption of a governmental accounting procedure recommended by GASB resulted in accrual of an extra month of revenue, or $285 million. Along with general obligation bonds, this allowed an extraordinary capital outlay package of

$490 million for 2,953 projects including a $10 million film education and training center. LFC analysis indicated the executive exceeded its share of capital outlay by $14 million. The governor vetoed $26 million of projects, and Republicans (and other political critics) bore the brunt of STB vetoes according to an LFC analysis requested by Senator Lee Rawson (R-Las Cruces). Representative Dan Foley (R-Roswell) lost 22 of 50 projects and Senator Jennings lost 23 of 54 projects. Co-Chairs of the Governor's Finance Council, Dave Contarino and James Jimenez, in a May 27 op-ed titled, "It's Still Pork, But It's Smarter Pork," described the 2005 capital bill as a "bold reform."

Other measures included expanding Northern New Mexico Community College in Espanola to a four-year institution, elevating offices of aging, veterans, Indian affairs and cultural affairs to cabinet status, and purchasing water rights on the Pecos River. Authorization of an empowerment zone in Gallup to control liquor sales did not pass, despite a march from Gallup to the capitol for a mass rally and participation of former Gallup Mayor Ed Munoz, Mayor Bob Rosebrough, President of the Navajo Nation Joe Shirley and hundreds of others.[129]

In April Representative Max Coll announced his retirement after representing Santa Fe County for 24 years. David Harris went to UNM as VP for Finance. Richardson hired Claudia Correra, wife and daughter in law of Richardson investment advisors as an "international protocol officer." On May 2nd District Chief Judge John Brennan resigned after arrest for DWI and possession. Health Secretary Pat Montoya, facing severe budget woes, resigned, replaced by Aging secretary Michelle Lujan Grisham. Representative Varela's son Jeff Varela resigned citing policy differences. Senate Majority Leader Manny Aragon was appointed President of New Mexico Highlands University.

16. David Abbey with Representative Max Coll outside the House chamber, January, 2004. (*Journal* photo)

LFC had an active interim beginning with questions about GSD's purchase of an airplane, bypassing the appropriations process by using $4 million of Road Fund revenue. The *Journal* criticized LFC for not acting, and the AG said the purchase required a legislative appropriation which they would enforce. Reports and hearings in 2004 included the Highway 44 warranty, a no-bid contract with Microsoft for e-mail service, state police time fraud, the closure of CYFD detention centers, gaming revenue losses due to video lottery machines mimicking class three machines and the need for a financial plan justifying the commuter rail initiative.

The State Investment Office replaced most of the private firms managing permanent fund assets, and six of the 11 new firms donated $105 thousand to Richardson's political committees. Investment Officer Gary Bland said, "People get access, but they don't get protection and contracts."[130]

LFC stumbled twice. Deputy Director Manu Patel used a state e-mail to negotiate a zoning issue for a motel in Ruidoso and dropped the names of key legislators. He was suspended briefly. An LFC auditor tried to sell parking spaces in the capitol lot for five dollars during Spanish market to raise money for a son's baseball team. He also was suspended and then resigned.

In the fall the revenue outlook improved $200 million due to higher oil and gas prices.

2005/Extortion by Treasurers. The LFC 2005 Post-Session Report said, "The revenue outlook caused a proliferation of spending initiatives from legislative executive and judicial branches as well as from advocates." The governor's recommendation had 140 initiatives. Richardson touted falling unemployment and a "flurry" of new business recruitments. LCS Highlights described, "smooth sailing on calm waters, reflecting healthy revenue and new legislative leadership."

Senator Altamirano was elected President Pro Tem of the Senate with Senator Fidel as SFC Chair and Senator Smith as Vice-Chair, and Speaker Lujan appointed Representative Kiki Saavedra HAFC Chair. HB2 had a General Fund increase of $320 million, or 7.3 percent, including 16 percent, or $80 million for Medicaid, although most of that was to replace Federal funds due to a lower matching rate. A $33 million junior bill also passed including some funding for pre-K, a top Richardson priority. Appropriators said the spending left no room for tax cuts, but Richardson insisted on his proposal for low- and middle-income tax cuts and threatened a special session. At the last minute, Richardson proposed delaying 2003 personal income tax rate reductions by one year to save $32 million and pay for the tax cuts and the measure passed.

In March the *American Journalism Review* reported that Richardson "hired a whopping 21 reporters, editors and producers from newspapers and TV and radio stations around the state to serve in his administration."[131] Government salaries were often sharply higher. The story said this showed "political savvy," but quoted blogger Joe Monahan saying, "If they think it's having no impact on coverage, they're drinking the Kool-Aid."

New Mexico Highlands President Aragon hired LFC's Manu Patel as VP for Finance and Dr. Bill Taylor as dean of the business school. Governor Richardson chaired the Democratic Governors Association which provided many national travel opportunities. The capital outlay bill included $5 million for GSD to purchase a state plane which morphed into a jet for $5.5 million with the difference funded with the sale of an aging GSD plane. Senator Rawson suggested that a jet was inefficient for instate travel. The number of exempt employees in state government grew from 292 in 2003 to 437 by July 2005 with the governor's office growing from 27 to 49. TRD paid for Governor Richardson to open an Albuquerque office in the Bank of the West tower on Central. In response to criticism, DFA Secretary Jimenez said, "Every time a new governor is elected, the boundaries of power are redefined."[132]

Richardson traveled to North Korea with a New Mexico delegation in an Air Force jet. In October CYFD Secretary Bolson announced a plan to close the New Mexico Boys School in Springer due to a decline in kids in custody. In the face of concerns over job losses, by December the plan changed to use Springer for adult prisoners. The Department of Transportation (DoT) reported the cost of Rail Runner would reach $318 million, including $76 million to purchase track to Las Vegas from BNSF. DoT Secretary Rhonda Faught said this wouldn't impair completion of other GRIP projects. Secretary Homans said a proposed spaceport could cost $100 million. New Mexico improved from 48th to 46th in the annual Kids Count rankings of child welfare.

DFA reported in the summer general fund revenue estimates were trending up sharply due to rising oil and gas prices, and discussions started about a special session with rebates of $100 million. Hurricane Katrina contributed to higher energy prices. Some senators suggested why not restore and accelerate the originally scheduled rate cuts for $100 million. So, at a special session in October the legislature passed both for approximately $200 million.

Meanwhile, on Friday, September 16 Treasurer Robert Vigil and former Treasurer Michael Montoya were arrested by the FBI and charged by the US Attorney for extorting $687 thousand from an investment advisor in exchange for contracts with the Treasurer's office.[133] The FBI acted on a tip from a disgruntled, fired employee. The extortion began in 1995 related to repurchase agreements, with a broker paying Montoya one sixth of his fees, $1.2 million in $100 bills. The kickbacks continued in 2003 when Treasurer Vigil took office. The *Journal*, profiling Wachovia broker Guy Riordan's services to the Treasurer, reported Riordan received one-third of the $1.2 billion of bond transactions for the prior year. This activity had been flagged by the Board of Finance and the legislative budget office in 2002 and 2003. Riordan contributed $28 thousand to Richardson.[134]

At the special session the legislature appointed a committee to study impeachment and scheduled a hearing October 26. Treasurer Vigil resigned on October 26, prior to the legislative hearing, and Montoya plead guilty on November 8. Vigil hired former Democratic party chairman and future district attorney Sam Bregman as defense attorney. Doug Brown, a retired California banker and New Mexico regent, was appointed to replace Vigil. In November the Board of Finance dropped Wachovia and other local brokers from the approved list and in December adopted recommendations of PFM's Barbara Fava to reduce trading costs and improve competitiveness. Fava said the recommendations would save the state $5 million. Board of Finance member Paul Blanchard expressed concern that brokerage commissions would not stay in New Mexico. The Board of Finance contracted accounting firm Deloitte and Touche and Washington, DC law firm Hogan and Hartson for a forensic audit of the treasurer's office, but State Auditor Domingo Martinez complained he was out of the loop even though he flagged investment concerns as far back as 2000.

Sixth Killing Fails. In early October Governor Richardson summoned all the Democrat members of the LFC and other leaders to the 4th floor and demanded my head so to speak. It was a short meeting. Senator Altamirano said, "Governor, we don't tell you who to hire and fire. And you don't tell us who to hire and fire. This meeting is over." He stood up and all the members walked out.

On October 7, Senator Altamirano, Senator Michael Sanchez, Senator Fidel and Senator Smith wrote a letter to Governor Richardson denying that I was "instigating" changes to proposed special session legislation and asserting that I was responding to legislative requests pursuant to statutory responsibility of

LFC. The Senators wrote they were counting on timely and objective responses from executive agencies and concluded, "the LFC Director and the LFC staff are held in high confidence by the Senate for their professionalism and quality of service. We look forward to your continued cooperation with the Senate and our staff." (See Figure 11)

2006/Pay-to-Play Rears Its Head. In January, Governor and Barbara Richardson rode on a float sponsored by the Tourism Department in the Rose Bowl parade. It rained and they wore plastic ponchos to keep dry. Washington lobbyist Jack Abramoff pleaded guilty to mail fraud and tax evasion and was sentenced to six years. In related cases two White House aides, a US representative and nine congressional aides, mostly Republicans were also convicted. Representative Heather Wilson received a $1,000 donation from Abramoff. GSD Secretary Ed Lopez and RLD Superintendent Art Jaramillo switched jobs in the wake of an LFC report finding "significant, lingering management problems in almost every GSD division." Lopez said the LFC report was a personal attack on the Richardson administration. Richardson proclaimed 2006 the "Year of the Child;" Representative Foley retorted, "It definitely is. Spend today. Make children pay for it tomorrow."[135]

Legislative Council Services' 2006 Legislative Highlights began, "Veterans often comment the more money, the harder the session. Veterans were proved right." New money was approximately $500 million and non-recurring approached $1 billion. Virtually every day, sometimes two or three times a day, the press reported a new spending proposal or initiative: $750 thousand for rodeo programs; $2 million added to a native American cultural center because NM SU President Mike Martin told Richardson they were short; $125 million for the spaceport; $300 thousand for foster children aging out of state custody; $290 million to build new schools; $15 million for UNM sports facilities (covered on the sports page); a mobile spray and neuter clinic for Albuquerque; and a $500 thousand planning grant for a state school for the arts. The proposals didn't seem strategic like the first session with a focus on education, health care and taxes. More like "no initiative left behind" or as Senator Smith often said, "the list goes on and on." When Governor Richardson promised an amount, it often was the total project cost with the expectation that proponents would procure half or two-thirds from legislators.

Senator John Grubesic (D-Santa Fe) penned a fearless op-ed in the *New Mexican* on February 1 describing a Friday evening at Jerry Peters' Rio Chama restaurant next to the capitol: "When I walked in, I noticed how everyone was strategically placed. Lobbyists positioned near the entrance to pick off the politicians as they walked in, attractive women in the second tier and then of course the governor's minions protecting his corner table until he arrived to hold court and have the fops approach to kiss his ring. ... The state cops place themselves between the crowd and Richardson. A curtain of muscle hiding the flabby king. ...Then the parade starts. This bootlicking is not partisan."

The legislature only passed 125 bills, the smallest number for a 30-day in two decades, but the General Fund budget reached $5.1 billion, up 8.4 percent or $393 million with $63 million or 11 percent for Medicaid, a ten percent increase for the judiciary, $23 million more, 16 percent for CYFD, and 7.6 percent more for schools. Capital outlay totaled about $850 million for over 2,200 projects. The legislature repealed the 2004 bed tax, passed an increase in the film tax credit to 25 percent and authorized tax increment development districts. But Richardson said the legislature overspent and it was his most frustrating, least productive session.

In early March Richardson summoned legislative leaders to the capital hoping for a special session seeking more PIT cuts, funding for GRIP, more for school construction and a minimum wage of $7.50/hr. With only speaker Lujan supporting a special session, Richardson vetoed $269 million, he said to bring reserves to ten percent: "There was a feeding frenzy. The legislature overspent and we fixed those problems."[136] Senator Smith said the spending complaint was "much ado about nothing," and if the revenue outlook improved, folks would remember his vetoes even more. Republican legislators and Senator Jennings again bore the brunt of vetoes.

The Board of Finance's $600 thousand forensic study of the State Treasurer was a whitewash. It focused on personnel transactions, travel expenses, absenteeism and timesheets and skipped addressing investment practices including churning and broker favoritism at the heart of allegations against treasurers Montoya and Vigil.

Key Donors in Spotlight. Legislators continued to question the feasibility and cost of the Rail Runner project including the purchase of right-of-way from Burlington Northern Santa Fe (BNSF) for $75 million. The *Journal's* Colleen Heild reported on the purchase and profiled Butch Maki, hired as BNSF lobbyist on January 1, 2003.[137] BNSF had a strong hand in negotiating the purchase price with the state, because Rail Runner had already purchased rolling stock. BNSF donated $23 thousand to Richardson. Richardson called Maki his "go to guy." Joe Monahan's New Mexico Politics blog routinely described Maki as Richardson's "buddy" and "favorite lobbyist." Maki also represented other key state contractors including Corrections Corporation of America, Northern Trust, Maximus, ResCare and Altria.

On February 2 the *Journal* reported a steakhouse dinner in Denver after a Broncos playoff game including Richardson and Jerry Peters. Peters, spurned for the Hobbs racino, was the only qualifying bidder to redevelop the Department of Transportation's campus in a $90 million transit/retail/office complex.

In April, the *Journal* reported the nation's largest payday loan company provided $17 thousand of travel costs for the Democratic Governors Association chaired by Richardson. Richardson proposed a compromise bill seen by consumer advocates as favorable to lenders. Senator Bernadette Sanchez (D-Albuquerque) filibustered against the bill on the last day of the session. She said the donations played a role in the governor's legislation. But Richardson spokesman Gilbert Gallegos said, "To suggest or imply a connection between any travel on behalf of the Democratic Governors Association and the governor's effort to protect consumers is insulting and flat wrong."[138]

State Jobs Too. On January 23 UNM President Louis Caldera resigned, receiving a $720 thousand contract buyout. VP David Harris was named acting president. When the session ended, CYFD Secretary Mary Dale Bolson announced her resignation, although it was submitted in January after an LFC report on juvenile justice. Former district judge Tommy Jewell was appointed to replace Bolson but dropped out before he started due to issues stemming from a domestic dispute. In April DFA Secretary James Jimenez moved up to chief of staff, replaced at DFA by Katherine Miller, director of the Mortgage Finance Authority.

A *Journal* editorial on March 8, "All Aboard the Governor's Gravy Train of Jobs," reported state agencies had 56 temporary exempt employees on the payroll at an annual cost of $3 million including the former mayor of Santa Fe Debbie Jaramillo and former lieutenant governor Roberto Mondragon. Representative Varela said the jobs should go through the appropriations process.

John Hendry, the marketing director for the tourism department, drew attention, because he also served as business agent for the screen actors local and owned a catering company serving the film industry. He resigned in March after an extortion charge related to legislative support for film tax credit legislation.

Billy Sparks left his job as communications director for the governor to take a $120 thousand job as a press chief at the University of New Mexico, prompting many letters to the editor that the job was not advertised, no interview was conducted, and Sparks lacked a college degree.

Spring 2006, A Black Eye for State Government. On March 15, the *Bond Buyer* reported that the FBI was investigating kickbacks from subcontractors for the $82 million Metropolitan Courthouse in Albuquerque. NMHU President Aragon was implicated, and he had a $200 thousand buyout in July.

On April 3 the *Journal* reported complaints about kickbacks from home sales to an entity run by Region 3 Housing Authority director Vincent "Smiley" Gallegos, a former legislator from Clovis. Gallegos' salary was $158 thousand. Governor Richardson directed the Board of Finance to conduct a review of all seven state housing authorities, and eventually Region 3 defaulted on a $5 million loan from the State Investment Council.

Drip, drip. On April 7, the *Journal* reported the suspension of Insurance Department superintendent Eric Serna following the recommendation of attorney general Patsy Madrid. Jerry Peter's Century Bank donated $124 thousand to the Con Alma Foundation, of which Serna was board president, while the Insurance Department awarded a no-bid $800 thousand contract to

Century Bank for custodial services required of insurance companies. Madrid said the inquiry was triggered by an October 2005 LFC audit of the Insurance Department that stated, "practices may give the appearance of favoritism." Serna retired in July.

On April 18 the extortion trial of former treasurer Robert Vigil opened with testimony of former treasurer Michael Montoya that investments were steered to Guy Riordan who would hand over cash to Montoya in mens' restrooms. Montoya said he collected between $2.5 million and $5 million from investment advisors during his two terms. A *Journal* editorial said Montoya sang, "louder and longer than most sopranos at the Santa Fe opera." Monahan wrote, "the full and fearsome prosecutorial power of the United States government set off more cries of Abandon Ship at the upper reaches of the New Mexico Democratic party." Richardson, Lieutenant Governor Denish, AG Madrid, Albuquerque Mayor Chavez and Reps. Al Park and Peter Wirth announced they were donating Riordan donations to charity. Richardson removed Riordan from the game commission. Monahan wondered why Riordan was not indicted, and a top Monahan gator (source) said it was likely due to the lack of physical evidence—"no phone calls, wiretaps, videos or checks." (But in a July 2008 civil proceeding, the Securities Exchange Commission banned Riordan from the securities business and imposed $2.2 million of fines and restitution.[139]) A lone juror held out for acquittal of Vigil. At an October retrial Vigil was convicted of one count and sentenced to prison for 37 months.

In the aftermath, Richardson appointed a 17-member task force to recommend ethics legislation. Representative Gary King, candidate for attorney general, recommended establishing a public integrity unit at the AG's office. State Auditor Domingo Martinez said a 1997 audit showed the Treasurer's office "was just part of a culture of public corruption." Representative Heather Wilson ran ads criticizing Madrid for failing to act in the Treasurer's case. The Association of Commerce and Industry reported, "a perception that New Mexico is a state where you have to pay-to-play has been allowed for too long."[140]

In July the LFC quarterly performance report for CYFD erroneously reported a foster care maltreatment rate of 40 percent, it should have been six percent.

The bad data came from CYFD, but we (LFC) should have caught it. CYFD blasted LFC, and Jimenez called me and said, "you need to know how incredibly angry Richardson is." Legislative leaders were summoned to meet with the governor's top aides who complained about LFC's "so-called audits" that veered from legitimate audit standards. Varela, Altamirano and Saavedra defended LFC and told staff to stay the course.[141]

At the November election Richardson crushed John Dendahl 69 percent to 31 percent. Despite a Republican wipeout in the US House, Representative Wilson nipped Madrid by 862 votes. The House Democrats lost almost their last toehold on the east side with the defeat of HTRC Chair Don Whitaker (D-Eunice).

In December Richardson was campaigning in coffee shops in New Hampshire.

## SECOND TERM

2007/Running for President. Richardson said it was The Year of Water, but it was more like the year of running for president which he announced on January 21 in the Sunday *Journal*.

On February 28 the governor and lieutenant governor honored Senator John Pinto, the Marine code talker and teacher, at a dinner at La Fonda. Senator Aragon loved to tell the story of driving to Santa Fe in 1977 after his first election. He stopped to pick up a Navajo hitchhiker and asked where are you going? The man said he'd taken a bus from Gallup and was heading to Santa Fe. Aragon said, "Oh yeah, what are you going to do there?" The hitchhiker replied, "I am a state senator." Aragon said, "So, am I." [142]

It was also another year of a lot of money, with oil climbing over $100 per bbl. For FY08, the legislature passed a $5.6 billion budget, increasing General Fund appropriations $537 million or 10.5 percent. This compared to an average increase for the previous ten years of 6.1 percent. Appropriations included

$7.5 million for the Kplus extended learning program adding 25 days to the school calendar, advocated by Representative Mimi Stewart (D-Albuquerque), supported by LFC and touted in a *Journal* editorial on January 31. Capital outlay totaled $722 million for 4,552 new projects with over 8,000 projects outstanding. The legislature passed revenue reductions of $80 million rising to $140 million in later years including a new working families income tax credit and phasing out transfers of certain insurance taxes from the fire protection fund to the general fund. The legislature also banned cockfighting, raised the minimum wage, authorized medical marijuana and tightened payday loan regulation.

Richardson said it was the most productive session ever but wanted more and called an immediate special session for Tuesday, March 20. He called for a $200 million local road program (GRIP II), an ethics commission and more and then headed to Oklahoma and Texas for fundraisers.

You can make 'em come, but you can't make 'em stay. The Senate met for ten minutes at noon on March 20 and then recessed for caucuses. Late afternoon, the Senate reconvened with President Pro Tem Altamirano presiding and Senators Michael Sanchez, Jennings, Smith and Ingle in the chamber. Jennings moved to let the record reflect that all those present in the morning session be shown as present which passed without objection. Jennings then moved that the Senate adjourn "sine die" which also passed without objection. Altamirano appointed Jennings to send a message to the House that the Senate was adjourned. Jennings walked over and relayed the message and invited Speaker Lujan to take up a similar motion.

By observation, I would say the Senators present appeared like cats who swallowed the canary, but Speaker Lujan was not pleased. The House continued in session and passed a handful of bills over the next three days. The House having not adjourned, the Senate had to return. On Saturday March 24, the Senate voted 18-17 to adjourn again with seven senators absent and three democrats joining all the republicans. On Thursday, March 29, the senate had to return again and passed two bills, a revised road package and public financing for election of judges. The road bill provided $180 million over three years with about half for GRIP I shortfalls and road maintenance. The Senate adjourned on Friday, and the

House concurred and adjourned an hour later. Speaker Lujan said Richardson, "should be happy with what he got."

Also on Thursday, March 29, the US attorney indicted Manny Aragon and former metro court administrator Toby Martinez on conspiracy and mail fraud charges and announced guilty pleas of former Albuquerque mayor Ken Schultz and two subcontractors. The indictments, secured with cooperation of Attorney General Gary King, alleged that the co-conspirators took $4.2 million from the $83 million project. Aragon, Martinez, Mike Murphy and two others later pleaded guilty.

Presidential Campaign. In January and February, the *Journal* profiled Richardson in a five-Sunday, 29-page series. Of note was Richardson's intersection with the Clinton impeachment, the focus of a four-hour interview with investigators. Deputy Chief of Staff John Podesta asked Richardson, then UN Ambassador, to interview Monica Lewinsky for a job in New York. Podesta said, "If you're in a war, you want Bill Richardson in a foxhole."[143]

The *Cook Report* said it would take about $50 million to get a presidential campaign through the primaries and be considered seriously. By July Richardson had raised about $13.2 million, including $4.2 million from New Mexico and $1.4 million from his second highest state, California. By comparison, Barack Obama had raised $8.4 million from California.[144] The Richardson campaign reported Richardson went on 83 trips to 22 states including 15 to California, seven to Nevada, six to Texas, six to Iowa, 11 to Washington DC, eight to North Carolina and six to New Hampshire.

Michelle Lujan Grisham. On March 7, the Journal reported criticism from health care advocates of DoH Secretary Michelle Lujan Grisham due to departure of key staff and lack of public health experience.[145] A former deputy secretary said, "It is a bizarre micro-management and manipulative style of leadership that is very destructive to the health of the public and the morale of the department." She was replaced in June by Taos physician Alfredo Vigil.

Transportation Headquarters. In July and August, the *Journal* reported that metro court co-conspirator Toby Martinez had been hired to work on the redevelopment of the Department of Transportation headquarters adjacent to the Rail Runner stop in Santa Fe. The *Journal* also profiled Johnny Cope, oilman from Hobbs, Chair of the Transportation Commission and lead investor in the ill-fated Lordsburg tilapia project that was defeated in the Senate in March. Other project developers linked to Metro Court also were working on the highway project and traveled with Cope and DoT Secretary Faught to a meeting with developers in Dallas. A superseding indictment on the Metro Court case alleged that some defendants also conspired to work on the Santa Fe DoT project. Further, DoT would not disclose the status of negotiations with a developer affiliated with Jerry Peters, a "major Richardson contributor." By September, the redevelopment was described as a $350 million to $400 million project. On September 9, Peters penned an op-ed for the *Journal*, "DoT Bid, Fundraisers are Beyond Reproach" detailing the timeline of the redevelopment procurement. Then, the *Journal* reported Mike Murphy, the latest indicted Metro Court coconspirator, also was called to work on the DoT project at the request of highway commissioners. Richardson ordered investigations into the headquarters project and related Santa Fe district office project, and DoT paid the Sutin firm $356 thousand for legal expenses on the projects.[146] With the GRIP project funding shortfall estimated at $500 million, the DOT headquarters project faded away. Secretary Faught retired in December.

LFC. In September the LFC traveled to Playas in Hidalgo County to inspect New Mexico Tech's homeland security project, crossed the border at Antelope Wells and then to Nuevo Casas Grandes, Chihuahua for two days of meetings.[147] Senator Smith said it was important for everyone to know their neighbors. Smith's district covered New Mexico's almost entire border with Mexico. Committee members and staff met with economic development experts and Mexican Senator Jeff Jones and toured the Paquime archeological site linked to Chaco Canyon in New Mexico, a Mennonite cotton farm and gin, Colonia Juarez and the village of Mata Ortiz, renowned for its pottery.

In October the committee celebrated its 50th anniversary in Santa Fe.

Senate Education Chair Cynthia Nava was appointed superintendent of the Gadsden school district.

In the fall Governor Richardson announced a plan to achieve universal health care coverage that was supposed to be cost neutral. But the cost estimates jumped by $200 million to $300 million. HSD Secretary Pam Hyde had a series of intense meetings with Senator Jennings and other legislators and staff to evaluate the proposal.

RIP Senator Altamirano. On December 27 Senator Ben Altamirano died unexpectedly of a heart attack at his home in Silver City. Beloved wife Nina and his dog King were home. Altamirano served in Germany in the US Army after WWII, ran a grocery store and served in the legislature since 1971, three years as Pro Tem and 17 years as Chair of Senate Finance. When I walked through the halls with Senator Altamirano, he'd nod to a passerby and I'd say who was that and sometimes he'd say I don't know, the veritable "he never knew a stranger." He loved bringing legislative committees to Silver and taking them to his home place in hardscrabble Pinos Altos for a steak dinner at the Buckhorn. Sometimes those functions were pretty rowdy. He rested in state at the capitol on New Years Eve. Thousands attended his funeral in Silver on January 3, lining the streets on the way to his interment at Memory Lane Cemetery, fire trucks hooking arches over US 180. Benny trusted us in a way that taught me what trust means. His family, David and Daniel Manzano, Kenny, his staff—Ron Forte, Mike Burkhart, Erlinda Campbell, Linda Kehoe, all LFC, all LCS, Freeport lobbyist Tony Trujillo, Dan Lopez, Senator Joe Fidel and many more loved him.

2008 / Fortunes Ride Rollercoaster. The events of 2008 were ominous. Richardson pushed relentlessly, he would say boldly, for his initiatives, especially universal health care, and he pursued his campaign for the Democratic nomination for president with the ambition to return to Washington. But the energy spiral collapsed, the Great recession arrived and play to pay caught up with him.

Obama won Iowa with Richardson at two percent. On January 9, Richardson reached five percent in New Hampshire and on January 11 suspended his campaign. By spring he was campaigning for Obama, and he was a primetime speaker on the last day of the Democratic convention in August.

Howie Morales, Grant County clerk and Cobre HS baseball coach, was appointed to replace Senator Altamirano, and Senator Jennings was unanimously elected president Pro Tem.

Senator Smith warned, "oil prices remain strong, but since the start of the session, many economists have concluded the nation is entering or already in a recession. … Fiscal prudence is not only recommended but critical. "Acting cautiously," legislators increased spending 6.3 percent with almost three quarters for public and higher education and Medicaid. The budget had extraordinary bi-partisan support passing the House 57-10 and the Senate 36-4. But Richardson said it was a "do-nothing session" and began a drumbeat for a special session focused on healthcare.

In March Bear Stearns, with excessive exposure to derivatives and subprime mortgages, collapsed. This marked the beginning of an extended financial crisis with Lehman Bros. failing in September, then Countrywide, then federal rescue of some financial firms and the Great Recession in 2009.

In the June 2008 primary, Senators Shannon Robinson and James Taylor were defeated beginning the decade long progressive resurgence.

In July while LFC was meeting in Cloudcroft, revenue estimators added $400 million to the FY09 outlook. The consensus oil price outlook rose from $80/bbl to $92/bbl, and the natural gas price forecast went to $9.60/mcf, even as natural gas prices were in freefall. I was aghast at the exuberance of the revenue estimators, but Senator Smith sort of blamed me. Richardson quickly added income tax rebates to the special session agenda he scheduled for August 15. But an August 12 update from DFA indicated the July surplus dwindled to $225 million. Senator Smith called for cancelling the special session saying, "these are imaginary dollars." He said it would take an additional $165 million of stable, recurring revenue to pursue universal health care. Senator Jennings said legislative experts thought the latest estimate was still $200 million too high. Richardson said, "I've been dealing with pessimists in the legislature, economists that keep telling me the economy is not going to grow, and we should be cautious. And I've been bold."[148]

Richardson downsized his rebate and road proposals. At the five-day special session, "mindful of plunging surplus revenue projections," the legislature passed $200 million for roads, mostly from severance tax bonds, rebates of $25 to $50 up to a $70 thousand family income, and $32 million to expand childcare and health coverage for kids but rejected most of the health care reform which "was the reason to call a special session."[149]

Richardson in an op-ed stated, when he was elected, he heard a string of "you can'ts" like touch the permanent funds, invest in rail, shift school funding from administration to the classroom: "Voters have rejected that entrenched way of thinking. They were tired of partisan bickering and the gridlock in Santa Fe that kept New Mexico at the bottom of so many lists. ...To some extent I learned to appreciate my annual debate with these so-called budget watchdogs. ... The media focus was on the political potshots from the usual suspects in the Senate who are more intent on criticizing me, rather than helping New Mexico families and moving the state forward."[150]

In September Senator Smith said the General Fund revenue surplus had "vaporized." Blanco hub prices were $4/mcf below the forecast with each ten-cent change worth $12 million. He asked me to meet with DFA secretary Miller to start working on a solvency plan. A *Journal* editorial on September 28, "New Mexico Budget Can Use a Cork-Screwed Pessimist" praised Senator Smith and urged the executive to put the brakes on spending. LFC analysts reported about $150 million of capital projects were inactive and could be reauthorized. On October 17 Richardson proposed "sweeping cuts" with a hiring freeze, halting work on $200 million in stalled capital projects and reducing spending on contracts, travel and supplies by five percent. On October 21, DFA told LFC revenues would be down another $350 million. On December 10 SPO Director Sandy Perez told LFC, in the month after the hiring freeze, state government hired 416 people with a net increase of 57. Senator Beffort said it was a red flag. The small jet startup Eclipse, which once had 2,000 employees, filed for bankruptcy in November. The state had a $19 million equity position in Eclipse. The value of permanent fund assets declined 25 percent in a year to $12 billion. By December Speaker Lujan and other legislative leaders had a $500 million solvency plan that they said needed to be first order of business at the 2009 session, including $125 million of one-time revenue, $137 million of spending reductions, $150 million from stalled capital projects and $95 million from restricted General Fund reserves. DFA Secretary Miller said the Executive plan was similar.[151]

At the November general election Obama led the Democrats to victory. The share of Hispanics voting for the Democratic candidate for president rose from 56 percent in 2004 to 69 percent. Republicans lost a few seats in the legislature, including Senator Rawson. Senator Jennings drew complaints from Senator Ortiz y Pino and others for a robo-call to Las Cruces voters supporting Rawson. On November 30 Senate Democrats caucused at a Los Lunas motel. Ron Forte, Mike Burkhart and I waited outside to brief on the budget, but we were never called. The caucus voted for Senator Carlos Cisneros (D-Taos) for president Pro Tem, but Senator Jennings said he would fight to keep his position. Senator Fidel told us, "Keep your heads down and do your job."

On December 3 President-Elect Obama introduced Governor Bill Richarson as his nominee for Commerce Secretary at a news conference in Chicago. This began a flurry of transition plans from Lieutenant Governor Diane Denish. But also, almost every day there was a story about a November 26 hit and run causing the death of a pueblo man near the Santa Fe rail yard. The driver was an attorney, former state government official and capitol hill aide, and the passenger was a State Police member of Governor Richardson's security detail who later took the 5th amendment related to the event. They had been drinking at the Rio Chama that evening, and Governor Richardson was there too, but they didn't meet according to a Santa Fe police report.[152]

Also escaping most notice in New Mexico was an FBI investigation into a Beverly Hills financial firm contracted by NMFA for financing $1.6 billion of GRIP bonds.

The *Journal* reported the CDR financial firm contributed $130 thousand to a Richardson PAC, Si Se Puede, to pay for the bills for the Democrat convention in Boston when Richardson was chairman.[153] CDR had been investigated for bid-rigging for at least two years in California and Chicago.

On December 30, the *Journal* published a color photo and maps of fighting in Gaza between Hamas and Israel Defense Forces that looked remarkably similar to the maps of 2023.

Journalist Dexter Filkins described a peace mission with UN Ambassador Bill Richardson. After a trip to Kabul, they flew to meet with Abdul Dostum, an Uzbek warlord. They visited a hospital, it was getting dark, and a "buoyant" Richardson announced a ceasefire: "As the engines on our Beechcraft started whirling, Dostum's men handed enormous handwoven maroon carpets into the hold of the plane."[154]

On Sunday January 4 Governor Richardson announced he was withdrawing as cabinet nominee due to a grand jury investigation.

2009/The Great Recession/Solvency/Pay-to-Play Erupts. To open the session on January 20, Governor Richardson proclaimed "The Year of Fiscal Restraint." (I didn't make that up.) The Senate elected Senator Tim Jennings as President Pro Tem 23-19 with eight Democrats joining all the Republicans. The Senate Committee on Committees kept things calm by leaving most Cisneros supporters in their previous positions, including Cisneros as Vice Chair of Senate Finance and Senator Nava as Chair of Education. There had been rumblings of replacing Smith as SFC chair based on seniority, but he said then he would want to be chair of Senate education, and some of his opponents lost their enthusiasm for a change.

Monahan had been calling Senator Smith "Dr. No", but he wrote, "He keeps saying the sky is falling. The problem is pieces of the darn thing have been spotted on the ground. ... He has been an incorrigible Nostradamus, correctly forecasting financial doom. Smith has become the state's reality check. No one likes to hear what he has to say, but they know they need to hear it."

The LFC 2009 Post-Session Report said, "rapid precipitous decline of the New Mexico economy grabbed the spotlight and forced intense focus on state spending." The first two weeks were all about solvency, fixing the FY09 budget with the four-pronged approach recommended by LFC and the executive: $148 million of additional revenue led by a speedup of corporate income taxes, $192 million of spending cuts, $158 million of capital savings and fund transfers to bring reserves to ten percent. (See Figure 12 presenting Senator Wirth's "rap" using the 2009 vocabulary of solvency.)

Then the focus shifted to FY10. A February revenue update cut the FY10 General Fund forecast by $282 million with natural gas prices around $3/mcf. The House passed a $400 million, 0.75 percent GRT rate increase to fund a school funding formula plan recommended by an interim task force by a vote of 37-31. Representative Heaton said he had concerns about raising taxes when the "economy is in the ditch." A study of the American Institute for Research figured public school funding was $300 million or 15 percent short, but LFC reported that economist Eric Hanushek called these "costing out studies ... political documents, not scientific studies."[155] The tax and school bills were non-starters in the Senate.

On a positive note, Federal stimulus funds under the American Relief and Recovery Act (ARRA) promised to bring $1.9 billion to New Mexico over three years, albeit with some onerous restrictions on supplanting state appropriations. The relief included an eight percent enhanced Medicaid match rate. The final appropriation for FY10 was $5.48 billion, down $539 million from FY09 pre-solvency and down $375 million from F09 adjusted post-solvency. The appropriations assumed use of $331 million of ARRA revenue in FY10. Accounting for the Federal funding, FY10 adjusted appropriations were down $200 million or four percent. The budget appeared to avoid layoffs and school and Medicaid cuts. Sounds easier than it was. A controversial "swap" of employer to employee retirement contributions passed; a bill to abolish the death penalty passed; and an appropriation to acquire the bankrupt College of Santa Fe failed, causing significant resentment from Speaker Lujan toward Senator Smith. (But later the New Mexico Finance Authority loaned the city of Santa Fe $30 million to acquire the college. A private operator went belly-up, and the campus remains mostly unused with much of the infrastructure beyond repair.)

The economy, energy markets and General Fund revenue worsened. New Mexico non-farm jobs declined five percent, or 42 thousand jobs from October 2008 to October 2009. The balance of the Unemployment Insurance Trust Fund fell by half from December 2008 to $260 million in November. Federal personal income tax revenue in FFY09 fell 20 percent. Fourth quarter US GDP declined six percent, the worst performance since 1978. Food stamp caseload was up 25 percent. The State Investment Office reported a loss of $320 million from securities lending related to the failure of Lehman Bros. The FY10 revenue shortfall compared to the 2009 session estimate grew from $150 million to $250 million to $300 million in three months over the summer. In August the governor and legislative leaders formed a solvency work group (including Varela, Smith, Saavedra, Miera, Neville, Stapleton, Hall, Cisneros, Bratton, Sapien, Ingle and Beffort) to fix an FY09 deficit and address solvency for FY10. At the onset, they agreed to take tax cuts off the table, at least until the 2010 regular session, but Richardson clashed with legislators about exempting public education from spending cuts. The *Las Cruces Sun News* reported that Smith and LFC staff had predicted the $450 million revenue shortfall in 2005 with "Kreskin-like accuracy."[156]

The October revenue estimate went down over $200 million from the August estimate, bringing the revenue shortfall to $650 million, or 12 percent of spending. Smith said it was a "pretty devastating picture." Speaker Lujan said the "increasing size of the shortfall makes leaving education untouched an unlikely proposition." But Richardson rejected the latest proposal of the legislative work group with education the sticking point.[157] The session began Saturday, October 17 without an agreement, but the Governor proposed a new $617 million plan that cut public and higher education 1.5 percent and most agencies 3.5 percent.

Legislators battled for a week. Progressive Senate Democrats (led by Feldman, Wirth, Ortiz y Pino, McSorley and Eric Griego) and Adair (R-Chaves) pushed for tax increases.[158] They argued the governor violated separation of powers by restricting the method to resolve the fiscal crisis. Repeated votes to blast tax bills out of committee failed 22-16. Republicans sought deeper recurring spending reductions. Representative Nathan Cote (D-Las Cruces) and Senator John Ryan (R-Albuquerque) sponsored bills to reduce Richardson's 760 exempt political appointees by 180 to save $19 million in the wake of a report that the Public Education Department had eight assistant secretaries. "Rank and file members spent much of the day lounging on the floor of the legislative chambers, waiting for leadership to bring forward revised budget proposals," according to the *Journal*.[159] Late Thursday and Friday, the legislature passed a package reported at $526 million which included $206 million of spending reductions. Governor Richardson vetoed $114 million of agency cuts ranging from two percent to 7.6 percent but issued an executive order to achieve smaller reductions. Schools were cut one percent. Richardson announced a five-day furlough of agency employees. Richardson also vetoed $59 million of authorization to use Federal American Recovery and Relief Act funds but said he would do it anyway. Other legislation swapped general fund appropriations for severance tax bonds to save $136 million and transferred balances of 48 other state accounts to the General Fund to bring in $117 million including $68 million from the College Affordability Fund. Altogether, LFC estimated reserves at 2.6 percent assuming the executive action. The big city papers featured Senator Smith and Speaker Lujan on the Senate floor shaking hands near the end.

LFC provided critical analysis and reporting on the fiscal options and outcomes of the 2009 regular and special sessions. In July I received the 2009 Legislative Staff Achievement Award for Fiscal Officers from the National Conference of State Legislatures.

Vendor Driven Investment Deals. Two separate investments exploded in January 2009. On January 5, the day after Richardson's withdrawal, the *Journal* reported on a $1.4 million New Mexico Finance Authority contract with CDR for advice on investing $1.6 billion of GRIP bond proceeds that seemed to have caught the attention of a federal grand jury.[160] This story generated many links to important people but started winding down in August with a no prosecution letter from the US Attorney of New Mexico to a number of attorneys working on the CDR inquiry. On January 15 the *Journal* reported on a fraud against taxpayer lawsuit filed by former Senator Victor Marshall on behalf of Frank Foy, retired investment officer for Education Retirement Board, alleging that political considerations led to a failed investment in a $90 million Vanderbilt Capital collateralized debt obligation.[161] Both the CDR and Vanderbilt stories evolved into broader investigations into the widespread financial industry practice of using third party placement agents that linked to New York and other states.

In just a few days, the CDR story quickly tied to Guy Riordan and the 2004 Boston convention, JP Morgan, the lead underwriter for the GRIP bond, investment bank UBS, Mickey Stratton, key political consultant for Richardson and contractor to JP Morgan, Colorado State senator Chris Romer, banker for UBS and son of a former Colorado governor, former NMFA director David Harris and VP for the University of New Mexico which used JP Morgan, Obama auto czar Steven Rattner and David Contarino, chief of staff.[162] They made big salaries, earned fees of millions of dollars and donated hundreds of thousands of dollars to Richardson campaign organizations. Former Transportation Secretary Faught claimed NMFA and bond experts found a way to lengthen bond maturities from 12 years to 20 years and use bond swaps and add money to the "pot." But it turned out that CDR entertained state officials at the time of the procurement, CDR had a low ranking in the NMFA procurement, and the variable rate bond swap performed poorly, requiring the state to boost its collateral. In May LFC had a hearing on investments and Senator Smith said, "As an elected official here, I am embarrassed to serve in New Mexico."[163]

The Foy lawsuit was dismissed by state investment officer Gary Bland as a "witch hunt" exploiting the world-wide financial collapse. But every story brought more scrutiny with reference to the $90 million Vanderbilt collateralized debt obligation (CDO) as worthless. Then, the story got even greater life when Aldus Equity Partners, a private equity advisor to ERB and SIC, was implicated in a pay-to-play investment scheme with a New York pension fund.[164] In April the *Journal* reported SIC and ERB paid Aldus $1.5 million to advise both SIC and ERB on private equity investments.

LFC scheduled a hearing in May on third party marketing to state investment agencies, and ERB and SIC released preliminary reports on use of third-party marketing agents by broker name, asset name and amount and investment bank. Marc Correra, son of Richardson contributor Anthony Correra, husband of a Richardson staffer and applicant for a Raton racetrack, was listed as making $11 million from SIC and ERB placement fees, a figure that rose to $22 million on over 40 deals in May. ERB reported Correra made $2 million on the Vanderbilt investment. The *Journal* also reported that Anthony Correra served on the search committee that selected Bland as investment officer, talked with Bland almost daily and regularly used an office at the Investment Council.

From there it was drip drip with the aggressive New York Attorney General Andrew Cuomo issuing subpoenas and indictments that rang in New Mexico, and with further investigation of the roster of New Mexico placement agents. Monahan on May 18 described another "tsunami of bad news" and recommended firing Bland.

Yet on August 27 US Attorney Greg Fouratt wrote to Paul Kennedy, Todd Wertheim, Luis Stelzner and three other attorneys representing possible grand jury targets, "As you know, the United States' investigation ... has revealed that CDR and its officers made substantial contributions to Governor Richardson's political organizations during the time that the company sought financial work from NMFA. This investigation further revealed that pressure from the governor's office resulted in the corruption of the procurement process so that CDR would be awarded the work. At this time, however, the United States will not seek to bring charges against your clients arising out of the NMFA's award of financial work to CDR. ... It is not to be interpreted as an exoneration of any party's conduct in that matter." A source told me the decision was made by Department of Justice officials in Washington, DC. In 2010 several CDR executives were convicted of bid-rigging in Federal court in New York, and the cost of unwinding the New Mexico swaps was estimated at about $70 million.[165]

Aldus founder Saul Meyer pleaded guilty to the New York kickback scheme on October 9. His plea said, "I ensured that Aldus recommended certain proposed investments that were pushed on me by politically connected individuals in New Mexico. I did this knowing that the politically connected individuals or their associates stood to benefit financially or politically from the investments and that the investments were not necessarily in the best economic interest of New

Mexico." Bland reluctantly resigned in October just before an SIC emergency meeting on personnel matters. (Bland produced a March 22, 2004 letter from Paul Blanchard asking him to raise $10 thousand from three or four donors "doing business with your office" in return for "access to the governor.")[166] Three other New Mexico placement agents pleaded guilty including Julio Ramirez who paid Marc Correra $900 thousand. In New York prominent Wall Street firms like the Carlyle Group started paying restitution to the New York pension funds.[167]

The SIC amended a 2006 $30 thousand legal services contract with San Francisco law firm Paul Hastings Janofsky to evaluate internal operations at SIC with the contract amount rising to $5.8 million.[168] LFC staff sought disclosure of the report to lawmakers and the public to enhance accountability.[169] Over a decade, State Investment Officer Steve Moise, appointed in March 2010, refused to provide the report, ostensibly to enhance SIC's restitution efforts. In February 2024 SIC again denied release of the Hastings report due to "outstanding" litigation. To me it seemed more like the movie Casablanca, "Round up the usual suspects."

Separately, sort of, in the course of research for this manuscript, I found in my personal files reference to an unreported March 2010 SIC suit against real estate venture CBA Investments (Cheslock Balker) for recovery of a $26 million investment. I say sort of because the Correras may have been a party. The lawsuit alleged the CBA principals distributed the bulk of proceeds to "themselves" the day the investment closed. SIC told me the lawsuit resulted in a $33 million judgment in 2012, but the judgment was uncollectible because of the bankruptcy of CBA. I wonder how many other poor, broker driven state investments failed or showed submarket returns and were lost in the turmoil.

No Deal Left Behind. In other news, former Secretary of State Rebecca Vigil Giron was indicted in August for awarding a marketing contract to a political operative with little work performed pursuant to a $6 million Help America Vote Act grant. Santa Fe Film Studio, whose principals included a childhood friend of Richardson's and Democratic party chair and former Santa Fe mayor Javier Gonzalez, received $16 million of state grants and loans. GSD worked on a land purchase and office development at Las Soleras south of Santa Fe.

On Labor Day, Brian Condit was driving the houseboat "Bloody Mary" along with Richardson and DFA Secretary Miller and two state police officers that crashed into the marina and two other boats. No one was injured.[170]

Illinois Governor Rod Blagojevich was impeached and then convicted with a 14-year sentence for "selling" an appointment to the US Senate. Like Richardson, he served in the US House before his election to governor in 2002.

The state auditor found the business manager of Jemez Mountain school district embezzled $3.4 million over a ten-year period including $700 thousand of district checks deposited to herself and family members. She pleaded guilty but committed suicide just prior to being sentenced.

2010. The 2010 LFC post-session report indicates a FY11 pre-session budget gap of $333 million. LFC reported progress in developing the budget, but the legislature ran out of time. Richardson quickly called an immediate special session to sustain progress. Senators Smith and Jennings still were skeptical about the revenue estimates, but DFA Secretary Miller and TRD Secretary Homans insisted they were good. It took a few days longer than Richardson hoped, but the legislature met on February 28 for a four-day special session. The legislature passed a budget of $5.339 billion, down 2.2 percent from FY10 post-solvency and seven percent from FY09 post solvency; $203 million of ARRA federal funds supplemented the general fund. Medicaid was up 0.8 percent, assuming Congress would extend the enhanced match for six months in 2011. The legislature voided 2,500 capital projects for $141 million and passed a recurring revenue package with a 1/8th GRT increase, PIT deduction changes and a 75-cent cigarette tax increase. Richardson vetoed a $60 million food tax provision leaving $186 million of additional recurring revenue. In an unprecedented move he also line-item vetoed part of the cigarette tax bill claiming that it was an appropriations measure subject to line-item veto because it made tax revenue distributions. Some legislators grumbled, but there was no legal objection. FY11 reserves were estimated at a skinny four percent.

Interim. Bernalillo Public Schools sent 32 people to a conference in Nevada. The superintendent said it was appropriate, because LFC criticized the district for not spending all the funding available.

In March Risk Management reported a $1.7 million settlement of a wrongful death involving the Children, Youth and Families Department. Former LFC analyst Bill Dunbar was appointed secretary of CYFD.

In June LFC objected to a BAR for $1.5 million for ERB to pay legal fees of the chairman, Bruce Malott, and Guy Riordan related to pay-to-pay allegations. The AG later ruled ERB could not cover the private legal costs. Malott quit in September when the *Journal* reported Anthony Correra loaned him $350 thousand in 2006 to cover an IRS tax lien.

Heath Haussamen reported the director of the Spaceport Authority attempted to buy a 30-thousand-acre ranch adjacent to the spaceport.[171]

Medicaid faced a potential $160 million shortfall if Congress didn't extend the enhanced FMAP rate for six months in 2011. I told LFC, "We're screwed in '11 if we don't get the extension. We have no reserves, we have no contingency funding, we have no funds we can transfer to Medicaid."

Workforce Solutions Secretary Ken Ortiz reported the unemployment compensation trust fund would run out of money by August 2011 because of the state's high unemployment rate, 8.2 percent in September.

A *New Mexican* editorial on September 18 suggested the gubernatorial candidates use LFC for fiscal policy, praised Senator Smith and said the director "has one of the finest fiscal minds in captivity." In October I received the 41st Annual Governor's New Mexico Distinguished Public Service Award.

In the fall my weekly activity reports to members started describing an uptick in drilling activity in shale formations in the Permian Basin, in hindsight foretelling New Mexico's incredible surge in oil production. Urenco opened a uranium enrichment facility near Eunice that would provide 230 jobs.

Richardson drew attention with his allocation of $40 million of undesignated ARRA money, notably a proposed $3 million allocation to purchase a Sandoval County ranch as a wild horse refuge but only $2 million to cover a childcare funding shortfall.

Richardson's approval rating was 33 percent.

On November 3, 3rd District Attorney Susana Martinez defeated Lieutenant Governor Diane Denish for governor by 54-46. She was the nation's first Latina governor. Former representative John Sanchez was elected lieutenant governor. Senator Dianna Duran was elected secretary of state, the first Republican in that post since 1930. Republicans gained eight seats in the house including the defeat of Representative John Heaton from Carlsbad and two democrats in Valencia County. Higher education general obligation bonds were narrowly defeated. The Democrats retained a 37-33 margin in the House.

Thom Cole, comparing pay-to-play convictions wrote, "New York eight, New Mexico zero." He added New York obtained over $100 million in restitution for its pension funds compared to $114 thousand in New Mexico.[172]

Paul Blanchard, President of Albuquerque Downs, proposed to build a racino at the Downs with a 25-year lease extension. Blanchard and Downs' partners gave $300 thousand to Richardson, but they also gave $70 thousand to Martinez and $54 thousand to Denish. The pay-to play scandal extended into the next administration.

Wrapping it Up. The December 26 *Albuquerque Journal* Richardson retrospective included notable observations. Carruthers said, "I would think he would be remembered for being the most aggressive on the big ideas. One has to give him credit for that." Senator Smith, "He's probably the hardest working governor that I've encountered in my 22 years up here. That's the plus side. I don't think he ever had a good grasp of the condition of state revenue. He couldn't see down the road very far." Brian Sanderoff, pollster, "His aggressive fundraising activities ultimately cost him popularity at home and a cabinet position in Washington, DC." Christine Sierra, UNM professor, "He was one of the most ambitious governors that we've seen in a while. He clearly wanted to put himself on the national map, and he did. Unfortunately, his ambition to run with influential people, in the state and nationally, ended up detracting from his policy successes."

Bill Richardson died on September 2, 2023, at 75. A memorial service at the capitol and the funeral mass at the cathedral drew thousands. Bill Clinton gave his eulogy. Senator Heinrich said he wanted big things for our state and never accepted mediocrity. Mayor Keller called him a "giant." Senator Cervantes blogged he, "learned most of what I know of governing from Bill Richardson." Senator Campos described how he could connect with elites and common people in small communities. Former DFA Secretary Debbie Romero said he was "genuinely concerned about the people."

For me his marquee investments—Rail Runner and the spaceport—stand out. What if he put all his energy into a couple marquee investments like improving early reading and math proficiency instead of trying to give everybody everything?

Pay-to-play hurts my heart. Henry Drummond, a Scottish minister, gave a sermon in 1884 to missionaries heading to Africa and China, "The Greatest Thing in the World," which is of course Love as explained in I. Corinthians 13. Discussing good temper, he said, "this compatibility of ill-temper with high moral character is one of the strangest and saddest problems of ethics. ... for him who is Love, a sin against Love may seem a hundred times more base."

For those in public service, corruption is the greatest sin.

# 11

# Susana Martinez 2011-2018

2011/Beginning the Lost Decade. Martinez tabbed former CYFD secretary and congresswoman Heather Wilson as head of her transition. Her first appointment was Rick May as DFA secretary. May, an Ohio native, worked in government relations for Sandia Lab and as staff director of the House Budget Committee under US Representative John Kasich. Keith Gardner, House Minority leader and owner of a physical therapy business, was chief of staff. Popular, former representative and Clayton grocer Brian Moore was deputy chief of staff. There was notable bickering during the transition between Martinez and Governor Richardson and their aides over matters ranging from the size of the budget shortfall to preventing Richardson appointees from moving to civil service positions.

The most notable and controversial appointment was 37-year-old Hanna Skandera, former deputy commissioner of education under Florida governor Jeb Bush to secretary of Public Education. Former astronaut and US Senator Harrison Schmitt was appointed to Energy and Minerals but dropped out after a few days, unwilling to submit a background check required by Senate Rules. Other cabinet appointments included Dr. Jose Garcia, NMSU government professor to Higher Education, Sidonie Squier, Texas human services official to HSD, Yolanda Berumen-Deines, a Texas social worker to CYFD and Retta Ward, an Arizona high school science teacher to Aging. Top cabinet pay was cut to $125 thousand from $188 thousand in the previous administration. The Executive hired five LFC analysts for key positions including Paul Aguilar deputy at PED, Brett Woods (aka the "voice of America") deputy at Energy and Minerals, Brent Earnest deputy at HSD, Gene Moser director of state personnel, Dr. Tom Clifford policy director at TRD and several others as division directors.

Despite state unemployment at 9.8 percent in November 2010, projected recurring revenue growth was seven percent; but with the need to replace Federal funds, the executive reported a shortfall of $400 million. LFC called the shortfall $200 million assuming extending one-time measures such as the retirement swap and diversion of tobacco settlement revenue earmarked to the tobacco permanent fund to the general fund. Both executive and LFC recommendations were similar, which was not surprising since the Executive asked Senator Smith to provide a preview of the LFC recommendation in late December.

Despite rumblings of a challenge from Rep Joseph Cervantes (D, Las Cruces), Speaker Lujan was reelected to a sixth term, 36-33. Rep Andy Nunez (Hatch) then switched from Democrat to independent.

The governor announced her top priority for her first administration was no tax increases. Schools and Medicaid should receive the smallest cuts. Governor Martinez proposed a cap on the film credit which exceeded $100 million in FY10 and proposed to sell the new state jet. Skandera led the charge on an education reform agenda with three key features: limiting social promotion, especially in early grades; assigning schools a letter grade; and a teacher evaluation system based on student progress.

Martinez also pushed other "wedge issues" that generated a lot of smoke and fire but didn't bear on the announced focus on the budget, notably restoration of the death penalty, disallowing drivers' licenses for undocumented immigrants (called then "illegal immigrants"), and unwinding Richardson era executive orders addressing climate change and energy efficiency. Before the days when all committee hearings and floor sessions were streamed and posted, governor's staff started videotaping committee hearings which triggered concerns about selective editing.[173] Martinez criticized Albuquerque Public Schools and Superintendent Winston Brooks for excessive travel and "unwillingness to keep cuts away from the classroom."[174] Brooks said he was "bewildered" by the governor's attacks. UNM professor Christine Sierra suggested the governor was adhering to a national GOP playbook with Martinez campaign strategist Jay McCleskey driving the agenda.[175]

In January the death of a three-year old in state custody presaged more than a decade of turmoil in the state's child protective service efforts. In February a severe cold spell led to power shutdowns and loss of natural gas for 32 thousand homes in New Mexico. On March 11, a tsunami destroyed a nuclear power plant at Fukushima, Japan displacing over one hundred thousand residents and releasing significant radiation.

After the Senate passed an amended budget 27-14 on March 17, the House concurred narrowly, 36-32. General fund appropriations for FY12 were $5.4 billion, down $152 million, or 2.8 percent from FY11 adjusted. Schools declined 1.5 percent with Medicaid up two percent. Further, the legislature continued the retirement swap with an increase from 1.5 percent to 1.75 percent and capped film credits at $50 million. The legislature also passed "Katie's law" led by Dave Sepich from Carlsbad requiring mandatory DNA testing after certain arrests, an exemption from GRT for locomotive fuel to benefit Union Pacific's investment in a switching yard near Santa Teresa, and the Governmental Conduct Act limiting certain campaign contributions. The Senate filibustered the capital bill. Except for letter grades, Skandera's school initiatives did not pass. All the budget saving agency consolidation proposals of Senator Tim Eichenberg's government reorganization task force failed. Four cabinet nominations failed, Skandera, Ward, Varela (Economic Development), and Bemis (EMNRD).

Many appropriators including Representative Varela said the pain was spread evenly. Minority Whip Don Bratton acknowledged communication issues with the fourth floor, and Speaker Lujan said, "The governor relied too much on campaign tactics to push a divisive agenda."[176]

Of special note the legislature passed two seemingly technical bills modifying the school calendar to help with cost controls while preserving learning time. The bills amended the same section of the public school code so only one could be enacted. Representative Rhonda King's HB 555 delayed the 180-day school year definition, passed in 2009, by one year. Senator Gay Kernan's (R-Hobbs) SB 145 defined the school year by hours rather than days. Two *Journal* editorials supported King's bill: On March 17, "Districts take advantage of flexibility by adding a few minutes to each day. The average number of instruction days is 176, according to a study cited by the Legislative Finance committee;" On March 30, SB145 "would define the school day in hours, not days, undoing the hard-won reform put forth by Representative Rhonda King in 2009 that 180 full instructional days, make a school year, not cobbled together half days and tacked-on minutes to make up snow days. ... LFC points out the foolishness of this backsliding, saying 'Time on task has been identified as a critical component of improved student achievement and an important element of this is more time in the classroom with highly effective teachers.'" Governor Martinez signed Kernan's bill paving the way for 2023 legislation that allowed professional development time to count as instructional time. (PED Secretary Arsenio Romero in November 2023 wrote to school districts lamenting the lack of progress in reading and math proficiency and proposed a rule to boost accountability for school instructional time.)


Of the 284 bills passed, Governor Martinez vetoed 98. An increase in the employer share of unemployment compensation to restore solvency was partially vetoed. A bill to provide LFC greater access to Medicaid data while protecting confidentiality was also vetoed. Representative Varela said, "It's not going to be a cooperative environment with this governor."[177]


In April, in the wake of a no-confidence vote from faculty, UNM President David Schmidly announced he would step down after the fifth year of his contract in June 2012. Schmidly berated me publicly at a legislative function at La Fonda, and UNM Regents Chairman Jamie Koch made him apologize to me first thing next morning.

In the wake of the failure of Skandera's teacher evaluation proposal, Governor Martinez issued an executive order creating a 15-member Effective Teaching Task Force including the LFC and LESC directors. The task force heard from national experts such as Ivy Alford of the Southern Regional Education Board and University of Southern California Professor Pete Goldschmidt on how to use student test data to evaluate teacher and principal effectiveness in improving student performance. The methods were highly technical and interesting, but it became clear the political challenges of teacher and school leader evaluation and performance-based compensation were great.

On June 23, in a challenge brought by four Democrat legislators, the Supreme Court struck down the partial veto of the numeral "1" in a $150 thousand appropriation for regional housing authority oversight. The court noted the 1974 *Sego* decision provided, "the power of partial veto is the power to disapprove. ... This is a negative power. It is not the power to enact or create new legislation by selective deletions."

In July deputy chief of staff and former LFC member Brian Moore moved to New Mexico liaison in Washington, DC. In August DFA Secretary Rick May moved to director of the New Mexico Finance Authority, replaced by TRD (and once LFC) economist Dr. Tom Clifford. The McCleskey faction on the 4th floor, led by Gardner and DFA deputy secretary Duffy Rodriguez, tightened their grip.

During the interim, Medicaid remained a preoccupation. HSD reported that expenditures in FY10 and prior years had been underreported, posing a General Fund deficiency in the range $60 million to $100 million. Senator Smith said he had been skeptical of Medicaid cost reporting, but there wasn't much choice but to pay up.

The legislature met in special session on September 6 for two weeks, primarily for redistricting. The governor vetoed house and senate maps leaving it to the courts for the second time in a decade. The legislature passed an $87 million capital outlay bill and an increase in the procurement preference for in-state businesses. Unemployment compensation bills, social promotion and immigrant drivers' licenses failed. Following a two-week impeachment inquiry, PRC Commissioner Jerome Block Jr. resigned and pleaded guilty to embezzlement.

By year-end, the state government workforce had declined about 14 percent or about 3,500 jobs, mostly by attrition. PED sought to RIF (reduction in force) 33 employees, but most were rehired in state government.

The Downs Lease and Racino. On July 27, Expo (the State Fair) issued a Request for Proposals to operate the racetrack and develop a racino with responses due August 25. Only The Downs at Albuquerque and Laguna Development Corporation (the operator of two tribal casinos) submitted bids. The Downs retooled politically for the new administration, moving Republican affiliated Louisiana partners to lead operations and hiring Darren White, former Johnson public safety head and Albuquerque sheriff, as security officer. Pat Rogers, Republican National Committeeman, represented the Downs for the procurement. An October LFC evaluation reported the Fair was "operationally insolvent," criticized racetrack contract management and found a scheduled lease payment of $400 thousand was offset by "in-kind-services." Governor Martinez appointed a three-member panel, a GSD division director, an aide to Mayor Berry and an Albuquerque economic development official, to recommend an award. At a November 9 meeting the Fair commission delayed acting on the panel recommendation to award the contract to the Downs. On November 19, Tom Tinnin, long-time Board of Finance member, resigned expressing concern about the Fair procurement. On November 22 at a special meeting the Fair Commission voted 4-3 to award the racino to Downs. Opponents expressed a range of concerns from a rushed process to possible conflicts of interest with commissioners.[178] On December 22 the Board of Finance approved the Downs lease. Monahan called it the "Down and Dirty Downs Deal." Over two years later, the *Journal* reported that Jay McCleskey's hands were all over the racino procurement. The Journal had texts between McCleskey and Andrea Goff, a Republican fundraiser and daughter-in-law of Fair Commissioner Buster Goff who changed his position to vote for the Downs on November 22. McCleskey's first text to Goff read, "Buster screwed us."[179]

2012, Centennial. On January 6, New Mexico celebrated the 100th anniversary of statehood with a grand ball in Santa Fe, issuance of a commemorative stamp and events throughout the year, including a cattle drive in Lea County.

Opening the session, Speaker Lujan dramatically announced he had battled cancer for two years, and this would be his last term.

The projected "new money" for FY13 was $250 million, up almost five percent with no significant "backfill requirements, the best fiscal outlook since the start of the Great recession." For context, oil prices in FY12 were around $80 bbl, about the same as FY22 and natural gas prices were pegged at $5.60/mcf, compared to $4 in FY22. But oil production was projected at 69 million barrels, a tenth of today's level and natural gas production was 1.2 trillion cubic feet, a third of today's levels.

The governor issued 80 messages for legislation, but members were determined to focus on the budget. John Robertson of the *Journal* wrote about budget development, touted LFC fiscal publications, and pondered tax breaks, natural gas price volatility and federal budget cuts. He called Senator Smith the Lone Ranger: "He is first of all a conservative. … a practical seat-of-the-pants kind of conservatism. And though he's a politician, he doesn't seem to worry too much about what people think of him. His big interest seems to be the bottom line." Smith said, "I'm not sure we should be doing anything this year. Because of the precarious economy until things are stabilized."[180] I used to dream about keeping the ship afloat, night after night.

The executive and the LFC had similar budget recommendations except the LFC left $35 million to be determined and the Executive recommended $55 million of economic development related tax reductions. The legislature found mathematically precise middle ground; the house passed the budget 70-0.

Robert Lamprecht Abbey. My mother broke her hip, and we kids realized what we sort of knew—she'd been carrying my father for some time. He first moved to assisted living in his senior care facility in Tucson and then to memory care. One night when HAFC went late and the capitol was deserted, he called, and I went out to the rail on the third-floor rotunda. He said he was in a transit camp in England trying to get home from the war. John Robertson of the *Journal* overheard and asked if everything was OK. Robertson wrote in his next column about life in the Roundhouse and how the world goes on while staff, legislators, lobbyists and others labor on trying to hold things together. The next call was from a hospice. I missed a chunk of the 2012 30-day session. Every day, I'd call Ron Forte, Senator Jennings' chief of staff, or Senator Smith and ask what's happening and they'd say don't worry about it, stay in Tucson. When I returned, Majority Leader Sanchez on the Senate floor asked for a moment of silence for my dad and family. It meant a lot to me.

The final budget increased $215 million, or four percent to $5.7 billion. The higher education appropriation reflected a new funding formula based partly on student completion and other performance factors. Revenue reductions were $50 million including GRT anti-pyramiding to aid manufacturing and higher distributions to small cities and counties. Only 77 bills passed, the lowest for a 30-day since 1976. (But at the 30-day session in 2024 only 71 bills passed.)

In April Tourism Secretary Monique Jacobson kicked off the $2 million *New Mexico True* marketing campaign which still has life a decade later with strategic goals, targeted investments and action plans.

PED Secretary Skandera proposed to implement by regulation a teacher evaluation method weighted 50 percent on student performance.

Two big wildfires shook the state, presaging things to come: the Little Bear Fire in Ruidoso which consumed 242 homes and the Whitewater Baldy Fire in the Gila, the biggest fire to date in state history.

Schott Solar, with 250 employees at Mesa del Sol, shuttered after $16 million of state aid.

In August a shocking financial scandal broke out at NMFA. The CFO inexplicably produced a fake audit for FY11. RLD Securities Division agents arrested NMFA's CFO and Chief Operating Officer at the office in Santa Fe, executed a search warrant and fears of financial losses exploded. NMFA director Rick May was put on leave. But external investigations revealed no money was lost, and allegations of fraudulently misreporting a $40 million sweep to the General Fund reversion lacked merit.[181] The CFO plead guilty to one count of securities fraud and received five years supervision with a conditional discharge; a grand jury failed to indict the COO; but May lost his job.

LFC produced a number of significant reports during the interim including: the need to cap a massive tax loophole for high wage jobs; improvement in student proficiency for the K3 Plus extended learning program; increasing footprint for state office space while state employment is declining; the failure of the dossier-based teacher evaluation to improve student performance and instead reward teachers based on attainment of advanced degrees and years teaching (99 percent of teachers were rated satisfactory); and easy admission standards and limited classroom training for colleges of education.

The biggest issue during the interim was whether to participate in Medicaid expansion pursuant to the Affordable Care Act. An LFC analysis projected that because of the initial 100 percent federal match (falling to a still generous 90 percent after six years) and the insurance premium tax on Medicaid managed care contracts, expansion would increase state revenue and grow the economy. The Journal and many advocates endorsed the expansion and cited LFC analysis. Other states later modeled their analysis on the LFC work. The share of New Mexicans covered by Medicaid was 25 percent in 2012 and is almost 50 percent today.

At the November general election, President Obama was re-elected, Michelle Lujan Grisham was elected to Congress and Senator Jennings and Senate Whip Mary Jane Garcia were defeated. Jacob Candelaria, a 26-year-old Princeton graduate and former LFC budget analyst, won a Senate seat in Albuquerque's South Valley. The Republicans picked up a few seats in the Senate but lost a few in the House.

2013/ Last Second Tax Cut and Behavioral Health Fiasco. On January 10, Governor Martinez announced that New Mexico would participate in expansion of Medicaid to an estimated 170 thousand low-income adults earning less than 138 percent of the federal poverty level. New Mexico was the first state led by a Republican governor to sign up. Health care providers, insurers and advocates were "universally pleased."

The 2013 session had 35 new legislators and elected new leaders, president Pro Tem Mary Kay Papen and Speaker Ken Martinez. Senator Pete Campos dropped out of the Pro Tem race to make support for Papen unanimous. Martinez's father, Walter Martinez, was Speaker during the "mama lucy" era. The Senate joined the House and OK'd webcasting committee meetings and floor sessions.

Like 2012, LFC and the executive had similar spending recommendations, around $230 million or four percent, but the Executive proposed $47 million of economic development-oriented tax cuts and the LFC proposed a one percent raise for all employees, the first since 2008. The consensus revenue estimate for FY12 reflected a $70 million charge to reconcile prior year revenue reports to cash in the Treasury, according to DFA, a problem dating to 2006 with the introduction of the SHARE accounting system.

Aging and Long Term Services Department Secretary Retta Ward moved to Health secretary in late January. Again, social promotion in schools and drivers' licenses drew a lot of fire and smoke but didn't advance. After years of struggling with poor actuarial condition of the teachers and public employees' pension funds, the legislature passed bills increasing contributions, scaling back cost of living adjustments and requiring longer service to an older age. (Of note was a sharp interchange between HAFC Vice Chair Patti Lundstrom and Representative Mimi Stewart, sponsor of the ERB bill. Lundstrom wasn't satisfied with the sponsor's answers and joined Republicans to temporarily table the bill 9-9. The *Journal* reported Stewart responded "testily" to Lundstrom.[182]) On Sunday March 10, the House passed a constitutional amendment to increase the Permanent Fund distribution for early childhood programs by 37-32, but the measure didn't get a hearing in the Senate. PED Secretary designate Skandera again was not confirmed.

HAFC passed a $5.9 billion budget with the raises 15-3 with nos from three Democrats identified as "progressives," a label seeing growing use. Representative Lundstrom, presenting HB 2 said "we're proud" that most of the new money went to education, but Representative Christine Trujillo said education funding was "hijacked" by HAFC. The House passed HB2 53-16 with all nos from "progressive" Democrats. SFC made minor amendments including removing a $3 million pilot for merit pay for teachers, and the Senate passed the budget unanimously on March 12. The House narrowly concurred on Wednesday 37-33 with Minority Whip Gentry leading Republicans to flip to opposition. Martinez "blasted" the Democratic majority for not adopting her proposed education and tax initiatives and threatened to veto the budget.[183]

Tax Cut/Senate Floor Amendment #1 to HBIC Substitute for HB64. John Robertson wrote, "One lawmaker looming large as the smoke clears from … the session is John Arthur Smith, chairman of the Senate finance committee."[184] He labored, likely with the Speaker, House Minority Leader Bratton, Senator Ingle, DFA's Clifford and others to find the 50-yard line on taxes. Late Friday night he brought a Senate floor amendment to Representative Moe Maestas' HB64 sub that boosted film credits. The amended bill passed 34-8. It reduced the top corporate income (CIT) tax rate 1.5 percent over five years; narrowed the high wage jobs tax credit loophole; phased out over 15 years food and medical hold harmless distributions to cities and counties; required combined CIT reporting for retail corporations; and allowed single sales CIT reporting to aid manufacturers. The bill went back to the House for concurrence sometime after 11:30 Saturday morning; only a draft fiscal impact report was available and Representative Maestas (D-Albuquerque) "handed Clifford the microphone" and asked him to explain the bill. He said it would increase revenue over five years. The bill passed 46-18 with Speaker Martinez and other leaders yes but progressive democrats no. Smith called the passage of the tax bill "true tax reform," it was praised by political leaders like Albuquerque Mayor RJ Berry and economic developers, and it averted a special session on the budget and who knows how many more items. Robertson called the bill a "master legislative stroke" and said Senator Smith reminded him of the late Senator Finance Chair Aubrey Dunn ("the old apple picker").

244   <small>FORTY YEARS IN THE NEW MEXICO ROUNDHOUSE</small>

There were legitimate concerns that the bill passed after noon when the session should have been over; that it was irregular to have a non-member (Clifford) testify on the floor; members didn't know what they were voting on given the pace of amendment process and absence of an FIR; and the fiscal information was overly optimistic.

Representative Stewart said the tax bill was a "royal screw job." According to Monahan on May 16, Clifford told a "stunned" LFC that the estimate provided to the House in March was based on a different bill and that revenue would decline $70 million by FY17.[185] The Center for Civic Policy, a non-profit supported by George Soros, the Kellog Foundation and others, launched an ad campaign criticizing the tax bill as a corporate giveaway and attacking Speaker Martinez and other legislators.[186]

Interim. Barbara Couture resigned as NMSU president and was replaced on a 3-2 vote by Garrey Carruthers, dean of the NMSU business school and former governor.

Steve Alford, popular UNM basketball coach, negotiated a ten-year contract extension. A week later the third ranked Lobos lost to #14 seed Harvard in the NCAA tournament, and Alford decamped to UCLA for $2.6 million per year.

The drumbeat for tapping the permanent fund continued all interim. Monahan said on May 16, "Santa Fe needs to halt its incessant and ineffective tax cuts as well as its money hoarding. It is time for bold change. A great gamble would be bipartisan support of a constitutional amendment to use a portion of the state's multibillion dollar fund for early childhood education and intervention."

In December at the annual Tax Research Institute pre-session warmup, I said, "the legislature probably has tax cut fatigue" and I added some tax changes "are pretty hard to prove to be of benefit." But GRT rates have climbed to the point that, "we're out of whack with neighboring states." Representative Harper concurred, "There is a burnout with putting new tax incentives in place," but suggested reform of the GRT, to broaden the base and lower the rates, is "in the air." Senator Smith said, "we cannot survive with an eight to ten percent GRT."[187]

The US Supreme Court ruled same sex marriages are protected by the US constitution.

Medicaid Behavioral Health. In 2012 HSD's behavioral health contract manager implemented a new software system that flagged potential problems of erroneous billing or even fraud. HSD contracted with Public Consulting Group (PCG) in February 2013 for $3 million to audit Medicaid behavioral health billings. PCG identified $36 million of potential overpayments, and HSD halted payments to 15 non-profits that served 30 thousand New Mexicans, 85 percent of behavioral health clients. HSD turned over the audit to the AG which ran the Medicaid Fraud Control Unit. The AG said the audit was confidential, so the non-profits couldn't respond to allegations of wrongdoing.

HSD contracted with five Arizona providers for $17 million, first to provide training and oversight to the New Mexico non-profits and then to replace them as most of the New Mexico providers laid off employees and eventually closed due to loss of revenue. Legislators were first puzzled and then outraged.[188] Senator Papen asked why wasn't it HSD's quality contractor's (Optum Health) responsibility to improve integrity and why didn't HSD work collaboratively with the providers to improve practices? Senator Ortiz y Pino said it seemed incredible that there could be such pervasive rotten practice. Senator Michael Sanchez said, "the behavioral health fiasco is an example of the administration using a sledgehammer as its tool of choice." LFC objected to a $10 million HSD budget adjustment to pay for the Arizona replacements. HSD said federal law required them to suspend payments when there were credible allegations of fraud. Litigation mushroomed regarding due process for New Mexico firms, and disclosure of the PCG audit to the State Auditor, the providers and the public. HSD and the Governor dug in defending their efforts to combat waste, fraud and abuse.

In December LFC's Pam Galbraith reported service disruptions were hard to assess in the short run but noted calls to the behavioral health hotline were up 72 percent beginning July. In the long run, HSD and Governor Martinez were blamed by many for destroying New Mexico's behavioral health system.

Daniel Libit (later a UNM watchdog with the *New Mexico Fishbowl*) wrote a widely circulated piece in *National Review* describing McCleskey's dominant role in 4th floor operations and policy. Former DFA official Duffy Rodriguez in an op ed argued it was racist and sexist to downplay Martinez's leadership. Monahan on December 2 reported a Rodriguez e-mail to Keith Gardner and McCleskey that said, "my whole end game was to protect the governor on all this kind of stuff and let the governor propose what she wants and not have it dictated by Abbey et. al."

On December 27 a nine-year old Albuquerque boy, Omaree, was kicked to death by his mother. It was quickly revealed that CYFD had received multiple referrals from schools and police. This case was one more of many leading to a spotlight on CYFD. CYFD had a 15 percent vacancy rate and reverted $6.6 million in FY13, including $2.2 million from Child Protective Services. Governor Martinez said CYFD was not to blame, and the harm was caused by the suspect, the victim's mother. For several years LFC evaluations had promoted early intervention or prevention or differential response strategies to reports of abuse and neglect rather than screening and investigation to "substantiate" referrals.[189] Senator Michael Padilla (D- Albuquerque) explained his passion for reform, referencing his youth in the New Mexico foster care system.

2014. New Mexico economic growth was only 1.2 percent, the lowest in the region, but strength in prior year revenue along with oil production climbing over 100 million barrels (up 50 percent in a few years) allowed five percent spending growth.

This was HAFC Chair Kiki Saavedra's last session. His son Marc, Bill Valdes, Representative Varela, Representative Lundstrom, Dan Lopez, and others united to maintain his dignity and make him successful. Democratic Party Chairman

Sam Bregman said, if Senator Smith didn't allow a hearing on a constitutional amendment to use the permanent fund for early childhood education, he should "join with the governor and become a republican," and if he blocks the bill again, he will be "primaryed." Senate Majority Leader Michael Sanchez defended Smith and declared the need for a "big tent" in the Democratic party.[190]

17. David Abbey, Representative Varela and HAFC Chair "Kiki" Saavedra, House floor debate on HB2, circa 2012.

The LCS' Highlights reported, "the 2014 session was dominated not by high profile bills but by the obscure but important method of precisely how schools are funded—specifically how much is appropriated "above the line" versus "below the line." Above the line means formula funding with distributions to districts determined by statute and with districts having discretion on how to spend the money. The legislature tends to favor formula funding, because it is predictable and equitable among districts. Below the line means special appropriations to the PED to make awards to districts for "reform" initiatives. Below the line funding is typically tens of millions of dollars. The executive tends to favor below the line funding, because it is an easy way to implement controversial initiatives like merit pay without amending state statute.

After passing HAFC 10-8, on Friday February 7, HB2 tied on the House floor 34-34 with two Democrats excused for the duration for health reasons and Representative Sandra Jeff (D-Crownpoint) voting no. Republicans said their requests for PED initiatives for low performing schools and merit pay were ignored. A governor's spokesman said, "Democrats tried to ram through a partisan budget after only negotiating with labor unions and special interests and not the minority party."[191] Minority Leader Bratton called for some adjustments, but the budget was sent back to HAFC. Senator Smith said the Senate wouldn't wait for the House bill any longer, and took up SFC sub for SB313, the 2015 GAA.

Guadalcanal. From August 1942 to February 1943, the Marines fought the Japanese in the jungle in the Solomon Islands. After Allied defeats at Singapore and Bataan, for the Allied forces it was like, we're not backing up any farther. Japan and the US threw everything they had at the end of their supply lines (read *Guadalcanal Diary* by Richard Tregaskis and *Into the Valley* by John Hersey). Sometimes the legislature gets stuck in a bitter partisan battle that turns into a near stalemate.

Senate Finance that year seemed like Guadalcanal. Members met for several days in the LFC conference room with a focus almost entirely on special appropriations to PED "below the line," especially merit pay for teachers. When the committee got bogged down, Smith sent Senator Steve Neville (R-Aztec) and Senator Howie Morales (D-Silver City) to work out the details in my office behind a closed door. They came to an agreement about the money first and then turned to implementing language. A few times, Smith would send me in to try for some kind of movement. I doubt Neville really cared about the issues that much other than to help Skandera come out with something. Senator Morales really dug in his heels. As a backdrop, on Saturday February 15, at least a thousand teachers and kids demonstrated at the Roundhouse against a social promotion ban and PED's teacher evaluations.

On Sunday March 16, SFC passed the budget 9-0. Compared to HB2, SFC sub for SB313 added $17.5 million to education funding, including $7.2 million for teacher training and retention, including up to $5 million for merit pay based on district applications. SFC consolidated many "below the line" appropriations into three buckets to provide flexibility to PED. To pay for the increase, a sanding adjustment of 0.275 percent on all FY15 recurring appropriations saved $17 million. Overall, General Fund appropriations increased $293 million or five percent and provided three percent raises plus more for state police, social workers and judges. The budget included $11 million to bolster the lottery tuition fund, $11 million more for early learning and K3plus and $8 million to expand nursing programs. Smith said, "We're working against time, but time can also be your friend."

On Monday, February 17 Senate Rules deadlocked on Skandera's nomination, and SFC tabled a constitutional amendment to boost the permanent fund distribution for early education.

On Tuesday the Senate passed SB 313, the GAA, unanimously, and on Wednesday the House passed it 58-8.

Seventh Killing. On March 12 after the 20-day bill signing ended, Ron Forte and I went to the Bull Ring for lunch. I told Ron I was going to retire after over 30 years' service. I got a call on my cell, and I couldn't hear clearly, and I said, "Excuse me?" The caller said, "This is Susana Martinez," and I about fell off my chair, but I said, "Hi governor." Generally, I am not on a first name basis with any elected official. Made sense she was in the Bull Ring, since I'd seen Keith Gardner walk in the back with some aides. The gist of it was that she told me I had to direct all requests for information from executive agencies to Gardner. I told her, "I don't work for you governor," and she said, "I don't work for you." I told her I would talk to members and got off the phone as quickly as I could.

I went back to the capitol and called Senator Smith and told him I had some good news and some bad news. The good news was that I was quitting, and the bad news was that the governor just picked a fight with me and the legislature. He told me he wished I wouldn't do that, and I was used to following his direction which was start calling members to rally support for LFC which I did and I'm sure he did too for the next couple of weeks.

I learned that the Executive was still sore from LFC's Medicaid behavioral health budget adjustment request (BAR) objection in August 2013. Further, the governor's folks picked up on the complaints from minority members of HAFC that LFC staff was partisan and just helped the majority and didn't involve them in budget development. Representative Bratton warned me about this undercurrent before the House vote on HB2.

Representative Bratton and Senator Smith advised me to focus on developing support at the LFC organizational meeting in April, including ensuring that leadership like Ingle, Bratton and Papen would attend. Smith said develop a "paper trail of written requests." Ingle told me, "We were exactly on the right track, and they didn't have a right to do that." But Larranaga said he shared the concerns of minority members and had discussed this with Clifford after the session. Bratton advised me to seek a private meeting with the minority members. Representative Jim White (R-Albuquerque) said we had the right to get information, and Representative Bill Gray (R-Artesia) said, "that's BS, that ain't right." Speaker Martinez dismissed the whole issue as "just politics."

On March 28 a *Journal* editorial stated, "lawmakers from both sides are puzzled and annoyed by this unnecessary flexing of executive muscle. ...It brings back bad memories of Richardson blasting the unfavorable SPO audit." The *Journal* described the credentials of LFC staff and listed 16 useful LFC studies on state government.[192]

I met with LFC analysts to discuss how to get information: use the sunshine portal, don't be afraid to ask just because you know you will be stonewalled, keep a log of requests, be prepared to escalate including use of subpoena power, keep management in the loop, use BARS as a tool to enhance cooperation, explain the analyst and evaluator work plans to agency officials.

On April 5 the Governor's spokesman announced a revised policy that would allow legislative requests in writing to agency heads, not just Gardner. LESC chair Rick Miera said, "I'm glad they've seen the wrong in what they've done," and Larranaga said, "this will work out."[193]

At an April 10 LFC executive session, Senator Ingle said, "this problem happens every election season. People in New Mexico support this committee. Don't beat this dead horse anymore." Senator Leavell (R-Jal) said legislators need staff help for constituents on regulatory and other issues and was concerned it would chill legislators getting their concerns addressed. Senator Munoz said the biggest rub was going to be education, and Representative White encouraged LFC staff to sit down with the education officials and try to repair a relationship.

Fishing Expedition. The dust hadn't settled, and I got snakebit. Representative Lundstrom asked me to get some information about a McKinley County man's possible violation of game and fish regulations which I asked an analyst to follow up. Turns out the man was a Lundstrom primary opponent, and the agency supposedly told my analyst to wave us off, but she didn't tell me. Then someone leaked the story to the *Journal* for an April 8 story and on April 10 Representative Monica Youngblood (R-Albuquerque) asked the attorney general to investigate Lundstrom and the LFC for abuse of power. An April *Journal* editorial said, "With legislative Power comes Big Responsibility. ... How much analysis does it take to figure out that asking the state's best and brightest finance analysts to reel in one guy's violations just might be, well, fishy? ... It also gives Governor Susana Martinez's office some high ground—albeit recently acquired—in directing LFC and LESC requests to the appropriate Cabinet secretary or agency." Speaker Martinez angrily told me it was really stupid.

During the interim, LFC participated in a couple taskforces with dozens of members: the J Paul Taylor memorial task force on child abuse prevention and another annual round of the higher education funding formula task force. These task forces and studies produced a lot of useful information but struggled to find a common policy direction.

In the wake of a doomed effort to recruit the 5,000 job Tesla battery giga-plant, Economic Development Secretary Jon Barela proposed an appropriation for a $50 million closing fund.

Albuquerque police shot James Boyd, a homeless, mentally ill camper, in the foothills. There were 37 APD shootings since 2010, and protests ensued.

My mother turned 97 on July 5—just before she went to a hospital in Tucson for treatment of COPD, an exceptionally rare event with her faith in healing and Christian Science. My son Clayton and I arrived as my brother and sister were visiting the hospital room. I tried to tell her that she didn't need to be at the hospital, that she could get up and go home. She said, "David, you can't talk to me that way. I am not the New Mexico legislature." We all laughed, but she knew it was the end, mercifully quickly.

Tourism Secretary Monique Jacobson was appointed to head the CYFD.

The Center on Law and Poverty and Mexican American Legal Defense Fund sued the state for failure to meet the constitutional requirement to provide a "sufficient education." School districts including Gallup and APS filed a similar lawsuit with a focus on the achievement gap and inequity of below the line funding. The two lawsuits were joined and moved to the First District in Santa Fe which likely paved the way to success.

In November Governor Martinez won reelection with 57 percent of the vote, defeating Attorney General Gary King. Republicans won the US Senate and gained four seats in the state House to take the majority for the first time in 60 years. Former representative and auditor Hector Balderas was elected AG, and Senator Tim Keller was elected auditor.

In December two of the Arizona behavioral health replacement firms that served southern New Mexico gave 90-day notice of pulling out.

## SECOND TERM

2015/Republican Majority in House. To open the session Governor Martinez asked, "that in every decision we choose courage over comfort, change-over stagnation, reform over the status quo." She proposed a "slew" of measures including the usual prohibition of immigrant drivers' licenses and social promotion. She added to the mix right-to-work legislation and a three-year road funding initiative from severance tax bonds. She appointed Dr. Barbara Damron, UNM nursing professor, as HED secretary.

Don Tripp, a Socorro businessman, was elected speaker, and Brian Egolf, a Santa Fe attorney became minority leader. Larry Larranaga and Jimmie Hall (R-Albuquerque) were chair and vice-chair of HAFC and kept Bill Valdes as chief of staff. Representative Mimi Stewart was appointed to the Senate, replacing Tim Keller. PED Secretary Hanna Skandera was finally confirmed 22-19 on February 16. It was Representative Varela's last term.

18. David Abbey and HAFC Chair Larry Larranaga, House floor debate on HB 2, circa 2015.

Following a complaint and quiet investigation of the Legislative Ethics Committee, Senator Phil Griego (D-San Jose) resigned on March 15. He received a $50 thousand commission on the sale of a State Parks building in an alley next to the capital. He asked Representative Jim Trujillo (D-Santa Fe) to carry the authorizing joint resolution, and the Senate record shows he voted for it. He was later convicted and went to prison.

The fiscal outlook for FY 16 fell by half on each report, from about $280 million new money expected in summer and fall 2014 to $141 million in December to $83 million in the 2015 mid-session review. There wasn't enough money to fight about initiatives. HB 2 increased General Fund appropriations by $82 million, or 1.3 percent, with modest increases for CYFD, public safety and education and most agencies flat. Only 191 bills passed, the lowest number for a 60-day session since 1941, with few of any significance. Despite Martinez's many initiatives, Republicans ordinarily don't favor a lot of bills anyway, and progressive Democrats knew they wouldn't get much through the House.

Capital. A major shortcoming was the failure of the $264 million capital bill on the last day. HTRC cut $57 million STB funding for courthouse security, higher education, native American schools and senior center renovations projects and added the $45 million for state roads. Smith had already objected to funding road maintenance with borrowed money (bonds), and Egolf on the floor blistered HTRC Chair Jason Harper (R-Rio Rancho) and the Republicans for the cuts. Twenty minutes before noon, the amended capital bill passed 36-32, but the Senate did not concur. A modest tax cut package of Harper's also failed in the Senate. Governor Martinez said, "Senate Democrats chose to obstruct, chose gridlock, chose partisanship and they chose not to compromise."[194]

For the next few weeks LFC spotlighted information on projects in the failed bill such as $12.5 million for an economic development closing fund, $4 million for a spaceport hangar and $16 million for the state hospital in Las Vegas as well as the projects eliminated in HTRC amendments. The Albuquerque Chamber of Commerce, Albuquerque Mayor RJ Berry and other local officials and labor leaders appealed for a special session to provide an economic boost from infrastructure spending.

On April 1 on the way home from spring break in Tucson, I visited Speaker Tripp at his *cantina* in Socorro. I told him the HTRC cuts were problematic and that I was confident LFC could find unspent funds in the Treasury to pay for both highways and restore the cuts. Thus started two months of shuttle diplomacy: developing high and low spending scenarios for Smith and Tripp, finding excess balances of other state funds to sweep, many meetings and phone calls with Smith, Ingle, Clifford, Michael Sanchez, governor's liaison Jeremiah Ritchie, and reporting compromise scenarios to caucuses. The tax bill and supplemental funding for DoH and the public defender were added sideshows. You can stick your neck out, but you can't freelance. Every move required approval and maybe a little cajoling with the chief legislative negotiators, Smith and Tripp. Except Ritchie, not much help from the Executive. One by one sticking points were resolved—fund roads with STBs and General Fund, restore HTRC cuts, don't increase General Fund spending, $4 million for DoH. Most legislators, especially appropriators, are really good compromisers. But the distrust and animosity between the Governor and Senator Sanchez rose, and by mid-May the Governor said she had no intention of calling a special session. At one point the governor hung up on Senator Smith. The breakthrough was Smith, Ingle and Tripp agreeing to a scaled back tax bill reaching $12 million by FY19 including PIT deductions for medical expenses and expansion of technology jobs tax credit.

On June 3, Governor Martinez and legislative leaders said they had a deal on a $295 million capital bill, tax breaks and supplemental funding and planned a special session. On June 8, the legislature passed three bills in four hours, a speed record and adjourned. The special session validated two LFC maxims: it ain't over 'til it's over; and once again, "spend your way to victory." That month I received the Spirit of Bipartisanship Award from New Mexico First.

Forty-five school districts were funded for K3 plus serving 21 thousand students for the 15-16 school year, perhaps the high-water mark of extended learning for the early grades.

LFC heard an update on Medicaid spending. Win Quigley of the *Journal* wrote, "David Abbey, who probably knows more about state finances than anyone else alive, said 216 thousand people have joined the state's Medicaid rolls since the expansion authorized under the Affordable Care Act." That was about 100 thousand more than initially projected. This led to discussion about growing pressure to offset Medicaid expenditure growth in other areas as well as the need to ensure that Medicaid clients are not only insured but getting services.

On August 5 an EPA monitoring crew inadvertently opened a plug on a drain at the Gold King mine near Silverton, Colorado, triggering a leak that turned the Animas River yellow, causing contamination as far as the San Juan River near Shiprock and initiating years of litigation. (In 2022 the Office of Natural Resources Trustee settled with EPA and others for $13 million for natural resource restoration projects.)

On August 29 Secretary of State Dianna Duran was charged with using campaign funds for personal use, notably gambling. She resigned and pleaded guilty in October.

In September the LFC, with the presidents of NMSU and WNMU and the secretaries of higher education and economic development, traveled to *Ciudad Chihuahua* to meet with Chihuahua legislators and officials and tour the university, a new hospital, a corporate headquarters, the massive food and produce wholesale market, and the apple growing Mennonite district at Cuahtemoc. (See LFC minutes, website) This continued the committee's and state's interest in forging stronger ties with our Southern neighbor.

LFC analyst Rachael Gudgel was appointed director of the Legislative Education Study Committee.

Just like in 2014, in Fall 2015 oil and gas prices and revenue estimates went down. Even after a $60 million reduction on Monday December 7, legislators were skeptical of the revenue estimates. Oil was $38/bbl on Monday, but the estimate was $44/bbl. On Thursday night Senator Neville called and expressed concern about the staff recommendation for pay raises. On Friday morning, the day the committee was supposed to vote on a recommendation, Vice Chair Hall called me at seven and asked me to meet him in his office. The other LFC House Republicans, Larranaga, Harper and Paul Bandy (R-Aztec) were also there. Hall launched into criticisms that I was Smith's guy, I never listened to them, not enough for public safety and across the board pay raises were unacceptable (not my first donkey barbecue from Hall). I called Smith and he called in all the LFC Democrats, and we quickly developed a compromise to reduce spending $78 million with the pay raise contingent on higher revenue. Neville agreed to that, then all the Republicans agreed and that morning the committee adopted the revised staff recommendation unanimously. It was a pretty slick audible, but events of the next year would make it seem like death by inches.

Governor Martinez wound down the year with a "holiday bash," also called "a pizza party" at the El Dorado Hotel in Santa Fe. The party got rowdy, leading to a 911 call from the hotel front desk, and SFPD, the Governor and the State Police security met in the lobby to talk it over. A December 23 *Journal* editorial lead: "The tone was testy. The attitude imperial. The conduct unbecoming of the state's highest elected official." Governor Martinez apologized, sort of, for the behavior of her staff.

2016, Finances Bad to Worse. Economic conditions beginning 2016 were weak: flat GDP, flat New Mexico jobs, rising unemployment, natural gas prices below $2/mcf and the New Mexico rig count down from 100 to 15, which battered GRT. Just like 2015, the revenue estimates cratered but more: the mid-session review was off $200 million to only $30 million "new money"; then in an extraordinary last week audible all parties agreed to lower the outlook another $125 million.

Beginning the session, Clifford sent me an e-mail criticizing me for not supporting the revenue estimates and assuming that I was egging legislators on. The state received favorable news from the state auditor that a *Share* accounting reserve of $100 million was not needed and that the US Department of Energy would settle a WIPP fine for payment of $50 million for state roads. Senator Smith introduced a bill to delay two years of corporate income tax cuts. Smith also let the early childhood constitutional amendment move out of the Senate, likely thinking Senator Padilla would blame Harper and the House Republicans for inaction. The House passed the budget on February 4, but Senators weren't buying the revised January estimate. On Monday February 8, Janet Peacock, Senate Finance economist requested a revenue status report from LFC. A table by revenue source showed YTD revenue down 5.9 percent or $125 million compared to the January FY16 forecast of 1.8 percent growth. Smith plastered the table all over the building, and on Tuesday made it the focus of his daily briefing to members on the floor about budget development. Tuesday evening Clifford privately acknowledged to Smith that we needed to scramble to update the revenue outlook again. Land Commissioner Aubrey Dunn Jr. told legislators the revenues were $800 million off. On Wednesday LFC staff developed a $125 million cut scenario for Smith's review and on Thursday presented it to key Senate fiscal staff including Ingle's outstanding team, Gasparich, Kormanik and Burch with 100 years of budget and legislative experience, HAFC's Bill Valdes and DFA deputy secretary Duffy Rodriguez. The group restored $6 million of agency cuts to address DFA concerns. Meanwhile, on Thursday the Governor's spokesman urged calm but Smith said, "We have a huge serious problem, and I think they're beginning to understand that."

Clifford told a bipartisan legislative leadership meeting on Friday to plan for $125 million reductions to the revenue estimate for both FY16 and FY 17 and everyone agreed. On Saturday SFC passed spreadsheets and LFC staff worked all weekend to prepare the amendment, every number in Section 4 changed. On Monday SFC passed amended HB2 and added $50 million more to HB311, the sweeps bill for total fund transfers of $130 million. The Senate passed the budget 39-1 and the House concurred 59-7 on Wednesday.

Total FY 17 appropriations were $6.228 billion, down $7 million: schools were flat, Medicaid, CYFD and public safety up two to four percent and most other agencies cut up to five percent. The governor vetoed authority to cut budgets one percent more if revenue fell short.

DFA secretary Clifford resigned in May with one week's notice, replaced by Duffy Rodriguez. On May 24 Monahan noted Clifford crowed about tax cuts:

He should have said, "I regret adhering to a rigid ideological line and advancing tax cuts and promoting budget austerity as the solution to New Mexico's long running economic stagnation."

*Journal* columnists echoed the tax theme, for example: "The legislature hasn't been exactly profligate. ... The problem is on the revenue side. ... Oil price declines are taking a huge toll. Gross receipts tax data are 'almost alarming' LFC said. ... The expected business expansion from (PIT cuts) never happened. ... Taxing ourselves enough to pay for the government we demand is not only common sense. It is the law."[195]

On June 20 I told LFC, "we're on fumes" after economists reported year-to- date revenue was down ten percent, or $454 million. On August 24 DFA reported to LFC that the General Fund was overspent in FY16 by $131 million, with revenue down 8.7 percent or $545 million. FY17 revenue was down another $223 million from the end of session estimate. Oil production in the first half of 2016 was down five percent. I told the committee, "The longer you take to address this issue, the fewer options you have."

Peabody, the nation's largest coal producer announced bankruptcy in March, and New Mexico mines near Grants and Farmington laid off hundreds of employees. Facebook received a $10 million LEDA award for a data center in Los Lunas. There were at least one thousand construction jobs but only 30 to 50 permanent employees. Representative Larranaga, and I'm sure the administration, were irritated that I reported this as an extraordinary $100 thousand or more cost per job.

The Supreme Court overturned a 12th District Court decision invalidating language in the GAA that prohibited hourly rates for contract public defenders, noting that compensation is not necessarily connected to the quality of representation.

NMSU and HED approved a tuition rate for students from Mexico at "1.5x" the in-state tuition rate, recognition of the value of these students to the university. The Burrell College of Osteopathic Medicine began its first class adjacent to NMSU's Arrowhead Center.

The gruesome murder of ten-year-old Victoria Martens in Albuquerque in late August left New Mexico reeling and hunting for accountability.

A month of talk and (sort of) negotiations about a special session heated up. On September 16 Auditor Keller wrote the governor New Mexico may have "violated" NMSA 8-6-7 by "paying warrants when funds were not available to support expenditures in FY15 and may be continuing to do so in the current fiscal year."The Senate Democrats caucused for six hours on Monday, September 26. LFC cancelled its September meeting. LFC staff had four scenarios, A-D. On Wednesday September 28 at 455 PM, Governor Martinez issued a proclamation for a special session to start on Friday at noon, five weeks before the general election. The proclamation included several crime-related bills including the death penalty for certain violent crimes and a mandatory life sentence for child abuse resulting in death. Lorraine Montoya Vigil, Senator Michael Sanchez's chief of staff, frantically called him to cancel a fundraiser which now fell in a blackout period. The executive didn't have a solvency plan much less an agreement, thought to be required for any special session. Senator Sanchez and Representative Egolf said the special session should focus on the budget crisis.

The session began with no bills, much less fiscal impact reports, no committee or floor agendas and minimal legislative staff. (Okay, LFC staff had FIRs on ideas about what bills might look like.) Legislators caucused, and then the Senate passed six solvency bills generating $418 million, including the corporate income tax delay which Martinez opposed by a vote of 22-21, and adjourned and most senators went home. House Judiciary passed two crime bills.

Over the weekend the House passed one crime bill. A governor's spokesman called the Senate solvency bills a "flawed hodge-podge cobbled together in the middle of the night so they wouldn't have to consider legislation to crack down on criminals."[196] Sunday night legislative leaders met, but the House wasn't in a hurry for a resolution. The House recessed late Monday afternoon forcing the Senate to return. Smith said he was going home but didn't and told me not to tell anybody.

For the next few days, I received lots of requests to generate lists with more savings. Majority Leader Gentry called and asked if I knew how to find middle ground and I said of course I did, I always had something in my back pocket and I told him. The lists were circulated and then members would call me asking why I didn't tell them that so and so detested this or that item or it was flawed for whatever reason (for example, cutting arts in public places). All college and university presidents attended the special session, protecting their turf. Some of the hottest issues were how much to cut higher education (Rs wanted deeper cuts), whether to cut UNM more, how much to credit school cash balances against school funding, scoring savings from closing the high wage jobs credit loophole and cutting earmarked funding for legislative retirement, adamantly opposed by Senator Ingle. Chief Justice Charlie Daniels was disconsolate, he thought he failed because judiciary cuts were three percent (when most agencies were five or lower.) All day Wednesday Smith and Gentry dug in their heels (deeply) over a half percent difference on higher education cuts, but lobbyist TJ Trujillo got them talking and Wednesday night the house passed spending cuts 36-32 and then spent the rest of the night on a death penalty bill, passing 36-30. The Senate concurred with House amendments to the budget cut bill and didn't take up the crime bills.

The final package cut spending $150 million with most agencies at -5.5 percent and raised $209 million, mostly non-recurring, from fund sweeps and capital outlay swaps (reauthorizing general fund to severance tax bonds). The new money outlook for FY 18 was negative $210 million.

On November 8 Donald Trump was elected president (although not endorsed by Governor Martinez). Greg Baca defeated Senator Michael Sanchez, but Democrats defeated five Republican representatives and three Republican senators.

TRD Secretary Demesia Padilla resigned in December following an investigation and search into alleged preferential treatment for a former tax practice client.

The US Supreme Court declined to hear a challenge to a Colorado sales tax applied to internet sales, paving the way to internet sales taxation in New Mexico.

2017/Higher Education Veto Debacle. The economic outlook was for moderate US GDP growth but flat employment and income in New Mexico. New Mexico had the second highest unemployment rate in the nation, 6.6 percent. The oil and gas sector was beginning to recover. New Mexico population also was flat with rising out-migration.[197] But prophetically, Daniel Fine, New Mexico Tech economist said, "the Permian is so geologically rich for future production that it could be what Alaska was in the 70s."[198]

Senator Peter Wirth was the new majority leader, Representative Egolf was elected speaker and Representative Patty Lundstrom was HAFC (and soon LFC) chair, the first woman in state history to head these important committees.

Senate Democrats caucused for six hours on January 11 and Senator Smith presented the solvency and budget plans in far more detail than usual. I thought he was like Moses guiding his flock through the wilderness. The governor's budget recommendation featured a take home pay cut/pension swap to save $100 million, and Senator Smith commented, "The governor's had a disdain for state employees and teachers, so that doesn't surprise me." The next day Governor Martinez said the LFC budget plan was a "cop-out." Nevertheless, Governor Martinez's state of the state address asked legislators to "embrace bipartisan solutions ... to the state's flagging budget and promote economic growth."[199]

The Senate passed four solvency bills in the first 24 hours with near unanimity, perhaps shocking Roundhouse watchers. After House action over the weekend and conference committees, on Wednesday January 25 three bills went to the governor, raising $216 million by sweeping cash balances, speeding up the collection of insurance premium tax revenue and taking credit for school cash balances. I figured out the insurance speedup, changing "July 1" to "June 30", one sleepless night about four in the morning. After a week, the 2017 session felt like the end of a 30-day session.

For the remainder of the session, fiscal focus was on the FY18 budget, a $350 million tax increase pushed by the majority (including $100 million from internet sales and a fuel tax increase) and a GRT tax reform plan pushed by Governor Martinez and Representative Harper. Martinez remained opposed to any tax rate increases but opened the door slightly to raising revenue through closing loopholes with tax reform. The GRT on food was a lightning rod for GRT reform legislation. Miffed by failure to confirm appointees and by the override of a vetoed bill sponsored by Senator Craig Brandt (R-Rio Rancho), Governor Martinez riled the legislature by vetoing ten bills in the last week without including a message explaining her "objection" to the bill(s). (Later the incomplete vetoes were determined unconstitutional.) Even in the last 48 hours, all three fiscal options seemed in play. A *Journal* editorial on Friday March 17 stated, "political payback is unbecoming of the governor", and wondered whether she'd forgotten her appeal for bipartisanship ("New Mexico doesn't need pettiness from governor, Lawmakers"). But ultimately the legislature passed only a flat $6.1 billion budget and the $350 million tax bill. Chief of Staff Gardner said a special session and vetoes were likely.

Grasping for a Response. Speculation mounted whether the governor would veto the tax bill and the budget, partial veto the tax bill or hack the budget. DFA was telling the governor there was a cash flow crisis, and on Tuesday March 22, Governor Martinez "warned park and museum closings possible," maybe furloughs too. But Lundstrom said, "we have more than enough money to get all agencies through the end of the fiscal year." On March 27 Governor Martinez reiterated these concerns to 400 business leaders, but a *Journal* editorial on March 29 quoted Smith and Egolf saying the solvency package is adequate and, "we can squeeze by … unless she's aware of other revenues that didn't materialize." ("Governor should produce data supporting drastic measures"). On March 30 Secretary Rodriguez said, "I know people think we're crying wolf, but we're not. I'm not sitting here making political decisions."[200] On April 5 the *Journal* reported the legislature sent the governor a menu of options, "and with a Friday deadline approaching, it's clear Martinez doesn't find the choices particularly appetizing."[201]

On April 7, Governor Martinez vetoed the tax bill and all FY18 appropriations to higher education institutions and legislative agencies, $766 million. She also vetoed 144 other bills, 52 percent of bills passed, the highest veto percentage ever. Senator Smith called this a lack of "fiscal competence. ... We're going to find out how many legislators are still going to be willing to walk in lockstep with her."[202] Senator Wirth questioned the constitutionality of vetoes that defunded an entire agency, and Legislative Council Service Director Burciaga initiated a legal review of the issue.

19. Director Abbey and Senator Wirth in LFC conference room planning for 2017 special session. Eddie Moore, (*Journal* photo, May 21, 2017.)

The next seven weeks were a whirlwind. Higher Education Secretary Damron said she wasn't in the loop on the higher education veto. Legislators started gathering signatures for an extraordinary session and filed a lawsuit challenging constitutionality of the budget vetoes. The monthly LFC revenue tracking report in April showed strength of about $55 million in year-to-date revenue compared to the December estimate. Governor Martinez announced that agencies should plan for furloughs. She also renewed her push for GRT reform to help resolve the budget impasse and said it would be on the agenda for a special session. On May 4 Governor Martinez said she had a budget plan, but legislators said they hadn't seen it. Again, on May 10 Governor Martinez said she had a plan to fund the legislature, but Egolf said, "saying you have a plan and actually having a plan are two different things." Senator Clemente Sanchez (D-Cubero) and Representative Candi Sweetser (D-Deming) questioned whether the legislature had good numbers on up to 100 tax reform options and whether tax changes could be executed in a short special session. NMSU President Carruthers, speaking for the Council of University Presidents in a *Journal* op-ed on April 16, appealed for funding colleges and universities at the vetoed HB2 level and said 133 thousand students and their families are left confused and wondering whether they should enroll in New Mexico. Jeremiah Ritchie resigned from the governor's office. On May 5, Smith, Lundstrom and Neville wrote the governor asking for a new revenue estimate, but the governor's spokesman called it a delaying tactic. The Supreme Court on May 12 ruled that the legislative petition challenging constitutionality of the vetoes wasn't "ripe", in effect saying, "keep working on it." On May 18 LFC revenue tracking indicated YTD strength of about $100 million. On the horizon TRD reported discussions with Amazon to collect GRT on internet sales. Governor Martinez complained to legislative leaders that I was doing unilateral revenue estimates and was uncommunicative.

20. L-R, Senators Neville, Cisneros and Smith and Director Abbey at LFC meeting, circa 2017.

21. Senators Cisneros and Smith, Director Abbey and Representative Lundstrom at LFC meeting, circa 2017.

The legislature met on May 24 and quickly passed the vetoed tax bill, the vetoed budgets for the legislature and higher education and a supplemental severance tax bond swap to raise $100 million. NMSU President Carruthers told HAFC failure to restore higher education funding would "essentially bankrupt the university."[203] On May 26 Governor Martinez signed the budget and vetoed the tax bill again. Legislators figured with strength in revenue, General Fund reserves would be about one percent. Two weeks later LFC economists reported Representative Harper's special session tax reform bill would have reduced General Fund revenue by $30 million to $44 million.[204] The governor's spokesman said the LFC analysis was "flawed" and "dishonest," but the Albuquerque Chamber said the analysis would help future debate.

Why We Call It the Lost Decade. A *Journal* editorial on May 27 said, "sixty days of negotiations later, there are no big changes, no big projects nothing that hollers New Mexico is an independent Western state that bucks trends or forges a path. Instead, it's a state stuck in the Great Recession (New Mexico has the worst unemployment rate in the nation) still banking on federal entitlements (almost half the population is on Medicaid and one in four receives food stamps) and finite energy revenues that fall victim to every Saudi prince's whim." Not just 60 days, the first five months of 2017. And for that matter since 2008.

UNM athletic director Krebs, who made $419 thousand per year, used UNM foundation money to travel to Scotland on a golf "fundraising" trip. He retired in June and later faced charges and was acquitted.

The *Martinez*-Yazzie school equalization trial took most of the summer in Santa Fe. Secretary Hanna Skandera resigned on June 8.

The State Auditor reported that health insurance companies owed $65 million for insurance premium taxes.

In August Chancellor Garrey Carruthers announced his retirement. Carruthers was a strong leader of both NMSU and the state's seven universities. In the spring he announced a restructuring initiative to reduce costs and boost enrollment along with a $125 million fundraising campaign. Brookings Institution listed NMSU as second highest among US public universities in generating research and promoting social mobility.[205] Carruthers' "retirement" clearly fell in the category of "let no good deed go unpunished." Senators Smith and Papen and Representative Bill McCamley (D- Las Cruces) unsuccessfully appealed to the NMSU regents to reconsider.

On September 2 former Representative Varela passed away. He had a memorial service in the capitol and the governor, legislative leaders and I praised his name.

On September 6 Monahan wrote that a Daniel Libit article on UNM operations shows, "the hallmarks of the now unpopular administration peeled back like scabs. The politics, the vindictiveness, and lack of interest in public policy, screwing your enemies and demanding fealty from all you encounter has been the governing principle."

Two kids were shot at Aztec High School in December. Senator Neville, an alum, led the LFC in a moment of silence when the shocking news came.

2018. The January session revenue estimate added $158 million to FY18 and $93 million to FY19. Eighty rigs were operating in January 2018, and New Mexico became the third highest oil producing state. Energy-related revenue accounted for 70 percent of FY 18 revenue growth, but the US economy had grown for 103 consecutive months.

LCS's Highlights reported the last Martinez session had a conciliatory tone. Senator Mimi Stewart was elected Senate Majority Whip. The legislature adopted an anti-harassment policy with mandatory training for legislative staff and members. Senator Bill Sharer (R-Farmington), of Scottish ancestry, jokingly asked how he should respond to comments about his kilt.

General Fund appropriations grew 4.3 percent to $6.3 billion including two percent raises for all, the first since 2014, targeted raises for state police and judges, a $5 million special appropriation for merit pay for "exemplary" teachers, $34 million more for early childhood programs, $45 million from various sources to repair a collapsed brine well in Carlsbad and $68 million for road and rest area improvements.

22. Senators Morales and Smith and Abbey, Senate floor debate on HB2, 2018. Gabriela Campos, *New Mexican* file photo, May 28, 2023.

In April, Katherine Freeman of United Way and the Early Childhood Funders Group presented to LFC a five-year plan for early childhood investment calling for increases of $16 million to $20 million per year. The plan included the creation of a new department responsible for workforce training and development. Dr. Jeannie Oakes, UCLA professor, recommended making K3 plus mandatory for low-income children. A *Journal* editorial on May 2 touted LFC research showing improved reading outcomes with K3 plus.

In July, UNM announced the termination of the UNM soccer program despite opposition from influential legislators, including Reps. Lundstrom, Larranaga and Maestas and Senator Munoz.

The *Journal* profiled Senator Smith: "It's not that I know so much. I've had pretty darned good luck listening to people. ... We don't need a deal. We need a sustainable plan that produces results."[206] He said one of his flaws is he looks too far down the road, "but there are some who don't even see the intersection they just drove through." He took exception to criticism of his record on early childhood education noting his wife taught the early grades, that he was a sponsor of full day K and that early childhood funding doubled since 2012, despite lean times.

On July 18 1st District Judge Sarah Singleton issued a "blistering" decision that New Mexico was violating constitutional rights of at-risk students and students of color because of inadequate funding and ordered the state to establish a new funding system by April 15, 2019. The decision did not specify a remedy.

In September the US received $922 million bonus payments to acquire oil and gas leases on 50 thousand acres. New Mexico received half for the General Fund. Historically federal lease sales netted less than $10 million.

At the November general election Michelle Lujan Grisham defeated US representative Steve Pearce with 57 percent of the votes. The Democrats also picked up eight seats in the House including almost wiping out the Republicans in Bernalillo County. Lujan Grisham picked former US Senator Jeff Bingaman to head the transition team.

The *Journal* on November 26 reported on the oil gusher in New Mexico.[207] Production for the first eight months of 2018 was up 38 percent and New Mexico received $467 million as a share of bonus payments for leases on Federal land. The December revenue estimate indicated new money for the FY20 budget was an eye-popping $1.1 billion.

Wrapping Up. The big accomplishment of the Martinez administration was to lead all Republican governors to participate in the expansion of Medicaid to working age adults. It paid for itself with additional federal funds and in the long run would lead to better health outcomes, especially for the homeless and individuals with substance abuse problems. Governor Martinez and Secretary Skandera had innovative ideas to improve educational outcomes and teacher quality, but they failed to gain traction or were quickly unwound like school grades. They can share with the legislature credit for growing investment in early childhood programs. Governor Martinez stubbornly clung to initiatives like social promotion that may not have made much difference. Fixation on tax cuts looked like a broken record. The Downs procurement, the crippling of behavioral health infrastructure and the higher education veto were great lasting sores from her administration.

RIP Reps. Varela/Larranaga/Saavedra. The historic confluence of these three Hispanic men is remarkable. They were born within two years—February 1935 (Varela), March 1936 (Saavedra) and December 1937 (Larranaga) and died within 16 months—September 2017 (Varela), October 2018 (Larranaga) and January 2019 (Saavedra). They were sons of the Depression, Varela at a Pecos ranch, Larranaga at a Red Hill ranch (near Encino) and Saavedra, son of a shoeshine man in Albuquerque. They were veterans and first-generation college graduates. Varela received a law degree in night school. Larranaga came home from the service and while working on a road crew, he took a class at Highlands. The professor threatened to flunk him if he didn't quit work and go to college full time. Larranaga seemed to always wear pressed Wranglers, Charletta by his side. Saavedra graduated from the University of Albuquerque. They had distinguished careers in New Mexico government, Varela state comptroller, Larranaga highway secretary and Saavedra running parks and recreation in Albuquerque. Larranaga was a principal of an engineering firm. They served in the New Mexico legislature a collective 92 years and led the House appropriations committee (Saavedra and Larranaga) and LFC (Varela).

They loved traveling to committee hearings around the state during the interim. At an LFC subcommittee meeting at the New Mexico School for the Visually

Handicapped in Alamogordo, Varela related that a cousin went there in the 1950s and went on to a distinguished career as a lawyer and advocate in California. Larranaga then said his sister went there for a couple years after a blow to the head until she recovered her eyesight. Their stories reminded us to support our neighbors and families in need and why we are in public service.

They were political opponents but allies, and their legacies are long. I think especially of the State History Museum (Varela and Saavedra), the new engineering building at UNM (Larranaga) and athletic facilities at UNM (Saavedra).

# 12

# MICHELLE LUJAN GRISHAM 2019—
# AT THE TIME OF PUBLICATION OF THIS
# BOOK

Michelle Lujan Grisham (MLG) graduated Santa Fe's St. Mike's HS and UNM and UNM School of Law. She served as aging and health secretary in the Richardson administration and two terms in Congress. Her first appointments included John Bingaman as chief of staff, Teresa Casados as chief operating officer, Dr. David Scrase for HSD and Olivia Padilla Jackson at DFA. Padilla Jackson was an LFC economist and board of finance director, my career path. Scrase was an executive for Presbyterian Health Care.

MLG greeted improved economic and fiscal conditions in her first two sessions with oil production up almost 50 percent in FY 19 to 300 million barrels and over 100 rigs operating. She said, "we will go big," and proposed an agenda including universal pre-K, controlling gun violence, higher teacher pay, addressing climate change and a "moonshot" for public education. General Fund appropriations increased 12 percent to $7.1 billion for FY20. Public school appropriations increased 16 percent including doubling the at-risk formula factor, and the legislature established the Early Childhood and Care Department. The 2019 legislature also enacted tax changes long recommended by LFC to raise $71 million: taxing internet sales, bringing non-profit hospitals into the gross receipts tax base and raising the motor vehicle excise tax. Governor Lujan Grisham also muscled through SB2, amendments to the film credit, paying off the credit backlog, more than doubling the credit cap to $110 million, and providing a five percent bonus credit for film spending in rural New Mexico. (The LFC FIR reported studies showed the state recoups only 40 cents for every dollar it spends through the film credit.) Capital outlay appropriations were $925 million, including an extra $250 million share for the governor to allocate to executive priorities like broadband and renewable energy. Projected reserves ending FY20 were 20 percent.

The Corrections Department took over operation of the 600-bed prison in Clayton from the GEO Group. (In 2024 the state appropriated $34 million to purchase the prison from Union County.) CYFD raised eligibility for childcare subsidies from 150 percent to 200 percent of Federal Poverty Level (FPL). The State Engineer committed $100 million of state spending as a share of the Aamodt water rights settlement in the Nambe Basin.

Deming Schools, under Superintendent Arsenio Romero, provided K5 plus for all students and reported summer attendance in the range 75-85 percent. Las Cruces and other districts planned for significant expansion of K5plus for the 2020-2021 school year.

On September 17, 2019, Senator Carlos Cisneros passed. He was stressed about the coming primary and anticipated a challenge from progressives. He was a molybdenum miner, served 34 years in the Senate, long-time LFC member and Vice-Chair of Senate Finance. He was a strong union man, a progressive but also a cautious ally of Senator Smith in addressing the state's volatile fiscal conditions. He was replaced by long-time HAFC member, Representative Roberto "Bobby" Gonzalez. Gonzalez' family had the school bus contracts in Taos County. He was a teacher and Taos superintendent. (My favorite Gonzalez story was his first-year teaching kindergarten at APS's Dolores Gonzales. They walked to the zoo for a field trip. On the way back to school, the kids ran off and he was alone. He got back to school and called the principal in a panic (no cell phones then), "What should I do?" The principal said don't worry about it, they've just run home.)

Speaker Egolf directed Majority Leader Sheryl Stapleton to lead an inquiry with LFC, LESC, and house leadership staff into the State equalization guarantee (SEG) credit for Federal PL874 revenue to school districts, impact aid. The credit had been reduced from 95 percent to 75 percent but still reduced the school appropriation requirement by $83 million. Most of the credit came from a handful of districts with high native student enrollment, Central, Gallup, Zuni and Grants. Stapleton led hearings in Roswell, Grants and Santa Fe. Legislative staff defended the credit in the interest of funding equalization, but districts and advocates were severely critical, verging on accusations of racism. As a transitional measure, the 2020 GAA included $18.9 million for above adequacy building projects at impact aid districts.

At the 2020 regular 30-day session the GAA appropriated $7.6 billion for an increase of 7.6 percent; but on Senator Smith's urging, Lujan Grisham vetoed $150 million of non-recurring appropriations in anticipation of economic deterioration.

## BUDGETMAKING DURING TWO YEARS OF THE PANDEMIC

During the 2020 session, there were reports of a rapidly spreading flu in China, but no one had time to pay much attention. After the session LFC staff had a briefing from HSD's Dr. Scrase, and he reported the situation was deteriorating quickly. LFC Deputy Sallee and I asked him if our March travel plans were in jeopardy, and he was noncommittal. I was about the last New Mexican to travel, to San Francisco to visit my sister. Sallee's trip to Disneyland a week later was canceled. New Mexico's first covid case was March 11.

Almost overnight in March and April 2020, New Mexico lost 80 thousand jobs, a ten percent decline. Oil rigs fell to 15, and one day in April the oil price was negative but settled around $15 barrel. The S&P 500 fell 30 percent. My weekly report to members on March 17 stated, "Economic developments are stunning every day."

New Mexico joined most states with emergency public health orders that closed almost everything—state offices, schools and universities and restaurants. Long lines formed to enter grocery and retail stores. If restaurants were open, it was for curbside pickup. For several months only a few stalwarts went to the capitol building—Mark Valenzuela, Micaela Fischer and me at LFC. Most others quickly transitioned to remote work relying on video conferencing, or "zoom." We formed the habit of scanning the county and state infection rates, then inoculation rates, to gauge the spread (and decline) of the pandemic.

On March 10 the word "special session" popped up, and on March 19 Governor Lujan Grisham advised legislators a special session was inevitable. For the next ten weeks, the economic and fiscal crises were on the front page every day. By mid-April the deficit was pegged at $2 billion to $3 billion. LFC staff were scouring the appropriations schedules looking for cuts, scouring the cash balance reports for funds to raid, and the capital outlay status reports for projects to cancel. School and university officials were losing their minds. Social service agencies were appealing for appropriation increases for health care and food aid. Some legislators were pushing for small business grants and low-income tax credits. Attention turned to what Federal aid would be forthcoming, and in late May Governor Lujan Grisham advocated tapping the Permanent Fund. Monahan reported on February 17 that Smith and Lundstrom had a tense relationship, fueled perhaps by Lundstrom economic development initiatives for McKinley County, but LFC staff talked to them almost every day, started developing scenarios and options, and then presented the scenarios to leadership. Then LFC briefed every Senator individually.

The legislature met June 18, 2020, in a four-day special session, mostly focused on solvency. (It was the first of five special sessions and two regular sessions over the next 22 months. Legislators don't get paid for this.) The capitol was closed to the public, and many members participated in committees and floor sessions from their offices.

The solvency effort was aided by a successful bet that Congress would pass significant relief to the state including $750 million for a state relief fund that could be deposited in the General Fund pursuant to the Coronavirus Response and Relief Supplemental Appropriations Act (CARES). The executive and LFC agreed on most remaining elements of a solvency plan. After the "lost decade", New Mexico was well practiced: four percent reductions for most agencies, the usual capital reversions and fund balance sweeps, voiding raises and special appropriations. Adjusted General Fund reserves ending FY21 were 12 percent.

In November covid cases averaged 1,900 per day but reached 3,675 on November 19. A one-day special session in November made appropriations from CARES/ General Fund for economic relief including supplemental unemployment benefits, small business grants and low-income rebates.

In January Conoco Philips acquired Concho Resources which was formed in 2004 with the acquisition of major independent producers in Artesia and Roswell, Chase and Marbob.

2021, the Year that Never Was. The 2021 session occurred with a fence around the capital, security checkpoints for entry, members participating mostly by video conference, everyone masked and long lines for covid testing. In early January a slow vaccine rollout began, targeted to at-risk populations. Charles Sallee and I scrounged up doses for every LFC staffer who wanted one, and most members also were vaccinated. LFC was apprehensive about preparing the GAA with many staff remote, but it worked, error-free. LCS's 2021 Highlights reported an "eerie quiet" at the Capitol.

The New Mexico and US economy had a pretty sharp recovery, sometimes called a "hockey stick" but also a "dead cat bounce" by Dr. Tom Clifford. New Mexico overtook North Dakota as the second biggest oil producer.

The Executive recommendation for FY22 was flat as a pancake for virtually all agencies; the LFC recommendations were in the range -three percent to flat with a 1.5 percent compensation increase. The legislature passed a $7.45 billion budget for FY22, up $378 million or five percent from FY21 adjusted but still below FY20. Appropriations for public schools were up seven percent including elimination of the impact aid credit. An Opportunity Scholarship program, free college tuition, was initiated with an $18 million appropriation. Governor Lujan Grisham vetoed a prohibition on five-day school districts shortening the week to four days, and some larger districts like Socorro and Central took advantage. After 15 years of trying, HJR1 increased distributions from the permanent fund for early childhood and public education. Other significant legislation included the New Mexico Civil Rights Act ending qualified immunity for law enforcement officers and other public officials, a requirement for private employers to provide paid sick leave, a 2.75 percent increase in the insurance premium tax to expand subsidized health insurance coverage, $200 million for grants to small businesses and a prohibition on fur trapping on public land. A special session in late March legalized recreational cannabis.

In March CYFD entered the *Kevin S.* settlement agreement to develop a "trauma responsive" foster care system. In July unemployment reached 12.7 percent. The Unemployment Trust Fund was depleted in September, and the state began to borrow from the federal government. In March 2022 Pattern Energy dedicated the 400 tower Corona wind farm delivering 1,050 megawatts to Los Angeles.

ARPA and Supreme Court Decision. Following up CARES, the American Rescue Plan Act, (ARPA) signed March 11, 2021, provided a $1.9 trillion economic stimulus package, including $1.75 billion to a New Mexico State Relief Fund. Anticipating passage, the 2021 General Appropriation Act appropriated $1.2 billion of stimulus revenue including $600 million to restore solvency for the Unemployment Trust Fund, $200 million for roads and $100 million for the lottery scholarship contingent on deposit of the Federal money to the General fund as required by state law. (The general fund shall get all revenue not otherwise designated, and no money can be spent from the Treasury without an appropriation.) The governor also vetoed the contingent ARPA appropriation challenging whether it was allowed by ARPA and referencing *Sego v. Kirkpatrick* that the legislature can't appropriate Federal grants to state agencies. But the ARPA funds were general revenue.

Legislative leaders, appropriators and staff questioned the constitutionality of the veto. On May 4 the LFC chairs advised the treasurer to deposit the $1.7 billion state ARPA payment in the general fund as required by Section 6-4-2.

LFC met in Las Cruces in May, the first in person meeting of the New Mexico legislators, and LFC staff confirmed the ability to deposit ARPA funds into the General Fund and appropriate with broad discretion.[208] MLG offered to work with legislators to determine an allocation of the funds, and despite analysis supporting legislative powers, leaders, especially in the House, were reluctant to challenge the governor. On September 20 Senator Greg Baca and Senator Jacob Candelaria petitioned the Supreme Court to bar the Governor from spending the unallocated ARPA funds.[209] State Treasurer Tim Eichenberg joined the lawsuit in October. At an NCSL meeting in Tampa, I discussed this issue with Senator Joseph Cervantes and Representative Ryan Lane (R-Aztec), and on November 10, four more senators joined the plaintiffs, Cervantes, Ivey Soto, Ortiz y Pino and Munoz. A *Journal* editorial on October 26 said the governor needs to turn $1.1 billion of federal aid over to lawmakers and cited concerns from Representative Patty Lundstrom and Representative Moe Maestas. On November 17 the Supreme Court decided unanimously in favor of the legislators. At the hearing Justice David Thomson said he learned in second grade that lawmakers control the purse strings.

At a December special session on reapportionment, the legislature also appropriated over $300 million for broadband and other infrastructure projects. Monahan on December 9 said Lundstrom was "leading the way."

Mike Gallagher of the *Journal* retired after 40 years.[210] A Brooklyn native and UNM grad, he was a fearless government watchdog and, in my view, public servant. Collen Heild continues to carry the torch for the *Journal*.

2022 Recovery. By February New Mexico had recovered three quarters of the jobs lost during the pandemic. Oil prices soared in the wake of the Russian invasion of Ukraine. Oil production rose over 500 million barrels. Projected revenue growth in FY23 was 11 percent to over $9 billion. FY23 General Fund appropriations were $8.46 billion, up 14 percent, about half of which replaced one-time federal funds used to prop up the FY21 budget. The legislature also passed an omnibus tax bill providing rebates, creating a child tax credit, reducing the GRT rate and exempting some social security and military pensions from the personal income tax.

Governor Lujan Grisham vetoed a supplemental General Appropriation Act, junior. To avoid an extraordinary session called by legislators, MLG called them back to pass a slightly adjusted junior bill and another round of rebates.

Following ARPA, two more federal bills provided great funding opportunities for New Mexico through funding formulas and competitive grants. The Infrastructure Investment and Jobs Act authorized $1.2 trillion over ten years and the Inflation Reduction Act authorized another $750 billion. The LFC issues regular reports on federal funding for New Mexico. (See LFC website, revenue report tab).

On February 23, 2022, my friend and mentor, Bob Lang, director of the Wisconsin Legislative Fiscal Bureau, received the Distinguished Public Leadership Award of the University of Wisconsin School of Public Administration. He was a Vietnam veteran, briefly a teacher, then worked for the Wisconsin legislature for 50 years with 40 years as director. He is revered by legislators and governors from both parties. Former governor and HHS secretary Tommy Thompson said, "No matter where you go, everyone wants Bob Lang on your side." I often wondered how Lang avoided friction with the executive branch. Perhaps I was too picky.

Political Change/Progressive Hegemony. In the June 2020 primary five moderate Democrat senators were defeated including President Pro Tem Mary Kay Papen, SFC Chair John Arthur Smith and Senate Corporations and Transportation Chair Clemente Sanchez. Former Senator Eric Griego, state director of the Working Families Party said, "a coalition of labor unions, environmental groups and reproductive rights organizations had worked together to oust the business-friendly incumbents."[211] Moderate Senator John Sapien did not run for reelection. In the November general election, Democratic primary victors over Senators Smith and Sanchez lost to Republicans, but Democrats picked up two seats in Bernalillo County. Senator Smith resigned in December 2020, just before the December LFC meeting.

Following Joe Biden's election, Governor Lujan Grisham figured in speculation as a cabinet appointee, notably for Health and Human Services.[212] Word on the street was that she was offered a different position, turned it down and then burned bridges with presidential staff.

In January 2021 Senator Mimi Stewart was elected president Pro Tem and Senator George Munoz moved to chair of Senate Finance. The changes obviously paved the way for the passage of the early childhood constitutional amendment and much more.

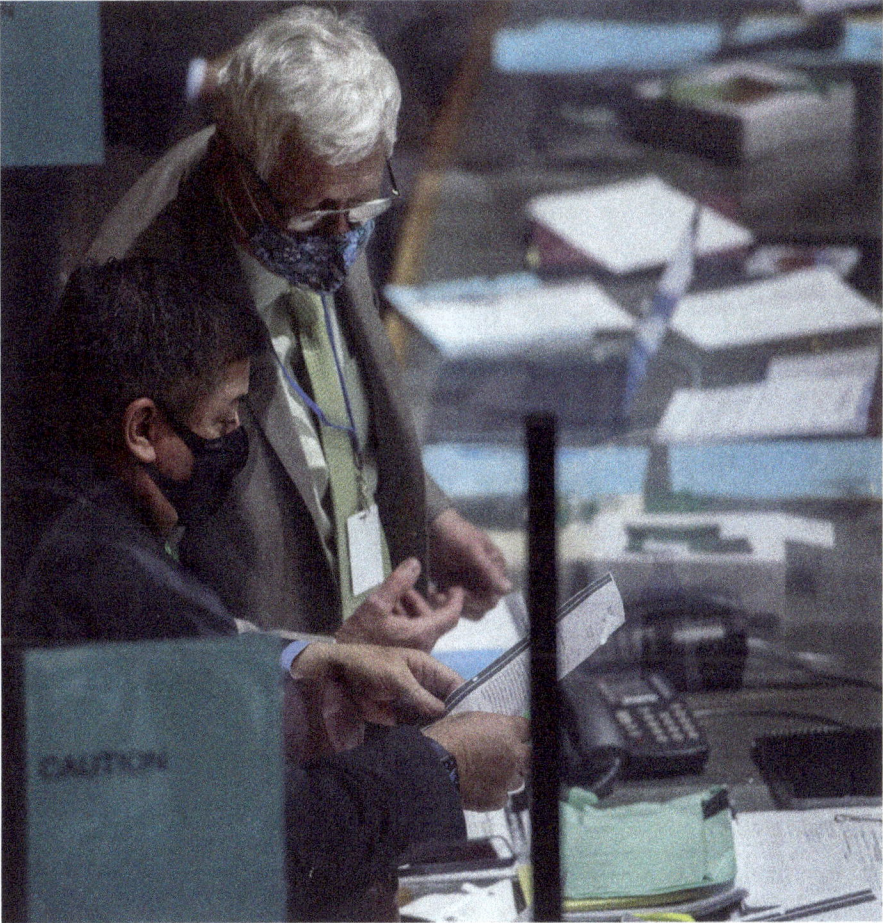

23. Senator Munoz and David Abbey, Senate floor debate on HB2. The pandemic session, 2021.

In February 2021, blogger Paul Gibson, Retake Our Democracy, put a target on my back ("How Fiscal Conservatives Clip the Wings of Eager New Legislators"). He said the FY22 budget was timid, the same kind that fiscal hawk Smith would advance. He quoted Monahan saying that "progressive ideals die as soon as newbies walk through those heavy brass doors… because they get the scare treatment and quickly learn to fall in line if they want to accomplish anything. … (Abbey) has done tremendous work for the state if you believe that pinching every penny is the right thing to do." Gibson said, "legislators have had their bandwidth narrowed at the same time that our collective vision has become increasingly bold. It's time for us to regroup and think about how to address these systemic problems."

In July 2021 House Majority Leader and Albuquerque Public Schools staff member Sheryl Stapleton became the target of an investigation into a kickback scheme with a school vendor. She resigned. In September, the Legislative Education Study Committee director, a former LFC analyst, resigned following complaints that she made remarks that were culturally insensitive.

Ending the 2022 session, House Speaker Egolf announced he would not run for reelection. Just days before the filing date, his chief of staff Reena Sczepanski was the only candidate. Incredibly, her Santa Fe precinct (and my precinct) was shifted into Egolf's district at the 2021 reapportionment. Sczepanski was elected majority whip in her first term in 2023. Sczepanski was a staffer for Emerge New Mexico, according to the website, "the state's premier organization to help Democratic women and non-binary individuals to run for office." Like me, she graduated from Brown University.

The Game and Fish Department purchased the 54-thousand-acre L Bar ranch on the east flank of Mt. Taylor for $34 million. (L-Bar is my father-in-law's brand, he won it in a poker game.)

The Calf Canyon/Hermits Peak fires in Mora and San Miguel Counties in April took two months to extinguish, threatened to crawl over the Sangres to Pecos and ruined the homes, livelihoods and traditions of thousands of families.

Distrust of government at any level grew when the US Forest Service admitted that the fires started in burn piles that were unwisely ignited in fierce spring winds or left unattended in severe drought conditions.

How Government Was Working. New Mexico's management of the pandemic tilted to protecting public health with relatively less emphasis on economic vitality, conditions for student learning and government services. On March 16, 2020, MLG issued a public health order closing all schools for three weeks, later extended to the remainder of the school year. As early as June 2020, LFC reported closures would result in learning loss of three months to a year, substantially more than the normal "summer slide".[213] LFC also reported at-risk students were likely to experience a greater learning loss due to lack of internet access or participation. In October LFC reported about half of K-5 children were still in remote instruction. The *Journal* said New Mexico was one of seven states keeping schools "partly to mostly closed."[214] LFC staff persistently recommended universal extended school year to make up learning losses. The 2022 legislature grew funding for the K5 plus program to $120 million for FY23, but participation was only 4,440 kids, down from 8,300 in FY22.[215]

On March 21, 2020, Governor Lujan Grisham issued an order closing "non-essential businesses," later extended through May. Public meetings were restricted. There was significant controversy about applicability, for example churches. Vaccination, available beginning December 2020, was required for most government, school and university employees but sometimes resisted. Some legislators expressed frustration to Economic Development Secretary Alicia Keyes regarding mask requirements and the slow pace of reopening.[216]

State employees were allowed to work remotely until summer 2022, when the State Personnel Office directed state agencies to authorize remote work only on a case-by-case basis. Unions resisted the return to work, but the telework policy was rescinded in November 2022 in the wake of an LFC report that the state was paying $18 million for unoccupied office space, mostly in Santa Fe.[217] Then agencies including DFA, HED and PED began to lease offices in Albuquerque and even Las Cruces to promote employee convenience and retention.

Most agencies struggled to hire and retain employees during and after the pandemic. For FY22 the average classified service vacancy rate was 23 percent. Agencies took 69 days on average to fill a vacant position, and almost 40 percent of new employees quit in their first year. State government employment challenges were no different than other sectors of the New Mexico economy with the unemployment rate, long above the US average, in October 2023 at only 3.8 percent, about the same as the US.

Attention also turned to labor force participation which by 2021 fell nine percent from the 2019 peak for workers aged 25 to 34, close to double the national decline. The 2021 workforce participation rate for men in New Mexico was the third lowest in the nation.

In August 2022 CYFD raised eligibility for childcare assistance from 250 percent to 400 percent FPL, over $100 thousand.

Recruitment and retention of cabinet members has also been "problematic." The first PED secretary resigned in 2019. The second lived in Philadelphia in the first year of the pandemic and didn't last much longer. The third PED secretary was a capable, experienced school superintendent, ditto for the fourth. The highly regarded DFA secretary resigned in April 2020 along with the HED secretary. Chief of Staff John Bingaman returned to investment banking in November 2020. The Departments of Health and Information Technology have had four secretaries and Veterans, Workforce, DFA, Aging, Personnel, GSD, Regulation and others have had three leaders. The issue rose to the fore in 2023 with the resignation of former Supreme Court Justice Barbara Vigil after a year as CYFD Secretary. Senator Craig Brandt said, "sounds like she's a little hard to work for."

The October 2021 LFC evaluation "Obtaining and Maximizing Value in State Procurement" said, "the pandemic highlighted holes in emergency procurement procedures that, in some cases, allowed for fraudulent purchases and waste of taxpayer dollars." The combined value of sole source and emergency procurements in FY21 was $314 million, up from $100 million in FY14.

In January 2023, HSD canceled the procurement of four-year contracts for Medicaid managed care organizations, with annual contract value approaching $10 billion. The excuse was the surprise resignation of HSD Secretary David Scrase. The Medicaid director and the Insurance Superintendent also resigned. The procurement scoring sheets revealed HSD's plan to award contracts to a firm that was not ranked in the top four and was a donor to the MLG campaign. The Ethics Commission, responding to a complaint, investigated the procurement. Using former Supreme Court Justice Judy Nakamura as a mediator, HSD and the Ethics Commission entered into a settlement agreement for HSD to revert to the original top ranked bidders. Monahan (August 21, 2023) called it a win for the Ethics Commission and an escape for "MLG and company." Also, it was a loss for the state of top caliber health administrators. Further, it was another reminder of the persistence of pay-to-play at the highest level.

GSD's Health Benefits Fund incurred increasing, illegal deficits. The fund balance was $6 million ending FY19 and was projected to fall to -$95 million ending FY23, despite the infusion of $43 million General Fund transfers. This reflected failure to raise premiums beginning FY21 until mid-FY24 and resulted in significant General Fund subsidies to universities and local governments.[218]

Periodic reviews of the state's tax system cast a spotlight on the gross receipts tax. New Mexico Tax Research Institute Director Richard Anklam told the interim Revenue and Tax Policy Committee, "In New Mexico we've narrowed our base, and we've raised our rates. That's been our policy history for the last 15 to 20 years." He described it akin to Sisyphus pushing the boulder uphill, only for it to fall back near the top. He said, "We've reached pretty much the absolute top of our capacity." Senator Wirth noted part of the problem is that it costs the state about $68 million per year to reduce the rate by just one eighth percent: "We've got ourselves into a really rough predicament."[219]

Other issues flagged by LFC included overpaying unemployment benefits by an estimated $250 million; misusing executive authority in disaster declarations; skimpy reporting to the Federal government on stimulus spending; failing to boost enrollment in infant home visiting for a decade after New Mexico was an early adopter; ever growing unspent balances of capital project appropriations, now at $5 billion; and deficient care at the New Mexico Veterans' Home in Truth or Consequences that led to Covid-related deaths of dozens of patients.[220] DFA Secretary Romero complained to Representative Lundstrom that LFC was "dingy", that we were constantly dinging agency efforts and not constructive.

I received the Earl Nunn Award from the New Mexico School Superintendents' Association presented by ally, director, and former Des Moines, Hobbs and Las Cruces superintendent Stan Rounds.

Progressive Legislators Gain Again and Revenues Surge. On November 8, 2022, Governor Lujan Grisham defeated weatherman and political newcomer Mark Ronchetti with 52 percent of the vote. Republican candidates in Bernalillo County failed across the board, and Representative Candy Sweetser (D-Deming) was defeated. The constitutional amendment to boost Permanent Fund distributions for education passed with 70 percent, despite the strong revenue outlook and the explosive growth in the Early Childhood Trust Fund, expected to reach $5.4 billion ending FY23.

The December 2022 revenue estimate indicated FY24 General Fund revenue of $12 billion, $3.6 billion over the FY23 operating budget. FY22 General Fund reserves were $3.7 billion, 49 percent of recurring appropriations. Oil and gas revenue accounted for 70 percent of the revenue growth. Finance officials acknowledged challenges in growing spending with the economy at full employment.[221]

## 2023 AND THE PROGRESSIVE AGENDA

On January 17, Governor Lujan Grisham outlined an aggressive agenda including more rebates, consolidating health agencies, and new funds for housing and environmental protection. The House elected Representative Javier Martinez as Speaker. An attorney, he was born in El Paso, raised at a young age in Ciudad Juarez and then Albuquerque. His first move was to appoint Representative Nathan Small (D-Las Cruces) to chair HAFC and assign Representative Lundstrom to the Transportation Committee. Monahan (1/25/23) reported a

"Senior Alligator" speculating about my future: "It's true that David has been deeply aligned with the conservative leadership of former Chair Lundstrom but in the end he is a staffer who will serve the legislature and expedite their agenda regardless of ideology. That's his job and that's also how you stay a top staffer for so many years."

24. Representative Gail Armstrong (R-Magdalena), David Abbey and HAFC Chair Small after HAFC hearing, February 15, 2023. Eddie Moore photo, *Journal*.

The General Appropriation Act of 2023 appropriated $9.57 billion for FY24 from the General Fund, a 14 percent increase. Highlights included funding child care up to 400 percent FPL income eligibility, fully funding the Opportunity scholarship free tuition for all program, restructuring extended learning to allow professional development to count for instructional hourly requirements, requiring free breakfast for all students regardless of income level, expanding the at-risk public school formula weight, doubling salaries for educational assistants, six percent raises for public employees, increasing the income level to receive

TANF benefits by 15 percent, and increasing the budget for Child Protective Services 14 percent.

Of special note, in my view two of the great legacies of the Lujan Grisham administration, were boosting Medicaid provider rates and funding elimination of the waiting list for services for the developmentally disabled. A December 2022 LFC report on Medicaid indicated only 13 percent of clients were able to get a timely appointment for general health care ("Program Evaluation: Medicaid Network Adequacy, Access and Utilization," which earned an Impact Award from the National Legislative Performance Evaluation Society). The GAA appropriated $100 million to boost nursing home and rural health care provider rates to 100 percent of Medicare and primary care, behavioral health and maternal health to 120 percent of Medicare. The intent was to boost health care provider recruitment and retention.

The GAA authorized the transfer of $475 million to the Severance Tax Permanent Fund and $200 million to other endowment funds including a new conservation legacy fund.

The legislature passed a $1.1 billion tax package including a phased gross receipts tax rate reduction, middle income personal income tax relief and transfer of the motor vehicle excise tax to road funds and more rebates. Except for rebates and an expanded child tax credit, it was mostly vetoed. The governor's veto message said, "I have grave concerns about the sustainability of this package. Cuts will impact our ability to fund important services and programs that our citizens depend on, such as education, health care, public safety and infrastructure."

The legislature passed HB 400 sponsored by the House leadership and others to expand Medicaid eligibility from the current top income eligibility level of 133 percent of the Federal poverty level up to 400 percent FPL. Premiums and co-pays could be required of the expansion group. A $500 thousand appropriation would aid HSD to develop recommendations by October 2024 with implementation by 2026. The legislature also passed a pilot project to modernize the legislature by funding district or field offices for legislators.

SB11 sponsored by Senator Stewart to implement paid family medical leave failed in the House. It would have appropriated $36.5 million to the Workforce Solutions Dept for startup costs, impose an employer/employee payroll tax of 0.9 percent and authorize 12 weeks leave for employees' personal health or maternity needs or to care for a newborn or other family member. Eleven states have such a program, but the New Mexico program offered longer leave for more expansive conditions than other states. An LFC FIR estimated a $500 million fund shortfall by FY28. Senator Stewart said the FIR was wrong. Senator Mark Moores (R-Albuquerque) said, "it's like we want California policies, without having California economic opportunities."

An LFC bill to require school districts to add instructional days failed. Under the calendar restructuring bill that passed, 40 percent of school districts reduced instructional days.

The December 2023 consensus revenue estimate is General Fund recurring revenue growth of $12.8 billion, up ten percent. FY25 "new money" is $3.2 billion.

Hanging It Up. On Monday March 27, 2023, a week after the 2023 session, I announced my retirement after 26 years as LFC Director and 40 years in state government.

The Journal reported I was "known as a prolific reader whose knowledge of state government often made him an annoyance to Democratic and Republican governors alike. But they also turned to his staff as a source of talent when they needed to fill high level positions."[222] Representative Lundstrom said I was the most valuable employee the legislature ever had. Senator Smith said I helped legislators see beyond their parochial interests: "When David looked at policy it had to be good for the entire state, in his mind. In the Legislature, you often have people thinking what's good for my district. David was uniformly for what was the best for the State of New Mexico." Speaker Javier Martinez said I helped steer legislators through enormous challenges and unprecedented opportunities— from the national financial crisis of 2008 to today's record revenue.

Monahan (March 28,2023) said I served with integrity, "was a cool head in a room of hot tempers", gave part time legislators a "patina of respect when it came to financial matters" and "did what he thought was best for New Mexico not what was expedient." But he said Abbey's record "gets mixed" in the 2010 decade and suggested LFC and its economists should have been more frank and expressed "misgivings" about "wrongheaded" economic and budget policy. "Cutting taxes and shaving budgets for vital social programs in a quasi-welfare state as it experienced deep recession was a calamity."

Phil Casaus, editor of the *New Mexican,* started with Senator Wirth's story about the time in 2008 when I told him I didn't know what to do and Wirth thought, "Uh, oh. Abbey doesn't know what to do" and then how I figured out a technical adjustment to raise $80 million. "New Mexico, cooked for sure, had its bacon saved." Abbey said, "That's sort of been my life in a lot of ways. ... I did it because I enjoyed it, and I helped people. It was challenging too." Casaus said, "that might explain the tectonic rumble you felt beneath the Roundhouse this Spring on the day Abbey officially announced his retirement. ... Abbey always seemed to be around: steady, driven, able. ... On the floor he was the gentle voice in the ear of a legislator as they spoke on financial matters: Cyrano with a spreadsheet. I told Abbey that there are a lot of people who thought he was on the medals stand as one of the most influential people in New Mexico."

On December 8, 2023, I received an honorary doctorate from Western New Mexico University.

# 13

# NEW MEXICO METRICS AND RANKINGS

"Show me your metrics." This is a stock challenge to both public and private organizations. Businesses and governments alike use performance metrics for operations and investments to set goals, to measure progress in reaching goals, to compare performance to similar organizations and just to report and explain organizational activity. In simple terms it means "how are you doing?" and is a tool for making results better.

The purpose of this chapter is to present the most important performance metrics for New Mexico past and present. The purpose is to determine whether New Mexico is making progress and identify challenges for the state going forward.

For the most part I've selected the "best" measures from LFC's quarterly performance reports and annual performance analysis in Volume 1 of LFC's Annual Report to the Legislature. What's best? LFC describes "elements of good performance measures": 1) Most important, *Useful* for policy analysis and budget development; 2) *Results-Oriented*; focus on outcomes for citizens rather than government activity levels like number of reports prepared; 3) *Clear, concise, understandable; 4) Meaningful* to legislators, the press and the public; no jargon, gobbledygook or bureaucratic exercises; 5) *Comparable.* Allows users to benchmark New Mexico government performance to other states or private or other public organizations that provide a similar service; 6) *Relevant and Economical.* Measures relate to the core agency function or the largest expenditures, in other words not in the weeds; and 7) *Timely, Valid Data.* Not ancient history, today's results.

I supplemented the LFC measures by reviewing dashboards of other states including Vermont, Colorado, Tennessee, Oklahoma and Washington suggested by LFC Deputy Director Micaela Fischer. All these reports are issued by the executive branch, usually the governor, and many tilt to governor's initiatives or just link to agency reports. I also reviewed reports focused on select expenditures, for example the education report card NAEP and the American Society of Civil Engineers' infrastructure report.

I organize the measures like LFC—Education, Child Well-Being, Economy and Workforce and so forth. I report the most recent annual data available for New Mexico and then try to report comparable historic data. I also report state rankings when available.[223]

TABLE 1: Economy and Workforce

|  | NM | US | Rank |
|---|---|---|---|
| Labor Force Participation, 2022 | 56.5% | 62.2% | 48th for men, 47th for women |
| Unemployment, 2022 | 4% | 3.6% | |
| Non-Farm Employment Growth, 2017-2022 | 2.2% | 4.1% | |
| Population in Poverty, 2021 | 18.3% | 12.6% | 3 |
| Population Change, 2017-2022 | 1% | 2.60% | |
| Median Household Income, 2021 | $54,020 | 75% of U.S. | |
| Per capita Income, 2022 | $32,667 | | 47 |

Source: NM 2023 State of the Workforce, Department of Workforce Solutions; Bureau of Census

New Mexico ranks near the bottom of states in measures of job growth, income, workforce participation and poverty. An exceptionally strong US economy lowered New Mexico's unemployment rate to four percent, only 0.4 percent higher than the US rate. But household income was three quarters of the US average. Population growth in 2023 slowed to nil.

Rachael Moskowitz, the capable Workforce Solutions economist, examined low workforce participation for men, women and New Mexicans with education less than a bachelors' degree. She reported low and decreasing participation rates of disabled persons. The number of disabled persons who did not participate in the workforce grew 16 percent from 2012 to 2020 in New Mexico, four times the US average. The percent of persons receiving social security disability benefits grew 67 percent in the US from 1999 to 2020 but 98 percent in New Mexico. Ms. Moskowitz noted New Mexico's relative dependence on lower wage service sector jobs might lower work incentives.[224]

TABLE 2: Education

| 4th Grade at or Above Proficiency | 1992 | 2013 | 2022 | 2022 Rank |
|---|---|---|---|---|
| Reading | 23% | 21% | 21% | 49 |
| Math | 11% | 31% | 19% | 51 |

Source: The Nation's Report Card, National Center for Education statisti

| K-12 School Year | 2013 | 2022 | 2023 | Rank |
|---|---|---|---|---|
| Enrollment | | | 305,600 | |
| K5 Plus Enrollment | | 8,334 | 4,934 | |
| Chronic Absenteeism | | | 35.8% | |
| High School Graduation | | 70.3% | 76.8% | 48 |
| Average Teacher Salary | | | $63,580 | |
| Students per Teacher | | 12.9 | | 29 |

Sources: Kids Count, NEA

| Higher Education School Year | 2017 | 2022 |
|---|---|---|
| Bachelor's Degrees Awarded | 12,400 | 11,137 |
| Associate degrees Awarded | 14,294 | 10,304 |
| Cost per University Award | $32,500 | $42,300 |
| Freshman Retention | | 50% |
| 6-year Bachelor's Graduation Rate | 64% | 49% |
| Required Remediation | 44% | 32% |

Source: LFC Public and Higher Education Performance, vol. 2, 2023 and 2024

Following declining birth rates, school and higher education enrollment has declined over the last decade. This trend will accelerate for schools, but perhaps stabilize for higher education due to free tuition. LFC evaluations show both schools and colleges have failed to reprioritize facility, instruction and overhead expenditures in the face of this trend.

New Mexico ranks at or near the bottom for reading and math proficiency, freshman retention and college completion. In the wake of the pandemic, funding for longer school calendars, K5 plus, has been significantly unused. For the 2023-2024 school year, PED figured almost half of districts and charters provided fewer instructional days. Teacher pay has moved near the top of the region in the last year. In 2022 a study.com survey showed New Mexico's median salary of $61,140 just below the US average of $62,360.

TABLE 3: Early Childhood Education and Care

|  | 2012 | 2022 | 2023 |
|---|---|---|---|
| Kids Count Overall Rank | 49 |  | 50 |
| Births | 26,992 | 21,000 |  |
| Childcare Slots |  | 20,000 | 25,000 |
| Childcare in Top Two Quality Tiers |  | 60% | 58% |
| Home Visiting Slots | 600 | 4,000 |  |
| Pre-K Kids Proficient in K |  |  | 61% |
| Repeat Maltreatment, Children in Custody |  | 14% | 13% |

Source: NM 2023 State of the Workforce, Department of Workforce Solutions; Bureau of Census

New Mexico continues at the bottom of the Kids Count rankings compiled by the Annie Casey Foundation. This mostly reflects underlying social and economic conditions. State funding and enrollment in early childhood programs have increased sharply over the last decade. Including high quality childcare and Head Start, LFC estimates that about 80 percent of four-year-olds and half of three-year olds receive early education services, a near universal pre- K program. Despite being an early adopter, less than ten percent of children 0-2 are receiving home visiting services. It is time to consider mandatory participation for some at-risk families. Childcare remains the focus of the ECECD, despite lack of evidence of learning gains for children.

TABLE 4: Health

| | 2010-2012 | 2020-2021 |
|---|---|---|
| Teen Birth Rate per 1,000 | 46 | 19 |
| Low Birth Weight | 8.8% | 9.4% |
| Medicaid Enrollment | 544, 000 | 986,000 |
| Uninsured Adults < 138% Poverty | 46% | 23% |
| Medicaid Children w Dental Visits | 38% | 57% |
| 2yr Olds Immunized | 57% | 74% |
| Children Overweight | | 36% |
| Overdose Death Rate per 100,000 | 25 | 51 |
| Suicides per 100,000 | 19.9 | 24.6 |
| Supports for Develop. Disabled Slots | 4,934 | 6,760 |

Source: 2023 Kids' count and LFC Vol. 1 2024

The game changer for health outcomes in New Mexico has been the steady expansion of eligibility for Medicaid, first children in the 2000s and then most low-income adults. Access to services remains problematic, but in the last couple of years Medicaid provider reimbursement has risen sharply. Also New Mexico has increased capacity for health care provider education and funding for loan repayment for service.

Table 5. Infrastructure

| | 2020/2021 | 2022/2023 |
|---|---|---|
| Pavement Condition Rating | 55 | 66 |
| Interstate Miles in Good Condition | 88% | 92% |
| Lane Miles in Poor Condition | 6805 | 2824 |
| Traffic Fatalities | 411 | 444 |
| Rail Runner Riders | 41,000 | 544,000 |
| Public School Facility Condition Index | 52% | 54% |
| Broadband Locations > 100 megabytes/sec | | 84% |
| Unspent Capital Appropriations (in billions) | $1.80 | $5.40 |
| Outstanding Capital Outlay Projects | 3,682 | 4,900 |

Sources: LFC Vol 1, 2024 and Vol. 2, 2023

Capital outlay appropriations have roughly tripled in the last six years, mostly due to using surplus general fund balances accumulated from soaring energy revenue. With tight labor markets, schools, universities, local governments and state agencies have struggled to boost project design and management capacity. Similarly, construction industry employment was unchanged from 2020 to 2023. LFC reports school and university construction costs have roughly doubled in a few years and highway costs are up 35 to 50 percent since 2020 (LFC Vol. 1, 2024). With 4,900 projects outstanding and unspent appropriations over $5 billion, infrastructure projects face a massive bottleneck. With growing Federal revenue and General Fund appropriations, state road conditions have improved modestly.

Aside from not completing projects timely, as reported in Chapter 4, many projects, large and small, have not been cost effective. Rail Runner occupancy is about 20 percent. You can see the empty cars traveling along I-25 even at peak travel times. Virgin Galactic suspended its commercial space flight business, and its share price plummeted from $50 to $2 in five years. Only 47 percent of DoH hospital beds are occupied, and the promised federal match for the new homes at the Veterans' hospital in T or C has not materialized. Both the Clayton and Santa Rosa prisons are half empty, yet the 2024 Executive recommendation is to purchase the Clayton prison for $34 million. With $85 million appropriations to date for a new executive office building, the 2024 executive recommendation proposed another $100 million. The needed space for elected officials mushroomed into a monstrosity with 700 underground spaces while the site remains in limbo at the City of Santa Fe's historic review board. Okay, enough.

TABLE 6: Natural Resources

|  | 2020-2021 | 2023 |
|---|---|---|
| Pecos Delivery Surplus (1,000 acre-feet) | 167 | 157 |
| Rio Grande Shortfall (1,000 acre-feet) | -96 | -93 |
| Abandoned Oil Wells Plugged | 49 | 76 |
| State Park Visits (in millions) | 4.4 | 4.8 |
| Forest Acres Treated | 14,637 | 15,735 |
| Population with Safe Drinking Water | 97% | 90% |

Source: 2023 Kids' count and LFC Vol. 1 2024

Most natural resource agency metrics show activity levels, notably number of inspections, but not environmental outcomes such as air and water quality. Further, current activity levels may require decades to provide adequate mitigation for wildland forests.

Public Safety. The transition to the new federal National Incident-Based Reporting System (NIBRS) on crime rates disrupted consistent and reliable crime reporting for New Mexico for several years.

LFC reported that violent crime in Albuquerque plateaued at the highest level in 20 years in 2017 and remains well above the national average. Property crimes, including auto theft, have declined over the 20-year period.[225]

The state inmate population declined about 13 percent from FY09 to FY23. Positive drug tests in state prisons in FY23 were 1.4 percent, down from three to four percent in the last decade. The recidivism rate within 36 months of release was 36 percent in FY23, down from 44 percent in FY21. Corrections provides the opportunity to enroll in Medicaid on release and will offer medication-assisted treatment to inmates, a best practice, beginning 2025.

TABLE 7: Government Finances

|  | FY21 | FY22 | FY23 |
|---|---|---|---|
| General Fund Balances | 35% |  | 48% |
| Early Child Trust Fund Bal ($ millions) | $314 | $3,462 | $5,508 |
| Classified Employee Vacancy Rate | 20% |  | 24% |
| Public Liability Fund Assets/Liabilities | 112% |  | 42% |
| Health Benefits Fund Balance ($ millions) | -$17 |  | -$6 |
| PERA Funded Ratio |  | 70.4 |  |
| ERB Funded Ratio |  | 65 |  |
| ERB Funding Period (years) | 42 |  | 27 |

298     FORTY YEARS IN THE NEW MEXICO ROUNDHOUSE

State finances are in good shape. General Fund balances are probably more than needed based on stress testing, and new endowments for opioid treatment and early childhood provide a significant backstop. Risk management funds are underfunded, because risk rates have not kept pace with inflation and payouts. The actuarial condition of pension funds has improved due to contribution rate increases, reduction in cost of living adjustments and other benefit changes.

# 14

## HOW TO IMPROVE PERFORMANCE

In 2022, New Mexico ranked 47th in per capita personal income. Mississippi was last, thus the long-time adage, "Thank God for Mississippi." A recent article in the *Wall Street Journal* attributed Mississippi's standing to the lowest workforce participation ranking, flat population, a "brain drain" of college graduates to vibrant southern cities like Atlanta and Nashville, dependence on government jobs and pensions, high disability rates, a high rate of incarceration, racial tension and a water supply crisis in the capital, Jackson.[226] Sound familiar? (But note recently Amazon, data centers, and Cummins, a battery factory, announced multi-billion dollar projects in Mississippi.)

In 2013, the most recent history of New Mexico prematurely declared victory in the final chapter: "New Mexico's transformation from a sparsely populated, agrarian-based, Spanish-speaking territory into an expanding industrial and technological community began in earnest after WWII. At every turn, a cadre of astute, well-seasoned congressional leaders positioned themselves to enable the state's political and economic metamorphosis. As the traditional post-war economy strengthened, New Mexico's indulgence in more volatile sources of revenue—heritage tourism, outdoor recreation, civic boosterism and the film industry—increased with measured confidence during each coming decade. ... As New Mexico continued to celebrate its one-hundredth year in 2012, state politicians, government administrators and local citizens pledged to capitalize on the promise of prosperity that enticed America's first European visitors to this remote desert frontier more than 400 years ago."[227] Reminds me of anthropologist Alfonso Ortiz's story at a LANL lecture. He was starting to tell schoolchildren, "About the time when dogs could talk," and one of the kids cracked, "Oh, those were the days."

## WHAT ECONOMISTS SAY

I took Economic Development in college 50 years ago, so I asked retired New Mexico State University (NMSU) Professor Jim Peach for a modern view of economic development principles and strategies. Peach emphasized the distinction between *economic growth,* the increase in income and output in a region, state or nation, and *economic development*. He referenced the work of Swedish Nobel prize winner Gunnar Myrdal, who defined economic development as "the movement upward of the entire social system."[228] Peach says economic development requires structural and social changes. Institutional barriers to economic development include "war, racism, sexism, income inequality, climate change and more."

Peach studied "Regional Income Inequality in the United States: 1967–2017" in the nation's lowest and highest per capita income counties.[229] He expected that institutional changes like welfare reform, NAFTA, low-income tax credits and technological changes like cell phones and the internet would reduce income inequality. But the poorest counties mostly remained poor. Half of the bottom 100 in 1967 remained at the bottom in 2017, and 88 percent of the bottom 100 were in the poorest 10 percent in 2017. These counties (including McKinley County in New Mexico) were predominantly very rural, with a high percentage of minorities, and were mostly in Appalachia, along the southern border, the Dakotas and the Deep South. The high-income counties, mostly along the coasts, changed even less over 50 years.

NMSU economists prepared the background report on economic development for New Mexico First in 2000.[230] They declared, "Creating high-wage jobs in non-metro areas of the state to close the rural-urban income gap is among the state's most challenging economic problems." They attributed New Mexico's low per capita income to the state's high share of low-paying industries such as tourism, high unemployment, low workforce participation, low non-wage income from dividends, interest and rent, and relatively low wages. They described the following strategies for economic development: targeting investment to poor regions or select industries or firms; specializing in investments where the region has a comparative advantage; promoting economic diversification; promoting industries that export goods and services (base industries); investing in social overhead capital such as educational systems and transportation and communication infrastructure; improving the business environment through changes in tax structure and regulation; and boosting in-migration including recruiting medical providers and other professionals. Peach and colleagues repeatedly cautioned about the analytic challenges in evaluating markets and investment opportunities and picking winners and losers.

One comment stands out in the report: "High technology, high productivity and globalization are incompatible with a poorly educated, undertrained workforce."

A Progressive Agenda. Former Oklahoma Senator and retired UNM political science professor Fred Harris compiled a blueprint for New Mexico's future with academic and other experts on the economy, education, healthcare, water and the environment, and even the arts.[231] Harris called it "a handbook for New Mexico's leaders and public officials." Former Senator Dede Feldman called the book a "sorely needed policy agenda to give future leaders the road map—if not the courage—to travel to a better future."

Professor Peach and Dr. Lee Reynis, retired director of the UNM Bureau of Business and Economic Research and former chief economist at DFA (and my boss), wrote the first chapter on the economy. They stated structural challenges, including lack of a leading economic sector and too much reliance on federal spending, allow poor educational outcomes, rural-urban disparities and racial and ethnic discrimination. A prosperous New Mexico economy requires, "substantial investment in physical and human resources, development of a leading sector, major changes in state and local policies and significant efforts to reduce income inequality and regional disparities." They recommend a new state economic development strategy, more public investment in education and technology, a systematic method to evaluate projects, greater investment in infrastructure and poverty and inequality reduction without offering specific actions.

Dr. Veronica Garcia, former superintendent of Santa Fe Public Schools, former state Secretary of Education and director of Voices for Children, presents a long education agenda. She begins linking the minority student achievement gap to income equality. She quotes Linda Darling Hammond, emeritus Stanford professor, "High achieving nations have transformed learning outcomes where government policies largely prevent child poverty by guaranteeing housing, health care and basic income security." Garcia highlights three recommendations of "education reformer" and USC professor Pedro Noguera to expand access to learning time with after-school and summer programs, universal pre-K and universal health care. Garcia advocates an eight-hour school day and 20 more school days. Other recommendations include more spending, a constitutional amendment to tap the state permanent fund, more instructional support services, improved bilingual education, free college tuition and improved bilingual education, higher teacher pay, and parental engagement.

Epidemiologist Nandini Pillai Kuehn on health care describes high rates of uninsurance and limited access to healthcare and correlates health status and outcomes to race, ethnicity and income. She focuses on implementation of the Affordable Care Act and universal health care.

What About Income Inequality? Former Texas Senator and Texas A&M economics professor Phil Gramm et al. reviewed federal statistics on poverty, income and transfer payments.[232] They report, "The number of Americans living in poverty has been largely unchanged since the war on poverty was implemented in the 1960s." But annual transfer payments to the bottom 20 percent (quintile) of income distribution grew from $9,677 in 1967 to $45,389 in 2017. Further, in 2017, the bottom 20 percent had household income of $13,525 but average consumption of $26,091. Gramm et al. report the Bureau of Census does not count two-thirds of the value of transfer payments in reporting household income. Excluded transfer payments include Medicare, Medicaid, food stamps, housing subsidies, Social Security disability payments, Supplemental Social Security (SSI) income and Pell Grants and refundable tax credits, for example, for children. The economists also note that calculations of income disparity are based on gross income, not net after-tax income, thus overstating disposable income of higher-income taxpayers. The economists figure that adjusting household income for transfer payments would reduce the 2017 estimate of percent of households in poverty from 12.3 percent to 2.3 percent. For the bottom quintile, transfer payments account for 86 percent of adjusted income and work and savings account for only 14 percent of income. They state, "In 1967, 67 percent of prime working-age adults in the bottom quintile had jobs, but by 2017, that percentage had dropped by almost half to 36 percent." They call this "Decoupling of Low-Income Households from the Workforce." After adjustments for transfer payments and taxes, average household income in the second quintile, $51 thousand, was only 2.5 percent higher than the lowest quintile. These households worked much more and paid more taxes but received far fewer transfer payments.

Gramm, Ekelund and Early conclude, "The path to the open field and fair chance that America has promised can best be found by getting all Americans back to work, dramatically improving the quality of primary and secondary education and removing artificial impediments to competition."

In 2021, an LFC Policy Spotlight examined the impacts of income support programs in New Mexico and "found for most family types, receiving all potential benefit types equates to a living wage ... But many potential income support recipients were not enrolling in programs for which they were eligible."

A 2023 LFC Progress Report figured state and federal income support programs increased by $2.6 billion, or one-third, from FY19 to FY23, mostly driven by Medicaid and higher earned income, low income and child tax credits. Poverty levels in New Mexico have remained stubbornly high, at 17.6 percent, the highest in the nation, 58 percent higher than the national average of 11.5 percent. However, LFC reports that the Bureau of Census supplemental poverty rate in 2022, adjusted for available benefits and cost of living, was only 10.2 percent, 0.4 percent above the national average. The average income support package in New Mexico, including SNAP (food stamps), Women Infants and Children (WIC) and state and federal tax credits, is 18 percent higher than the US average.

If New Mexico workforce participation was about 5 percent higher, or about at the national average, 50 thousand more adults would be working. Only 38 percent of working families below the poverty level have a household member working full time. Further, "To improve systemic poverty, families may need to make more money so they can earn a living wage without utilizing income support programs."

The LFC report recommends prioritizing greater enrollment for the lowest income families rather than expanding benefits, better connecting some benefits programs to work and training and adjusting the benefit structure to reduce cliff effects where more work results in benefit reductions with minimal net income gains.

Improved Financial Conditions and Policy Changes Lead to Quick Achievement of Some NM 2050 Goals. Following the "lost decade" of the 2010s, growing ranks of progressive legislators and initiatives of Governor Lujan Grisham led to speedy implementation of some 2050 goals proposed in 2015. This occurred because of broad economic prosperity and low unemployment, exceptional state revenue growth due mainly to explosive oil production, court decisions, notably *Martinez-Yazzie*, creation of new trust funds dedicated to early education and health care, the constitutional amendment to boost spending from the permanent fund, and declining birth rates and school enrollment.

Public school appropriations grew $1.3 billion from FY19 to FY24, up 49 percent. Enrollment declined 21 thousand over this same period. The State Equalization Guarantee per student rose from $7,905 to $12,991 or 64 percent. The website Statis reports New Mexico school spending in FY23 ranked 19th, higher than all states in the Southwest. LFC's education analyst says teacher salaries ranked 22nd, also the highest in the region. School reforms in this period included tripling the at-risk formula weight, full art and physical education formula funding, near-universal eligibility for full-day pre-K, free meals for all students and sharp pay boosts for the lowest-income school personnel.

According to *LFC Volume 1*, the State Higher Education Executive Officers Association ranked New Mexico fourth in FY22 for state and local appropriations per full-time student. For FY24, New Mexico fully funded free tuition for all residents.

Almost half of New Mexicans are on Medicaid, and an insurance premium tax increase and the new health care affordability fund are bringing services to residents ineligible for Medicaid. Access remains challenging, but some Medicaid provider rates are up to 120 percent of Medicare. By comparison, California Medicaid rates are in the range of 85 percent of Medicare. New Mexico is also boosting state support for rural hospitals.

Beginning FY21, New Mexico offered subsidized childcare up to 400 percent of the federal poverty level, or $120 thousand for a family of four.

As described in the previous section, transfer payments and tax credits for low-income families have increased significantly.

In sum, since the 2016 report, New Mexico has implemented many spending recommendations for education, health care, childcare and income supports recommended for 2050.

## WHAT ABBEY THINKS

I have often been asked what I think is holding the state back and what we need to do to improve our performance. A couple disclaimers: first, it won't be one thing, one magic bullet but a combination of actions; second, I believe in evidence-based policymaking. This book covers a lot of territory, and any recommendations are worthy of more analysis and validation.

Education Trumps Everything

New Mexico has been mired at the bottom of reading and math proficiency rankings for decades. In the 2024 *Nation's Report Card*, New Mexico ranked last in the percentage of fourth graders proficient in math and reading at 23 and 20 percent, respectively. One might speculate that New Mexico's prospects will remain low in 10 to 15 years when today's fourth graders leave school and enter the workforce.

NCSL studied education in ten top-performing countries and in 2016 issued a report, *No Time to Lose*, that identified four key features of education reform: early childhood readiness; high quality and selective teacher preparation programs; rigorous career technical education; and coordinated and aligned education reforms. New Mexico legislators, notably Senator Stewart, embraced this reform agenda, and LFC effectively adopted it too, with adjustments including extended learning, appropriate curricula such as bilingual education and accountability systems. Since 2019, *LFC Volume 1, Policy and Performance Analysis for Public Education* has reported the status of this reform agenda.

For several reasons, New Mexico seems to have lost focus on the big picture and the structure of reform. First, leadership instability at the Public Education Department makes messaging about priorities and effectiveness hard to discern. One can find the NCSL themes in the PED strategic plan posted on its website, but the plan dates to 2022, two cabinet secretaries ago. Second, after the *Martinez-Yazzie* decision, the executive and legislative focus shifted to compliance without clearly articulating the reform goals. Third, without a clear reform agenda, the Legislature, the executive, districts and advocates rushed to implement new programs akin to taking 100 buckets to 100 fires.

Early Learning, School Readiness and Extended Learning. New Mexico is a leader for investment in early childhood education, first full-day K, then home visiting and pre-K, now three-year-old and four-year-old full-day.

But extended learning time has gone backward. It started with the proliferation of half-day Wednesdays or Fridays. Then, it continued with four-day weeks in almost half the districts. I don't quibble with four days in New Mexico's small, isolated districts like Quemado and Reserve and especially those like Des Moines with a track record of high college matriculation. But what about Las Vegas and Socorro? How does the calendar affect recruiting at NM Tech and Highlands when potential professors with families learn there is no school on Friday?

I've been on the extended learning bandwagon since hearing Paul Vallas in New Orleans in 2006. LFC joined Senator Stewart in pushing the K plus, then 3, then 5, then 12 plus initiative with 25 extra days. The state was on the verge of widespread implementation, from Deming to Arrey Elementary in the Truth or Consequences District to south-side Santa Fe elementaries, until implementation was interrupted by the pandemic closures and fiscal crisis. LFC reported in *2024 Volume 1* that extended learning enrollment fell short of appropriations, leaving hundreds of millions unspent. Teachers said they were tired, and some parents resented encroachment on other summer opportunities like camp or travel. Former Education Secretary Arsenio Romero became almost a pariah for proposing a rule requiring at least a 180-day calendar that was challenged and eventually overturned by school district litigation.

The extended learning movement certainly lost momentum, maybe even failed. Education leaders should return to the original focus on implementation at low-performing schools. The funding formula makes funding available.

High-Quality Teachers and School Leaders, Teacher and Leader Preparation. Every child deserves a good teacher. There are 20 thousand teachers in New Mexico. Stanford economist Paul Hanushek reported, "Students of an ineffectual teacher learn on average half a year's worth of work in one school year, while the students of a very good teacher learn 1.5 years' worth—a difference of a year's worth of learning in a single school year." (*2017 LFC Volume 1*).

Teacher pay gains should contribute to better quality. The minimum salary for a beginning teacher is $50 thousand, and the level 3 minimum is $70 thousand, with additional pay for special duties or extended learning.

Schools of education suffer from a disproportionate share of adjunct professors and low university funding, but enrollment reportedly is on the rise.

There has been a myriad of teacher professional development, recruitment and retention initiatives, including district "grow your own," paid student teaching, teacher and principal first-year residencies, endowments for scholarships, teacher loan repayments for service, educator fellows, salary differentials for special education and hard to staff positions, media campaigns, a literacy institute, a leadership academy, alternative licensure, micro-credentials for licensure and mentorship.

The Lujan Grisham administration replaced a teacher evaluation system based partly on student test scores with reliance on school administrator observation and teacher-prepared portfolios.

The challenge with these teacher quality initiatives is to determine what works, replicate what works, train administrators in administering successful programs, ensure the best teachers stay and perhaps most important, cause the less effective teachers to improve or move on.

Accountability and Coordinating Reform. As noted above, PED is on its fourth secretary in six years. Frustrated legislators proposed a constitutional amendment to remove the PED from the cabinet and governor's control and return to an independent elected commission overseeing public instruction. This would be reactionary.

The Legislature, the executive and the public need a bird's eye view of performance by school and district. School grades were discontinued early in the Lujan Grisham administration, and student testing was discontinued during the pandemic. The replacement system results in a numerical score for each school with uncertainty about the meaning of the number and doubts about data reliability. A transparent school reporting system is a precursor to managing school improvement initiatives.

The 2024 GAA provided PED with an increase from $36 million to $147 million non-recurring appropriations for the general fund for 21 school improvement initiatives and $200 million from the public education reform fund and other funds for 33 more initiatives. History shows a sprawling reform agenda from Santa Fe is unmanageable, unsustainable and inequitable. However, left to their own devices, New Mexico's 180 districts and charter schools haven't realized widespread learning gains. New Mexico needs stable state leadership with a streamlined agenda and greater control over district academic programs.

Excellence in Higher Education. As reported earlier, New Mexico is near the top of higher education spending per student. *US News and World Report* ranks UNM 236 and NMSU 296 among US universities, and UNM 129 and NMSU 132 among public universities. New Mexico has seven four-year universities and 20 two-year colleges, branches and special schools. That is another sprawling infrastructure and overhead system to maintain along with public education's almost 200 districts and charter schools. Think of all the presidents, CFOs, and HR managers, architects and deans. Tuition provides minimal support.

Professor Peach reminded me why the University of Texas is excellent, ranked 32 among national and 9 among public universities. Revenue from oil production in the Texas Permian basin is earmarked to UT.

Since the 1980s, New Mexico has dabbled with various centers for technical excellence—cybersecurity, a brain institute, high-tech materials, and sustainable agriculture. Funding has been inconsistent and modest. Why not establish a supplemental endowment for New Mexico's three research universities? The 2024 GAA established an almost $1 billion trust fund for the opportunity scholarship program, perhaps a good start except it was already mostly funded in the base state budget.

Tax Reform

Chapter 2 reviewed New Mexico's tax structure. In general, we want the tax system to: 1) yield a diverse, stable, adequate revenue stream; 2) impose a tax burden on individuals and industries that is like goldilocks, not too high, not too low; and 3) treat similar taxpayers the same; and 4) not be complicated for tax filers and tax administrators.

Stability and Adequacy. Due to the energy windfall, New Mexico has overdone it in adequacy. The New Mexico tax structure is not diverse, but it sure beats the alternative (not having energy wealth). New Mexico has achieved fiscal stability for at least the mid-term by having ample general fund reserves, 30 percent or more and establishing trust funds that can replace oil and gas revenue in future years and be tapped in an emergency.

State treasury accounts were about $9 billion in 2023. The sovereign wealth permanent funds at the State Investment Council, the permanent fund and the severance tax permanent fund were $39 billion ending 2023. In addition, excluding the tax stabilization reserve in the general fund, the State Investment Council managed other expendable trust funds, including $5.7 billion in the early childhood trust fund, $341 million in the tobacco settlement trust fund, and over $300 million in the water project fund, the new conservation legacy trust fund, the new opioid settlement fund and the rural library fund. In 2024, $1.3 billion was transferred to create or expand trust funds.

If the government collects more revenue than it needs, it may promote uncontrolled spending or deprive New Mexico citizens and the economy of income that they could use more productively or at least decide for themselves how to spend it. In 2023, the estimated "new money" was $3.6 billion for FY24; the governor vetoed tax reductions of $280 million that would have reached $900 million in FY27. In 2024, "new money" for FY25 was estimated at $3.5 billion, but the Legislature passed FY25 tax reductions of a mere $192 million. It's as if New Mexico is a hoarder.

GRT Too High. Aside from over-collecting revenue, the tax structure is out of whack. The Tax Foundation reports in 2022 New Mexico ranked 25th in both effective tax rate and tax burden as percent of state income, which is good. But the Tax Foundation ranks New Mexico 35th for the sales tax (a higher number represents higher tax burden and economic distortions; see *2024 State Business*

*Climate Report*). New Mexico has the 16th highest combined state and local GRT rate and taxes many business inputs, leading to pyramiding and effective tax rates nearing 20 percent for some sectors. The GRT structure is also nearly unique in New Mexico. NM Tax Research Institute Director Richard Anklam calls it "weird," which can't be a great selling point. Recently, the Legislature passed some anti-pyramiding provisions; a quarter percent GRT rate reduction passed in 2022, but a phased-in 1 percent GRT reduction in 2023 was vetoed.

New Mexico ranks 36th for the personal income tax. New Mexico has the highest personal income tax rate in the region at 5.9 percent with Arizona at 2.5 percent and Texas with no PIT. LFC reports 26 states cut income tax rates since 2021. Also, while New Mexico has expanded low-income credits, almost half of New Mexico taxpayers fall in the second income bracket, resulting in a relatively flat tax and creating a disincentive to enter the workforce. (See *2024 LFC Volume 1*).

New Mexico ranks first (low) for the property tax, reflecting the history of loss of property at tax auctions, especially in northern New Mexico in the cash-poor economy of 100 years ago.

Horizontal Inequity. According to LFC, "various tax credits, deductions and exemptions have narrowed the tax base and encouraged high tax rates … which results in inequities in taxation across demographics or income levels and creates uneven playing field for businesses providing the same products and services." (*2024 LFC Volume 1*). Boilerplate language in LFC FIRS on revenue measures includes, "LFC has serious concerns about the substantial risk to state revenues from the proliferation of tax expenditures and the increase in revenue volatility from erosion of the tax base. … Narrowing the base leads to continually rising tax rates and increases the volatility of the state's general fund revenues. Higher rates compound tax pyramiding issues and force consumers and businesses to pay higher taxes on all other purchases without an exemption, deduction or credit."

In 2022, there were breaks for nurses, military retirees, social security recipients, solar projects, sustainable building developers, sale of feminine hygiene products and dialysis. In 2023, it was income tax credits for kids and film. 2024 brought a green Christmas tree with credits for energy storage, geothermal heat pumps, geothermal electricity, solar projects and electric vehicles. Other new credits or exemptions in 2024 were for rural health care providers, "angel" (venture) investors, home modification for health care, special needs children, teacher expenditures for school supplies, diesel fuel used in agriculture, childcare providers, oil and gas stripper wells and lawyers' receipts settling claims for the Las Vegas fires.

To recap, lower PIT and GRT rates could boost the state's tax rankings and economic prospects.

### Edifice Complex/Capital Outlay Reform

I had the honor to speak at the dedication of NMSU's agriculture modernization building in November 2023. I told the crowd I was reminded of the bluegrass song by the Carter family, covered by Patty Loveless and dozens of others, "I'm Working on a Building:" If *I was a sinner, I'd tell you what I'd do, I'd quit my sinning and work on a building too, a holy ghost building for my lord.*" I said the building was an exciting and important project for New Mexico's agriculture livestock community. But more important than the building were all the people I knew working on ag projects at the farmers' markets and at the demonstration stations in Corona and Velarde. I met a scientist at Navajo Agricultural Products Industries (NAPI) near Farmington cultivating a low-cholesterol potato that he hoped would conquer obesity and save the world.

We have $4.7 billion appropriations for capital projects unspent in the state treasury, and in 2024 we'll add $1.3 billion more. The problems of minimal vetting, piecemeal funding, poor design, ineffective project management and waste were covered in Chapter 4. My poster child for 2024 is $30 million for a building to house a reading institute. There is merit to investing in better instruction, training and professional development in the science of reading. However, with both school and college enrollment on a long downward trend, it is hard to imagine that we need a new facility to do this work.

Every year, there is a call for capital outlay reform, in particular changing the method of dividing the pie at the Legislature, a third a third a third, with the governor trading the executive share for votes for other initiatives. I know there are areas where the state is underfunding infrastructure, notably water supply and wastewater treatment. But overall, I recommend slowing down the gravy train and investing more in people and operations. Specifically, the Legislature could reduce the severance tax earmarked to the severance tax bonding fund and increase the school tax going to the general fund.

Public Integrity

There have been times when you pick up the paper and wonder what will it be today? 2008 was the worst of it with the foxes in the henhouse of the state investment office.

For the last few years, things have been quieter on the pay-to-play front. The Ethics Commission, the Judicial Standards Commission and the current Attorney General have increased vigilance for integrity. But, procurement irregularities were identified for a $10 billion Medicaid managed care contract; the chair of the public defender commission and at least three Albuquerque policemen pleaded guilty to fixing DWI charges for decades; Monahan (November 20, 2023) flagged the 33 percent contingency fee agreed by a former attorney general with his "favorite law firm" for opioid settlements, almost triple the rate in other states; a former legislator is embroiled in litigation related to the failure of a family business that included prominent citizens as co-investors and obtained economic development grants from state agencies and local governments; and a former university president filed a wrongful discharge lawsuit after flagging way below market interest earned on $40 million university funds invested in a local bank.

In addition to more aggressive enforcement, paying legislators, at least for part-time service, might enhance their independence.

Boost Workforce Participation

The 2023 LFC Program Evaluation, *Improving New Mexico's Workforce Participation*, reported New Mexico ranked 44th among states. Compared to the US average of 19 percent, 28 percent of New Mexicans are disengaged from the workforce, not going to school or actively seeking employment. The report notes workforce centers are under-utilized and have limited employment outcomes and recommends the Workforce Solutions Department improve case management services for job seekers, adopt evidence-based practices for training programs and co-locate centers with college or other agency partners. The report also identifies a "benefits cliff" and recommends a targeted expansion of the working families and earned income tax credits. Central New Mexico College President Tracy Hartzler (and former LFC analyst) notes research of the Federal Reserve Bank of Atlanta that finds benefit cliffs are a barrier to career advancement for low-income adults.

No Initiative Left Behind/ Better Vetting/Listen to Experts

Mark Moore of Harvard's Kennedy School of Government describes how government executives should develop spending plans, what data and analysis they should use, how to manage political interests and how to innovate.[233] Moore uses the Kennedy School's case studies to show what works. The basic framework was mentioned in Chapter 8: Capacity (government has funding and can administer the goal or project), Values (it's worth doing, the people want it) and Support (legislators and bureaucrats will get behind it).

In New Mexico, the principal method of budget development by the executive branch seems to be to survey what advocates, constituents and agency heads want and then compile lists to present in the budget document. This is particularly the case in the financially flush times of the current administration, with numerous initiatives proposed in the special appropriations section of the GAA. Special appropriation requests are due after the September 1 statutory deadline for budget submission. Unlike requests for the operating budget, special appropriation requests require minimal budget justification. The requests are lumped together for review at one LFC hearing in November and then one HAFC hearing.

The executive special appropriation request for the 2024 Legislature totaled $1.6 billion from the general fund for 171 items each described in a phrase; 109 items are greater than $1 million, including $771 million for 12 initiatives at DFA, $500 million for housing, $42 million for broadband, 20 million for renewable energy loans, $100 million for health clinics, approximately $250 million for 39 initiatives for public education, $86 million and 17 initiatives for higher education (*State of New Mexico Executive Budget Recommendation FY25, Department of Finance and Administration*). The LFC and the appropriation committees try to figure out which items are priorities for the Governor, how the cost was estimated, whether the item is recurring (most of them), whether there is duplication, whether the agency has the funding and personnel to administer the initiative and what outcomes are expected.

The House funded about $400 million for these Executive items, and reportedly, after the governor threatened to veto the budget and force a special session, the Senate funded another $400 million for a total of 41 items. Total general fund special appropriations in the 2024 GAA were $1.14 billion. Compare the special appropriations total to growth in the general fund operating budget for all of government, $652 million or 6.8 percent. After LFC hearings on each agency all fall, HAFC heard all the budgets again over 3 weeks. Appropriators claimed they held down the budget growth below 10 percent, but counting the special appropriations, it is about 15 percent. This budgeting process reminds me of the Woody Guthrie song Deportee (Plane Crash at Los Gatos Canyon): *Is this the best way we can grow our big orchards? Is this the best way we can raise our good crops? To fall like dry leaves and rot on our topsoil. And be known by no names except "deportees."*

Separately from the budgeting process, I confess to some disappointment that expert recommendations are occasionally lost in the wind. Sometimes, staff have a worms-eye view of the gutter in the face of the steamroller of special interests or entrenched bureaucrats. I have in mind, for example, the failure to expand infant home visiting, the failure of procurement reform to limit emergency or sole source procurements or elimination of the cap on the film tax credit. I know that policy choices are not clear-cut and that we are staff and not elected. Still, it is painful to watch the influence of money in politics.

## Leadership

Judging from metrics covered in Chapter 13 alone, New Mexico performed poorly over the last 40 years. The practices and activities of executive leaders and some legislators have been at fault. Anaya, Johnson and Martinez stand out for "unwillingness to compromise." During their terms, Johnson and Martinez and some legislative leaders stand out for "failure to communicate"—not even a pretense of talking sometimes. The terms of Anaya and Richardson stand out for misuse of public funds and power at the highest levels, also known as corruption. The $10 billion Medicaid managed care procurement under Lujan Grisham drew the attention of the Ethics Commission. During their administrations, Anaya, Johnson and Martinez were often characterized by non-stop bickering, chaos, turbulence, feuding and power struggles. Some of the governors seemed vindictive and petty. King was notable for his easygoing efforts to build consensus but also perhaps for a lack of strategic vision.

The most recent four governors, Johnson, Richardson, Martinez and Lujan Grisham, seemed preoccupied in their second term, especially the last year or two, with a national agenda and their ambition. Many New Mexicans thought they were bored and disinterested, hence their low favorability at the end of their terms.

Every topic in this section requires leadership. It is paramount for better outcomes, efficient government and good public policy and budgeting. Obvious attributes of leadership include strategic vision, setting good goals and communicating them to the public, the Legislature and agencies, maintaining a performance measurement system, picking good managers and staff (not their pals), and letting them do their job without standing over their shoulder. You need a thick skin and need to take responsibility, probably for more than you can reasonably influence.

I was a natural analyst but not a natural manager. I learned on the job, I had support to be a better manager, I had elected officials who stuck their necks out for me, and I worried and planned through the night.

At the end of my legislative career, Governor Carruthers, Representative Lundstrom, Senator Munoz, Senator Cervantes and others said I was a great leader. I am proud of that, yet disappointed that I didn't do enough.

I hope this book inspires many people in different ways to make New Mexico better.

# ACKNOWLEDGMENTS

I started this manuscript immediately on retirement from the New Mexico Legislative Finance Committee in June 2023. My wife Lorin helped me set up a home office with a new computer, printer, old furniture and a great view of the Sangre de Cristo Mountains. I was used to having a robust support staff and had to learn the most basic activities like using "Word," file management and finding archival material. Lorin, who works from home, regularly reminded me that she was not my staff and to keep quiet.

Rick Hendricks, PhD, Director of State Records Center and Archives, and Colonel Robert Himmerich y Valencia, retired Marine and University of New Mexico history professor, provided invaluable advice on simply starting.

Staff of the Legislative Finance Committee provided a wide range of support every step of the way from brainstorming state history and politics to fact finding and fact checking to document style to printing and moral support. Thank you to Director Charles Sallee, Deputy Directors Jon Courtney and Micaela Fischer and Jeannae Leger, Assistant Director and Administrative Manager. Micaela, on her own time, was my lead supporter in producing the innumerable drafts of the manuscript. Thanks to all analysts, notably Kelly Klundt, Connor Jorgenson, Sunny Liu, Ismael Torres, Jennifer Faubion, Cally Carswell and Joey Simon. Thanks to support staff Sharon Boylan, Adreena Lujan, Rene Lopez and Christina Tapia. Legislative Council Service librarian Joanne Montague found decades old records of legislative action.

LFC's Helen Gaussoin, Richard Bosson, and Michael Weinberg read early drafts and helped to sharpen my objectives.

Professors Jim Peach and Jose Garcia, retired from New Mexico State University, University of New Mexico professor Barbara Damron, and UNM Director of Public Administraion, Patria de Lancer-Julnes and Valerie Plame provided constructive comments on late drafts and suggestions for a path to publication.

House fiscal analyst Rick May, lobbyists Dan Weaks and Scott Scanland, campaign expert Chris Brown and Linda Kehoe were good sounding boards for the state of government and politics. Joe Thompson encouraged me every step of the way.

I am grateful to the many executive, judicial and legislative leaders who supported me over my career and contributed to a better New Mexico. At risk of leaving many out, I recognize Garrey Carruthers, Bruce King, Richard Bosson, Kay Marr, Willard Lewis, Jerry Sandel, Ben Altamirano, Kiki Saavedra, Larry Larranaga, Lucky Varela, Brian Moore, Don Bratton, Peter Wirth, Michael Sanchez, Mary Kay Papen, Pat Woods, Patty Lundstrom and John Arthur Smith. Legislative staff Bill Valdes, Ron Forte and Mike Burkhart were great allies.

Lorin sacrificed a lot for my career over the last twenty years and I am grateful to her.

# Timeline

## Anaya Administration (1983–1986)

### 1983

    2 percent budget cut for FY83
    $112 million tax increase for FY84
    Abbey starts as DFA economist

### 1984

    Failure of Penny for Education campaign
    Eight-day special session on budget
    Investment officer and deputy treasurer indicted

### 1985

    Conservative coalitions in both chambers
    Natural gas deregulation
    Kerr McGee closes uranium mine
    Legislative Finance Committee (LFC) vetoed twice
    Capital filibuster by Senator Victor Marshall
    Seven-day special session
    Anaya's aide Ramming indicted
    Savings and loan industry collapse
    LFC analyst Ed Howard flees to Russia

### 1986

    Gross receipts tax and personal income tax rate increases and teacher pay increase
    Oil falls to $10 per barrel
    Attorney General opinion disallows deficit spending and forces special session
    Special session tax increase and budget cuts
    Senator Houston dumped as Pro Tem

## Carruthers Administration (1987–1990)

### 1987

$99 million tax increase

Natural gas tax reform, reduced bonding revenue

Special session on superconducting supercollider

Supreme Court rules against New Mexico on Pecos River delivery to Texas

### 1988

One-day special session on capital

Supreme Court clarifies line-item veto (*Coll v Carruthers*)

### 1989

First time General Appropriation Act vetoed in entirety

New budget increases 7.5 percent

### 1990

Carruthers chairs Education Commission of States

Carruthers requests tax increase and recommends extended school year

Solid waste landfill legislation enacted

Two special sessions—Gross receipts tax increase and workers comp reform

## King Administration (1991–1994)

### 1991

Persian Gulf war

Capitol remodeling

Tourism and Environment Departments created

Federal court directs facilities for the developmentally disabled to close

Azscam rocks Arizona legislature

Representative Ron Olguin indicted

### 1992

Children, Youth and Families Department created

Abbey goes to Harvard's Kennedy School of Government

### 1993

Santa Teresa border crossing opens

Intel expands in Rio Rancho

Six cent gasoline tax increase

100 bills vetoed

Abbey appointed State Board of Finance director

1994

General Fund revenue soars

General Fund appropriations up eight percent; $47 million tax cuts

$487 million capital outlay

Lieutenant Governor Luna opposes King in primary

Former Lieutenant Governor Mondragon runs for governor on Green Party ticket

## Johnson Administration (1995–2002)

1995

Johnson fires most exempt employees on New Year's Eve

Supreme Court rules Johnson's gaming compacts illegal

Johnson vetoes 200 bills

Abbey fired as Board of Finance director; goes to Treasurer's office

1996

Rest in Peace (RIP) Senate Majority Leader Edward Lopez

Special session on capital

Johnson proposes private prisons in Hobbs and Santa Rosa

Representative Coll sues to halt private prison plan

1997

Senator Aragon moves executive budget plan

Abbey hired as LFC director

Supreme Court rules Johnson's welfare reform plan illegal

Four lanes for Highway 44, borrow and spend

1998

Johnson vetoes cigarette tax increase for cancer hospital

Johnson vetoes LFC staff expansion

Special session for Budget Adjustment Request authority and Johnson initiatives

First veto override since 1970; cigarette tax veto override fails narrowly

Drive-up liquor windows banned

Tobacco settlement brings $40 million per year for perpetuity

1999 (Johnson Second Term)

Johnson vetoes all LFC staff , General Appropriation Act and capital outlay

Oil falls to $5.65/barrel
Johnson seeks school vouchers; May special session on budget
Prison riot in Santa Rosa, guard killed; Independent Board of Inquiry
Koch contract for Hwy. 44 scrutinized
LFC moves to new capitol annex
*Zuni* decision, school financing unconstitutional

2000

Feed bill for legislature vetoed; General Appropriation Act vetoed twice
Full-day kindergarten authorized
Senator Carraro filibusters capital outlay
Eight-day special session on budget and capital
Johnson advisor David Harris retires
Speaker Sanchez and Representative Sandel defeated

2001

Senator Richard Romero's coalition takes over Senate
Johnson vetoes $90 million from the General Appropriation Act and a tax cut and capital
Legislators don't take the bait
Varela chairs LFC
State treasurer investments scrutinized for bidding favorites
Johnson advocated decriminalization of marijuana

2002

The General Appropriation Act is vetoed twice
Legislature calls extraordinary session on budget
New General Appropriation Act with $8 million increase vetoed; then veto overridden in hours

## Richardson Administration (2003–2010)

2003

Constitutional amendments for school reform and permanent fund revenue
70-cent cigarette tax increase and PIT rate reductions
Lorin Abbey fired
Special session for $1.585 billion road projects (GRIP)

2004

LFC staff vetoed, House overrides 66-0
Gross receipts tax on food eliminated

$490 million capital outlay
Four new state agencies and cabinet heads
Senator Aragon is president of New Mexico Highlands
Representative Coll retires after 24 years

2005

Altamirano is senate president Pro Tem
General Services Department buys jet
State Treasurer Vigil and former treasurer Montoya indicted for extortion
October special session authorizes $100 million rebates
Senators defend Abbey

2006

Jack Abramoff scandal in Congress
$500 million in new money
Richardson donors scrutinized
Metro Court and Region II Housing Authority scandals
Insurance Superintendent Serna resigns
Montoya "sings" and implicates Richardson associate Riordan

2007 (Richardson Second Term)

Richardson running for president
Oil price reaches over $100/barrel
Budget grows 10.5 percent
LFC audit of state personnel office
Special session, local road projects, GRIP2
Department of Transportation headquarters pay-to-play
LFC travels to Chihuahua
LFC celebrates 50 years
RIP Senator Altamirano

2008

Great Recession
Richardson fizzles in Iowa
Natural gas soars, August special session, more rebates and roads
Natural gas prices collapse and LFC focuses on solvency
Eclipse bankruptcy, state loses $19 million
Richardson nominated by Obama to US Commerce secretary
CDR/New Mexico Finance Authority contracts probed
War in Gaza

2009

    Richardson pulls out of presidential run

    FY09 solvency first at regular session

    $1.9 billion federal stimulus funds to New Mexico

    Pay-to-play erupts for state finances, New Mexico brokers plead guilty

    State faces $650 million budget shortfall

    October special session to cut spending, Smith saves the day

    Investment officer Bland resigns

    Secretary of State Vigil Giron resigns

2010

    Budget fails at 30-day session

    February special session passes 2 percent cuts and tax increases

    Looming insolvency of New Mexico unemployment trust fund

    Richardson's approval rating 33 percent

    Higher education general obligation bond fails

## Martinez Administration (2011–2018)

2011

    Education secretary pushes school tuition vouchers and merit pay

    Capital filibustered

    98 bills vetoed

    Teacher evaluation task force

    Special session on redistricting and capital

    Public Regulation Commissioner Block pleads guilty to embezzlement

    State agency employment down 14 percent

    State fair racino contract awarded to donors

2012

    New Mexico centennial

    Speaker Lujan retires

    New Mexico True tourism marketing campaign initiated

    Gila and Ruidoso fires

    New Mexico Finance Authority fake audit

    Senator President Pro Tem Jennings defeated

2013

    Kenny Martinez, son of former speaker, elected speaker

    Session ends with last second tax bill

    Carruthers to New Mexico State University president

Harvard beats Lobos in basketball tournament and Coach Alford decamps
Medicaid behavioral health contractors replaced by Arizona firms
Another death in Children Youth and Families Department custody
Fracking revolution in Permian basin

2014

Representative Saavedra retires
Senate runs General Appropriation Act; sanding used for budget savings
Abbey tries to quit, Martinez picks fight with LFC
LFC evaluations under fire
Republicans win House

2015 (Martinez Second Term)

Tripp is speaker, Larranaga House Appropriations and Finance Committee (HAFC) chair
Skandera confirmed for public education
Senator Griego quits after kickback allegation
Capital fails at regular session, but LFC gets capital on track for special session in June
Secretary of State Duran resigns, misused campaign funds
Martinez Christmas pizza party out of control at hotel

2016

Oil prices and revenue estimates crater during session
Legislators scramble to cut budget
Revenue estimates lowered repeatedly
Ten-year-old Victoria Martens murdered
September special session, six solvency bills, 5.5 percent budget cuts
Senator Majority Leader Sanchez defeated, Varela retires
Taxation and Revenue Department secretary quits, tax preparation fraud in private practice

2017

Egolf speaker, Lundstrom first female HAFC chair
Solvency again, four Senate bills in four hours
Martinez vetoes LFC and higher education to leverage a tax cut
May special session funds LFC and higher ed at vetoed level
Carruthers pushed out at New Mexico State University
Representative Varela RIP

2018

> New Mexico third highest oil-producing state
> UNM dumps soccer
> First district judge rules school funding unconstitutional
> Representative Larranaga RIP

## Lujan Grisham Administration (2019–present)

2019

> General Fund appropriations up 12 percent
> At-risk school formula factor doubled
> Early Child Education and Care Department created

2020

> Covid epidemic
> Ten percent job losses, oil drilling collapses
> June solvency special session
> Ubiquitous telecommuting and mandatory masks
> November special session for economic relief
> Senators Smith, Papen and Clemente Sanchez defeated in June primary

2021

> Senator Stewart senate president Pro Tem
> Video conferencing for regular session; capitol building access restricted
> Vaccines roll out in January
> Hockey stick (sharp upturn) economic recovery
> New Mexico Civil Rights Act ends qualified immunity for certain public officers
> New Mexico gets $1.9 billion federal American Rescue Plan Act revenue
> Supreme Court rules legislature must appropriate emergency federal funds
> December special session on reapportionment and broadband

2022

> Oil production grows over 500 million barrels per year
> Russia invades Ukraine
> Gross receipts tax rate cut and personal income tax exemptions and credits
> Pattern dedicates 400 wind towers for electricity transmission to Los Angeles
> Special session, PIT rebates, and "junior" appropriations
> Pecos fires
> Constitutional amendment to use permanent fund for early childhood

2023
> Speaker Javier Martinez
>
> Representative Small replaces Lundstrom at HAFC
>
> General Fund appropriations up 14 percent; free college tuition, free school breakfast
>
> Childcare subsidy at 400 percent federal poverty level and elimination of developmental disabilities waiting list
>
> Tax cuts mostly vetoed
>
> Abbey retires after forty years at capitol

# FIGURES

Congressional Boxscore: MAJOR LEGISLATION IN 88TH CONGRESS
The Washington Post, Times Herald (1959-1973); Jun 17, 1963;
ProQuest Historical Newspapers: The Washington Post
pg. A2

# Congressional Boxscore

## MAJOR LEGISLATION IN 88TH CONGRESS

|          | Dem. | GOP | Vacancies |
|----------|------|-----|-----------|
| House Line-up | 256 | 178 | 1 |
| Senate Line-up | 67 | 33 | 0 |

▲ SCHEDULED
☼ IN PROCESS
● COMPLETED

As of June 14, 1963

| | HOUSE | | | | | SENATE | | | | | FINAL ACTION | SIGNED | VETOED |
|---|---|---|---|---|---|---|---|---|---|---|---|---|---|
| | HEARINGS | REPORTED | DEBATE | PASSED | ELECTED | HEARINGS | REPORTED | DEBATE | PASSED | REACTED | | | |
| Tax Cut and Reform | ● | | | | | | | | | | | | |
| Corporate, Excise Tax Extension | ● | ● | ● | ● | | | | | | | | | |
| Debt Limit | ● | ● | ● | ● | | ● | ● | ● | ● | | ● | ● | |
| Foreign Aid Authorization | ● | | | | | ☼ | | | | | | | |
| Medical Schools | ● | ● | ● | ● | | | | | | | | | |
| Mental Health | ● | | | | | ● | ● | ● | ● | | | | |
| College Aid | ● | ● | | | | ☼ | | | | | | | |
| Youth Employment | ● | ● | | | | ● | ● | ● | ● | | | | |
| National Service Corps | ☼ | | | | | ☼ | | | | | | | |
| Mass Transportation | ● | ● | | | | ● | ● | ● | ● | | | | |
| Transportation Rate Changes | ● | | | | | ☼ | | | | | | | |
| Airport Grants | ● | | | | | ● | | | | | | | |
| Voting Rights | ☼ | | | | | | | | | | | | |
| Civil Rights Commission | ☼ | | | | | ● | | | | | | | |
| Conservation Fund | ● | | | | | ● | | | | | | | |
| Wilderness System | | | | | | ● | ● | ● | ● | | | | |
| Cotton Controls | ● | ● | | | | ● | | | | | | | |
| Feed Grains | ● | ● | ● | ● | | ● | ● | ● | ● | | ● | ● | |
| Civil Defense Shelters | ☼ | | | | | | | | | | | | |
| Draft Extension | ● | ● | ● | ● | | ● | ● | ● | ● | | ● | ● | |
| **APPROPRIATIONS** | | | | | | | | | | | | | |
| Agriculture | ● | | | ● | | ● | | | | | | | |
| Defense | ● | | | | | ● | | | | | | | |
| First Supplemental '63 | ● | ● | ● | ● | | ● | ● | ● | ● | | | ● | |
| Independent Offices | ☼ | | | | | | | | | | | | |
| Interior | ● | ● | ● | ● | | ● | ● | ● | ● | | | | |
| State, Justice and Commerce | ● | ● | | | | | | | | | | | |
| Labor-HEW | ● | ● | ● | ● | | ● | | | | | | | |
| Treasury-Post Office | ● | ● | ● | ● | | ● | ● | ● | ● | | | ● | |
| District | ☼ | | | | | | | | | | | | |
| Foreign Aid | ☼ | | | | | | | | | | | | |
| Legislative | ● | ● | ● | ● | | ☼ | | | | | | | |
| Military Construction | ☼ | | | | | | | | | | | | |
| Public Works | ☼ | | | | | ☼ | | | | | | | |
| **DISTRICT OF COLUMBIA AREA** | | | | | | | | | | | | | |
| Corporal Punishment | ● | ● | ● | ● | | | | | | | | | |
| Urban Renewal | ☼ | | | | | ● | ● | | | | | | |
| Federal Payment | ● | | | | | ● | | | | | | | |
| Chancery Zoning | | | | | | ● | ● | | | | | | |

Figure 1.

# Prioritize Funding to meet state's challenges

Let's not take 100 buckets to 100 fires

New Mexico needs to take 100 buckets to 3 fires

Figure 2.

## General Fund Financial Summary and Reserves

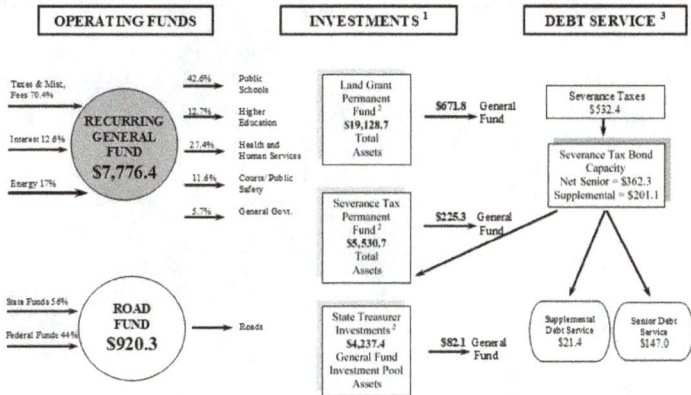

**OVERVIEW OF NEW MEXICO FINANCES: FY20 OPERATING BUDGET**
(in millions of dollars)

C. Structure of State Finances

Figure 3.

## Figure 4.

## Figure 5.

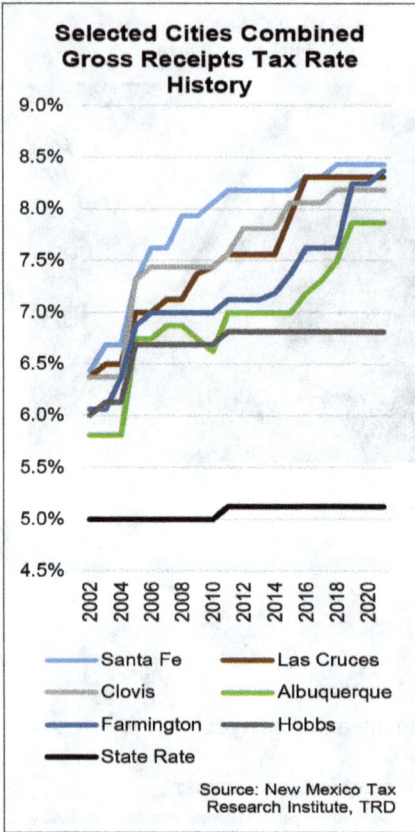

**Selected Cities Combined Gross Receipts Tax Rate History**

Santa Fe — Clovis — Farmington — State Rate — Las Cruces — Albuquerque — Hobbs

Source: New Mexico Tax Research Institute, TRD

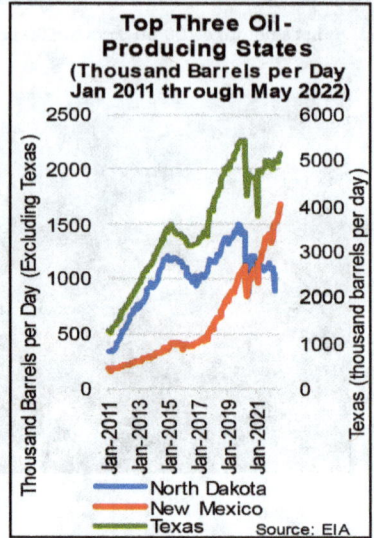

**Top Three Oil-Producing States** (Thousand Barrels per Day Jan 2011 through May 2022)

North Dakota — New Mexico — Texas    Source: EIA

Figure 4. and Figure 5.

# State funding prioritizes education, health and public safety.

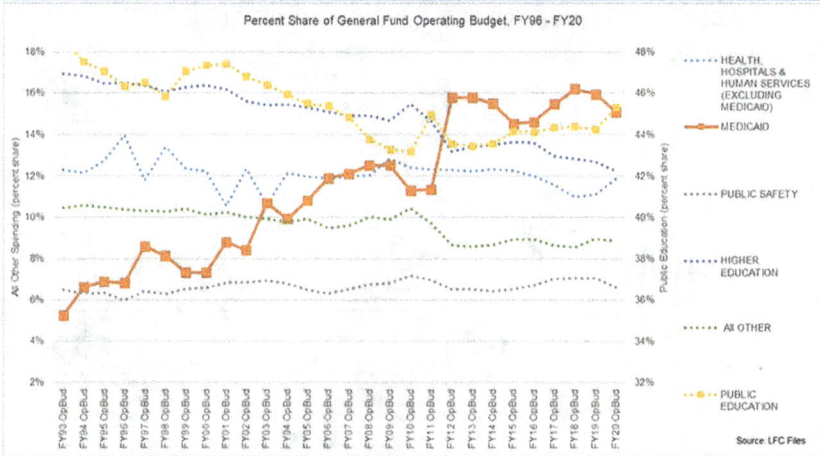

Figure 6.

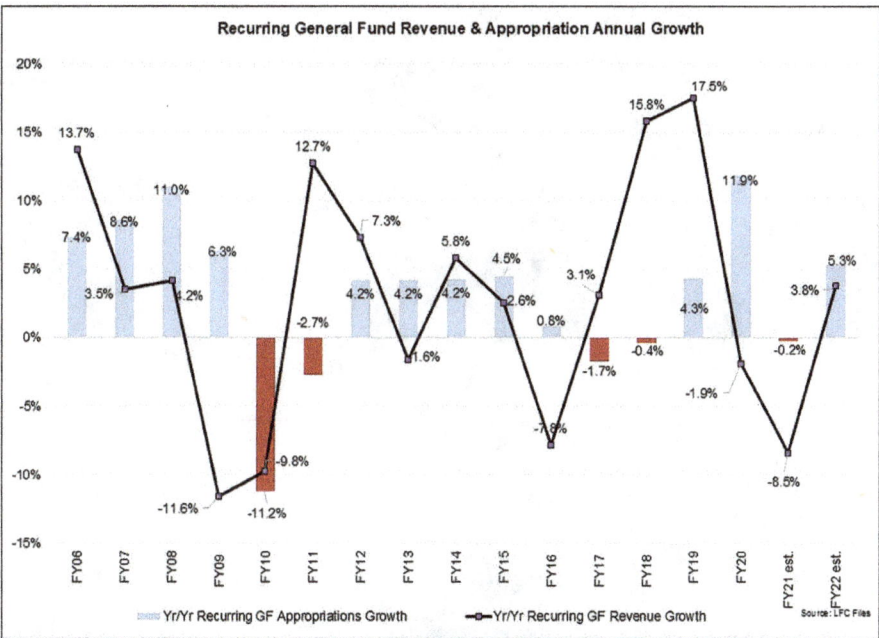

Figure 7.

# Stress testing informs reserve needs.

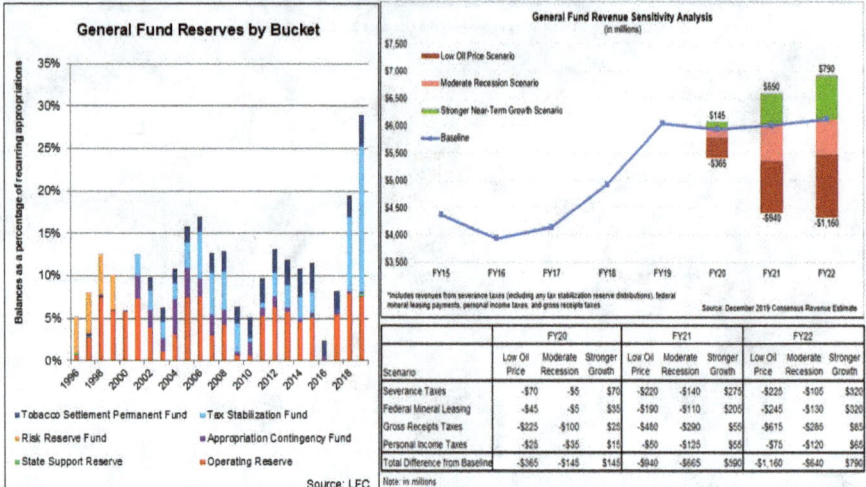

### General Fund Reserves by Bucket

Balances as a percentage of recurring appropriations

(bar chart, years 1996–2018, values 0%–35%)

- Tobacco Settlement Permanent Fund
- Risk Reserve Fund
- State Support Reserve
- Tax Stabilization Fund
- Appropriation Contingency Fund
- Operating Reserve

Source: LFC

### General Fund Revenue Sensitivity Analysis
(in millions)

- Low Oil Price Scenario
- Moderate Recession Scenario
- Stronger Near-Term Growth Scenario
- Baseline

(chart FY15–FY22 with values: -$365, $145, $650, $790, -$940, -$1,160)

*Includes revenues from severance taxes (including any tax stabilization reserve distributions), federal mineral leasing payments, personal income taxes, and gross receipts taxes

Source: December 2019 Consensus Revenue Estimate

| Scenario | FY20 | | | FY21 | | | FY22 | | |
|---|---|---|---|---|---|---|---|---|---|
| | Low Oil Price | Moderate Recession | Stronger Growth | Low Oil Price | Moderate Recession | Stronger Growth | Low Oil Price | Moderate Recession | Stronger Growth |
| Severance Taxes | -$70 | -$5 | $70 | -$220 | -$140 | $275 | -$225 | -$105 | $320 |
| Federal Mineral Leasing | -$45 | -$5 | $35 | -$190 | -$110 | $205 | -$245 | -$130 | $320 |
| Gross Receipts Taxes | -$225 | -$100 | $25 | -$480 | -$290 | $55 | -$615 | -$285 | $85 |
| Personal Income Taxes | -$25 | -$35 | $15 | -$50 | -$125 | $55 | -$75 | -$120 | $65 |
| Total Difference from Baseline | -$365 | -$145 | $145 | -$940 | -$665 | $590 | -$1,160 | -$640 | $790 |

Note: in millions

**D. General Fund Financial Summary**

17

Figure 8.

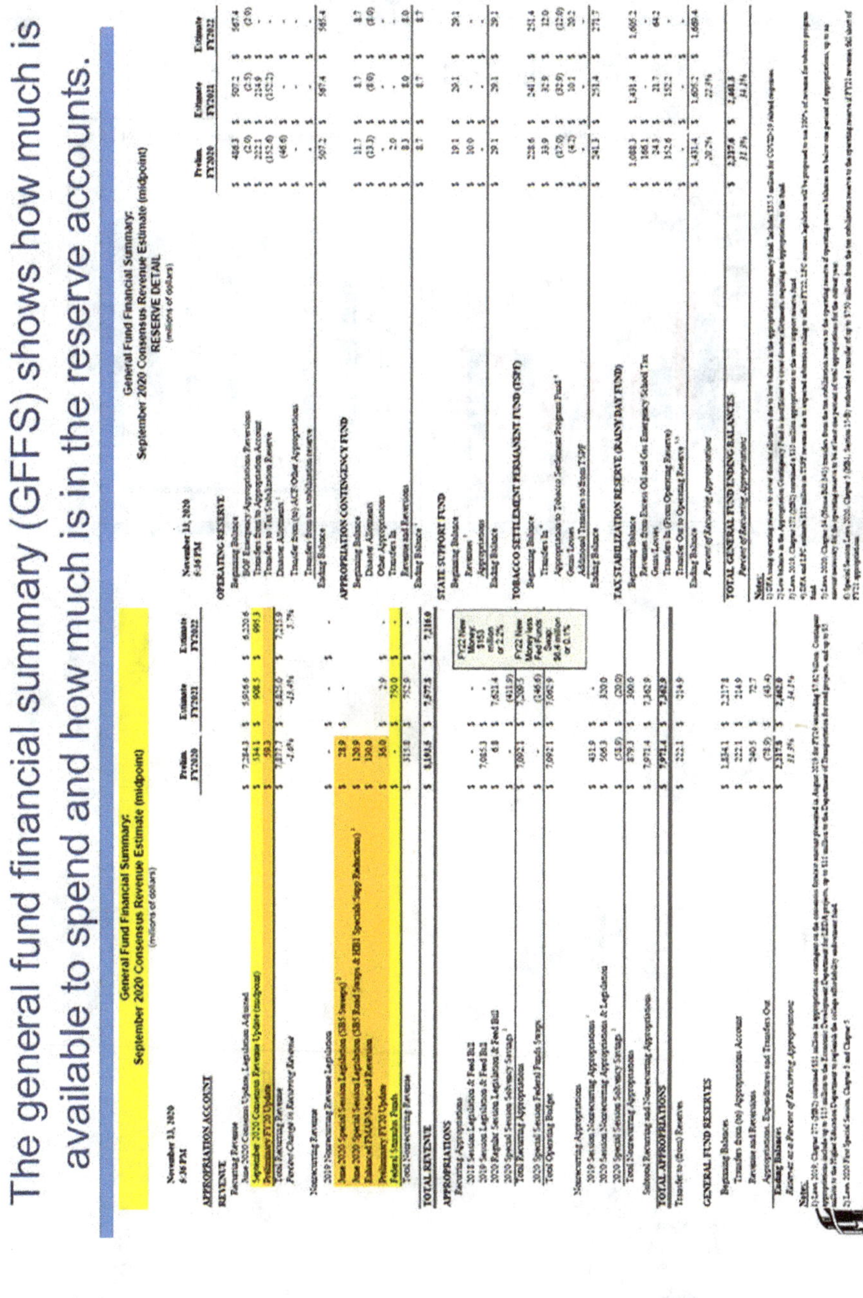
The general fund financial summary (GFFS) shows how much is available to spend and how much is in the reserve accounts.
General Fund Financial Summary:
September 2020 Consensus Revenue Estimate (midpoint)
(millions of dollars)
APPROPRIATION ACCOUNT
REVENUE
TOTAL REVENUE
APPROPRIATIONS
TOTAL APPROPRIATIONS
GENERAL FUND RESERVES
General Fund Financial Summary:
September 2020 Consensus Revenue Estimate (midpoint)
RESERVE DETAIL
(millions of dollars)
OPERATING RESERVE
APPROPRIATION CONTINGENCY FUND
STATE SUPPORT FUND
TOBACCO SETTLEMENT PERMANENT FUND (TSPF)
TAX STABILIZATION RESERVE (RAINY DAY FUND)
TOTAL GENERAL FUND ENDING BALANCES
D. General Fund Financial Summary

Figure 9.

# The AGA focuses budgeting on outcomes for New Mexicans.

### Examples of LFC Report Cards:

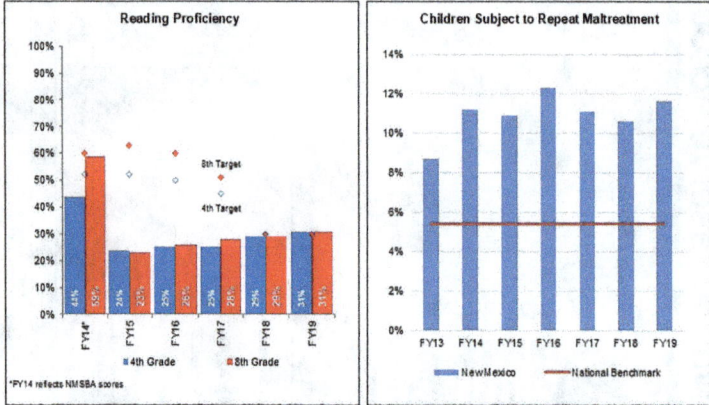

A. Principles

Figure 10.

# New Mexico State Senate

### State Capitol
### Santa Fe

COMMITTEES:

CHAIRMAN:
· Committees' Committee

MEMBER:
· Conservation
· Rules

**SENATOR BEN D. ALTAMIRANO**
PRESIDENT PRO TEMPORE
D-Catron, Grant & Socorro-28

1123 Santa Rita St.
Silver City, NM 88061

Home: (505) 538-3525

October 7, 2005

Honorable Bill Richardson
New Mexico State Governor
State Capitol
Santa Fe, NM 87501

Dear Governor Richardson:

I received a call this morning from your staff reporting concern about the activities of the Legislative Finance Committee staff. Apparently, there was a misunderstanding that the LFC Director was instigating changes to your proposed legislation for the Special Session, which is not true.

The fact is, that last night the Director and his staff were responding to Senators' requests for information. Section 2-5-3 NMSA 1978 authorizes the LFC to "examine the laws governing the finances and operation of departments, agencies and institutions ... the effect of laws on the proper functioning of the government units, the policies and costs of government units as related to the laws."

It is imperative, especially during fast-moving special sessions, for your staff, your cabinet heads and agencies to provide timely and objective responses to requests for information from legislators and legislative staff.

Finally, please have no doubt the LFC Director and the LFC staff are held in high confidence by the Senate for their professionalism and quality of service. We look forward to your continued cooperation with the Senate and our staff.

Sincerely,

Senator Ben D. Altamirano
President Pro Tem

Senator John Smith
Vice-Chair
Senate Finance

Senator Joe Fidel
Chairman
Senate Finance

Senator Michael Sanchez
Senate Floor Leader

Figure 11.

*"Mindblow"*

*The Lost Deal*
*(An Appropriator's Rap)*

In 2009, there was a $454 million revenue shortfall. In order to try to maintain reserves at 10%, these were some of the tools used from the solvency toolbox:

*Sn. Peter Wirth*
*Lorraine Montoya Vigil*

**Sweeping**

**Swapping**

**Sanding**

**Shifting**

**Sponge bonds**

**Cutting**

**Transferring funds**

**Reauthorizing**

**Voiding general fund capital outlay projects**

**Postponing distributions**

**Accessing contingency funds, including lockbox**

**Changing reporting dates for taxes**

**Authorizing adjustments of agency budgets**

**Using federal stimulus money**

Figure 12.

# NOTES

1. See *The Passage of Power: The Years of Lyndon Johnson*, Robert Caro, 2012; and *An Unfinished Love Story: A Personal History of the 1960s*, Doris Kearns Goodwin, Simon and Schuster, 2024.

2. There is a Madonna in Albuquerque and another in Springerville, Arizona next to the McDonalds.

3. See *Rising from the Plains*, John McPhee, Noonday Press, 1986 about the geomorphologist Love.

4. "An Election Last Week in Remotest New Mexico Retained the Status Quo," Molly Ivins, *New York Times*, Nov. 12, 1978.

5. *Adobe: Build it Yourself*, Paul Graham McHenry, UAP, 1973.

6. For a complete cultural, natural and anthropological history see *Legends of the American Desert: Sojourns of the Greater Southwest*, Alex Shoumatoff, Knopf, 1977.

7. *New Mexico Politics*, ed. Paul Hain, Chris Garcia and Gilbert St. Clair, University of New Mexico Press, 2006.

8. See Rystad forecast, LFC Volume 1, 2023.

9. "State Land Trust," LFC Finance Facts, website.

10. "Oil and Natural Gas Prices and Production Effects on Permanent Fund Inflows," State Investment Council, April 2023.

11. "For New Mexico's Revenue Estimators, Goal Is to Be on the Money," Jens Gould, *New Mexican*, August 24, 2019.

12. See "The Economics Profession and the Making of Public Policy," *Journal of Economic Literature*, 1987 for commentary on the role of economists in public finance. Notable Legislative Finance Committee economists included Bill Taylor, Norton Francis,

Stephanie Schardin Clark, Olivia Padilla Jackson, Scott Smith, Dawn Iglesias, Ismael Torres, Jennifer Faubion. Other experts who advised the legislature on revenue included Franklin Jones, Dr. Tom Clifford, New Mexico State University economics professor Jim Peach, University of New Mexico's Dr. Brian McDonald, Richard Anklam of the New Mexico Tax Policy Research Institute, TRD alumnae Jim O'Neill and Janet Peacock and Legislative Council Service's Pam Stafford and Gary Carlson.

13. LFC Progress Report, "Addressing Pandemic Impacts on Learning," September 2021.

14. The yearly Partnership for Assessment of Readiness for College and Careers (PARCC) test was established by a state consortium. The National Assessment of Educational Progress (NAEP) test is administered by the US Department of Education to a representative sample of students.

15. LFC Program Evaluation, "Impact of Childcare and Head Start on Student Achievement," September 2013.

16. In Wikipedia, Mark Tracy, March 28, 2015, *New York Times*.

17. "The Appropriations Process," prepared for LFC by Maralyn Budke, June 1964 and PowerPoint, "Legislative Finance Committee Diamond Jubilee," prepared by Helen Gaussoin for LFC, 2007.

18. *A Fly on the Wall*, Tony Hillerman, Harper and Row, 1971; a highway procurement scandal and a murder at an unnamed state capitol.

19. See for example, Chairman Varela's letter, "On the Road Again," LFC Newsletter, June 2001 and Chairman Altamirano's letter, "Travelin' Shoes," LFC Newsletter, April 2004.

20. See "Making Results-Based Government Work," Blaine Liner, Harry Hatry et. al, the Urban Institute, April 2001.

21. See "The Crime Buster," David Remnick, *New Yorker*, February 16, *1997,* about Chief William Bratton.

22. See "Applying PerformanceStat to a Legislative Context: Initial Observations from the Launch of Legistat in New Mexico," Andrew Feldman, April 2022.

23. LFC Performance Evaluation, "Obtaining and Maximizing Value in State Procurement," October 2021.

24. See page 55 General Fund High Level Appropriations Summary, LFC Post-Session Review, May 2023.

25. See agency high level spreadsheets in May 2023 post- session report, for example

Department of Public Safety showing budget increases including a state police pay step increase, targeted pay increases for dispatchers, records management contracts and a new law enforcement officer certification board.

26. Notable leaders of the FIR operation have included retired LFC deputy director Cathy Fernandez, former deputy attorney general Betsy Glenn, former assistant attorney general Marty Daly and former chief economist Laird Graeser. See "Inside the Boiler room of Legislative Analysts During the Session," Jens Gould, *New Mexican*, February 12, 2020.

27. 2004 LFC Post-Session Fiscal Review.

28. Volume 1, LFC Recommendations to the Legislature for FY08, January 2006.

29. See *Ambassador, Lessons from a Life of Service*, Frank Ortiz and Don Usner, University of New Mexico Press, 2005.

30. Department of Transportation report card, Volume 1, and 2004 LFC Recommendation.

31. "Richardson Woos Imus Over Controversial School Project," NBC News, March 22, 2007.

32. "Review of Selected Water Pojects," LFC Performance Evaluation January 2008; and "Office of the State Engineer, Department of Environment Capital Outlay, Review of Select Projects," LFC Performance Evaluation, December 2014.

33. In 1599, Onate's nephew attacked Acoma Pueblo leaving 880 dead and then amputated one foot of male survivors. See *Indigenous Continent*, Pekka Hamalainen, Liveright Publishing, New York, 2022.

34. "Congressional Oversight," Elaine Halchin and Frederick Kaiser, Congressional Research Service, October 17, 2012.

35. "State Tax Refund Going to the Dogs," Wren Propp, *Albuquerque Journal*, October 17, 1998.

36. "Veto Sparks New Fight in Capital," Barry Massey, *Albuquerque Journal*, February 1, 1999.

37. "Controlling Stationary Source Emissions in the Four Corners Region," Winston Harrington and David Abbey, *Southwestern Review of Management and Economics*, Summer 1981.

38. "Early Childhood Accountability Report," August 2021 and "Prekindergarten Quality and Education Outcomes," June 2020.

39. LFC Performance Evaluation, "Department of Health Facilities Oversight, Capacity

and Performance," July 2021 and LFC Progress Report, "Challenges at Some DoH Facilities Deepen," September 2022.

40. Letter David Abbey to CYFD Secretary Deines, April 12, 2013.

41. See for example, "CYFD blamed in child's 2020 death," Colleen Heild, *Albuquerque Journal*. August 14, 2023.

42. "Governor-elect wastes no time," Robert Storrey, *New Mexican*, November 3, 1982.

43. "LA Voters Buck State Democratic Trend," JW Schomisch, *New Mexican*, November 3, 1982.

44. "Anaya's Keeper of the Door," David Steinberg, *Albuquerque Journal*, June 26, 1983.

45. The Roundhouse replaced the Bataan memorial building in 1966. It is designed after the zia symbol, widely displayed on the orange and red state flag. The house and senate chambers are underground on the first floor with a three-story atrium at the center on ground level.

46. "Bold Efforts of Governor Anaya Meet Reality in New Mexico," Iver Peterson, *New York Times*, March 21, 1984.

47. "LFC Has Lost Its Zip," David Steinberg, *Albuquerque Journal*, August 19, 1984.

48. "Quiter Education Association Remains on Alert," Leah Beth Ward, *Albuquerque Journal*, February 3, 1985.

49. "Legislature Consumed by Politics," Bill Feather, *Albuquerque Journal*, February 24, 1985.

50. "Kraft Called on Bank Tickets," Betty Golden, *Albuquerque Journal*, August 18, 1984.

51. "State Auditor Mounts Challenge to Refunding Plan," Leah Beth Ward, *Albuquerque Journal*, July 7, 1985.

52. See *The Quiet Americans*, Scott Anderson, May 2021 and *The 4th Man: The Hunt for a KGB Spy at the Top of the CIA and the Rise of Putin's Russia*, Robert Baer, May 2022.

53. "Right Wing Waging War, Anaya Charges," John Robertson, *Albuquerque Journal*, September 22, 1985.

54. "Anaya's desire to strengthen office often led to trouble," Doug McClellan, *New Mexican,* December 28, 1986; "Anaya Years Marked by Controversy, Achievement," David Staats, *Albuquerque Journal*, December 28, 1986.

55. "New Governor Promises Positive State Tone," David Staats, *Albuquerque Journal*, January 1, 1987.

56. "Carruthers Learned the Session Game," David Staats, *Albuquerque Journal*, February 28, 1988.

57. "Change Comes Slowly to State Budgets," David Staats, *Albuquerque Journal*, March20, 1988.

58. "Promising Ventures Yield Costly Failures," Leah Beth Ward, *Albuquerque Journal*, December 4, 1988.

59. "Selling New Mexico," Larry Calloway, *Albuquerque Journal*, October 9, 1988.

60. "Last One Out Lock the Era," Larry Calloway, *Albuquerque Journal*, December 17, 1989.

61. "Few Missteps Mar Carruthers' Tenure," Ed Moreno, *Albuquerque Journal*, December 31, 1989.

62. "Governor Offers Budget, Chance of a Tax Hike," John Yeager and Jackie Jadrnak, *Albuquerque Journal*, January 7, 1990.

63. "Legislators raise Taxes, Close Session," Jackie Jadrnak, *Albuquerque Journal*, March 21, 1990.

64. "King, Bond Differ on Where State Should Put Its Nest Eggs," Leah Beth Ward, *Albuquerque Journal*, October 28, 1990.

65. See *Cowboy in the Roundhouse: A Political Life*, Bruce King as told to Charles Poling, Sunstone Press, 1998.

66. "Family Tree Spreads Over New Mexico Politics," John Robertson, *Albuquerque Journal*, December 29, 1991.

67. "Workers Fight Budget War in the Trenches," Jackie Jadrnak, *Albuquerque Journal*, January 27, 1991.

68. "School Levy Dies Amid Chaos," Jackie Jadrnak, John Yeager and Leah Beth Ward, *Albuquerque Journal*, March 17, 1991.

69. "Shrinking Pie Leads to Squabble Over Slices," Jackie Jadrnak, *Albuquerque Journal*, September 5, 1991.

70. See *What's In It For Me: How an Ex-Wiseguy Exposed the Greed, Jealousy and Lust That Drive Arizona Politics*, Joseph Stedino with Daryl Matera, Harper Collins, 1992.

71. "Az Texas Area Report," Larry Calloway, *Albuquerque Journal*, December 20, 1992.

72. "Democratic Control Doesn't Guarantee Leadership Vision," Bill Hume, *Albuquerque Journal*, January 3, 1993.

73. "Plains Speaking," Fritz Thompson, *Albuquerque Journal*, January 31, 1993.

74. *Cowboy in the Roundhouse: A Political Life*, op. cit.

75. "Governor Shakes Off Criticism," Jackie Jadrnak, *Albuquerque Journal*, June 27, 1993.

76. "Guns, Welfare, Teacher Pay on New Mexico Plan," Thom Cole, *Albuquerque Journal*, September 30, 1993.

77. "Only a Week and Already a Crisis," Larry Calloway, *Albuquerque Journal*, January 23, 1994.

78. "On a Highway to the Stars," and "It All Comes down to Highway Money," Larry Calloway, *Albuquerque Journal*, February 24 and 27, 1994.

79. "Ethnic Comments Not New to New Mexico Politics," Kate Nelson, *Albuquerque Tribune*, October 25, 1994.

80. "Johnson May Tap Budget Wiz," Thom Cole and Jackie Jadrnak, *Albuquerque Journal*, December 2, 1994.

81. "King Led with a Steady Hand," John Robertson, *Albuquerque Journal*, December 26, 1994.

82. "Lawmakers Want Dibs on Bond Millions," Jackie Jadrnak, *Albuquerque Journal*, February 4, 1995.

83. The governor must act on legislation within 72 hours of the enrolled and engrossed bill being clocked in to the governor's office; except the governor has 20 days to act on legislation received in the final 72 hours of the session. The appropriators sometimes threaten to jam the governor with quick action on the budget leaving the governor little time to examine amendments or language or to cut deals for other bills. But since 2009, this has been an idle threat.

84. See "Governing to the Beat of His Own Drummer," John Robertson, *Albuquerque Journal*, May 21, 1995.

85. "Johnson Will Meet You at His Place," In Brief, *New Mexican*, August 18, 1995 and "Help Me Out There," Larry Calloway, *Albuquerque Journal*, November 19, 1995.

86. "Bruised Governor Returns to Court," TJ Sullivan, *Albuquerque Tribune*, November 8, 1995 and "Johnson Faces Diminished Prospects in 1996 Legislature," Bill Hume, *Albuquerque Journal*, December 1995.

87. "Rocking the Boat," Jackie Jadrnak, *Albuquerque Journal*, December 31, 1995.

88. "Mama" Lucy Lopez ran a Las Vegas restaurant that catered to students and *politicos*. In the 1970s a group of House democrats took the name Mama Lucy Gang and pushed school reform and other liberal policies.

89. "Old Santa Fe's Sense of Place," Larry Calloway, *Albuquerque Journal*, January 23, 1996.

90. "Government by Men of Letters," Larry Calloway, *Albuquerque Journal*, August 13, 1996.

91. "The King of the Senate," John Robertson, *Albuquerque Journal*, March 17, 1997.

92. "AG Nixes Investment," Mike Gallagher, *Albuquerque Journal*, June 3, 1995.

93. See "Johnson Takes Night Tour of N.Y," John Robertson, *Albuquerque Journal*, June 16, 1995.

94. "New Mexico Targeting Longer Yields to Lock in Rates," Valerie Carlson, *Bond Buyer*, January 22, 1996.

95. "Legislators Skeptical of NM 44 Financing", Carla Crowder, *Albuquerque Journal*, July 24, 1997.

96. "Talking About Money and NM 44, and Money and Fatherhood," Larry Calloway, *Albuquerque Journal*, July 26, 1998.

97. "Another Judicial Brick Hits Johnson," Bill Hume, *Albuquerque Journal*, September 14, 1997.

98. "Prison Subpoena Riles Aragon," Barry Massey, *Albuquerque Journal*, November 22, 1997.

99. "Credibility Blight Hits All Branches," Bill Hume, *Albuquerque Journal*, January 25, 1998.

100. "Driveup Battle Fiery to the End," Larry Calloway, *Albuquerque Journal*, May 5, 1998.

101. "A Different Breed," Loie Fecteau, *Albuquerque Journal, August 30, 1998*.

102. "State Awash in Unappropriated General Fund," Bill Hume, *Albuquerque Journal*, Oct. 4, 1998.

103. See reference to his service in *We Were Soldiers Once—and Young: Ia Drang—the Battle that Changed the War in Vietnam*, Lieutenant Gen. Harold Moore and Joseph Galloway, Random House, 1992.

104. See "Panel Aims to Salvage Archeology Agency," Wrenn Propp, *Albuquerque Journal*, February 2, 1999.

105. "LFC Oversight of Government Operations Indispensable," Larry Calloway, *Albuquerque Journal*, February 2, 1999.

106. "'Worst Ever' Budget Bill," Loie Fecteau, *Albuquerque Journal*, March 17, 1999.

107. "History of New Mexico Prisons Written in Blood," Mike Gallagher, *Albuquerque Journal*, September 19, 1999.

108. "Drug Debate Fizzled in Inane Sound-Bites," Editorial, *Albuquerque Journal*, October 10, 1999.

109. "New Mexico on Fast Track, $420 M Project Raises Questions, Criticism," Mike Gallagher and Colleen Heild, *Albuquerque Journal*, December 5, 1999.

110. "Budget Impasse Brews at the Capitol," Barry Massey, *Albuquerque Journal*, February 17, 2000.

111. President Trump also practiced chaos theory. See Chapter 8, "Chaos as a Way of Life," in *The Room Where It Happened: A White House Memoir*, John Bolton, Simon and Schuster, 2020.

112. "Court Pays High Price for Land," Thom Cole, *Albuquerque Journal*, April 2, 2000.

113. "Finance Ace to Advise Senate GOP," Loie Fecteau, *Albuquerque Journal*, December 10, 2000.

114. "State Auditor Formally Questions Treasurer's Practices," Larry Calloway, *Albuquerque Journal*, September 2, 1999.

115. memo LFC analyst Arley Williams to David Abbey, September 14, 1999.

116. memo LFC analyst Jeff Eaton to David Abbey, October 6, 1999.

117. "If Pigs Could Fly," David Miles, *Albuquerque Journal*, February 21, 2002.

118. "Governor Plans 3rd Budget Veto," David Miles, *Albuquerque Journal*, May 22, 2002.

119. "Governor Enjoys National Stature," Loie Fecteau, *Albuquerque Journal*, July 6, 2003.

120. "Money Shortfall Predicted," Barry Massey, *Albuquerque Journal*, March 4, 2003.

121. "Governor Says He Can Dole Out Federal Aid," Loie Fecteau, *Albuquerque Journal*, July 18, 2003.

122. "Richardson's Crossing of the Line Remains Unresolved," Larry Calloway, *Albuquerque Journal*, June 15, 2003.

123. "Restore Limitations on Governors' Power," Editorial, *Albuquerque Journal*, July 6, 2003, and "Commission Reports Second Threat," Larry Calloway, *Albuquerque Journal*, July 20, 2003.

124. "Ready to Deal," Thom Cole, *Albuquerque Journal*, August 10, 2003, and "Track Hopeful Helps Governor's Gala,"Thom Cole, *Albuquerque Journal*, November 11, 2003.

125. "Racino Applicant Has Ties to Governor," Thom Cole, *Albuquerque Journal*, November 26, 2008.

126. "Amendment Voting Says Much About Governor," Larry Calloway, *Albuquerque Journal*, September 28, 2003.

127. "Legislature May Make Quick Exit," Loie Fecteau, *Albuquerque Journal*, October 26, 2003.

128. "Lobby Stung by Governor's Wrath," Shea Anderson, *Albuquerque Tribune*, February 6, 2004.

129. See *A Place of Thin Veil: Life and Death in Gallup New Mexico*, Bob Rosebrough, Rio Nuevo Press, 2002.

130. "Funds' Managers Gave Big to Governor,"Thom Cole, *Albuquerque Journal*, August 1, 2004.

131. "Stockpiling Journalists," Leanne Potts, *American Journalism Review*.

132. "Governor's Duke City Office Irks Critics," Mike Gallagher, *Albuquerque Journal*, June 12, 2005.

133. "Kickbacks Spanned a Decade," Thom Cole, *Albuquerque Journal*, September 18, 2005.

134. "Insider Lands State business," Thom Cole, *Albuquerque Journal*, September 25, 2005.

135. "Obstacles to Opportunities," Trip Jennings and Gabriela Guzman, *Albuquerque Journal*, January 18, 2006.

136. "Governor Slashes 'Feeding Frenzy," Trip Jennings and Gabriela Guzman, *Albuquerque Journal*, March 9, 2006.

137. "Plan on fast Track," Colleen Heild, *Albuquerque Journal*, Jan. 8, 2006 and "Go-to Lobbyist," Colleen Heild, *Albuquerque Journal*, January 22, 2006.

138. "Under the Radar," Jeff Jones, *Albuquerque Journal*, April 2, 2006.

139. Initial Decision No. 353 Administrative Proceeding, File no. 3-12829, Securities Exchange Commission in the Matter of Guy P. Riordan.

140. "Ethics Reform Top Priority," ACI Focus Report, Vol. XVI, 2005.

141. "Discontent Brewing in the Roundhouse," David Roybal, *Albuquerque Journal*, August 22, 2006.

142. "Man of the People," Leslie Linthicum, *Albuquerque Journal*, February 25, 1997.

143. "The Rising Star," Thom Cole, *Albuquerque Journal*, January 28, 2007 and "Lewinsky Spotlight Casts Shadow," Leslie Linthicum, *Albuquerque Journal*, February 4, 2007.

144. "State Workers Pitch in for Governor," Jeff Jones and John Fleck, *Albuquerque Journal,* July 29, 2007.

145. "State Health Secretary Under Scrutiny," Leanne Holt, *Albuquerque Journal*, March 4, 2007.

146. "Tycoon Backs Governor All the Way," July 8, "Suspects Involved in DoT Project," July 22, "Plane Trips Courtesy of DoT Project," August 5, "Donor Linked to Sole DoT Bidder, August 26, "Defendant Had Ties to DoT Project," September 30, 2007, *Albuquerque Journal*; Heath Haussamen, New Mexico Politics blog, Oct. 1, 2007

147. See field trip minutes/report, September 2007, LFC website.

148. "Oil Prices Still Tumbling," Barry Massey, *Albuquerque Journal*, July 26, 2007.

149. "Governor's Proposal Cut, But Passed," Dan Boyd and Win Quigley, *Albuquerque Journal*, August 20, 2008.

150. "Governor, New Mexico Won't Settle for Gridlock," Bill Richardson, *Albuquerque Journal*, August 24, 2007.

151. "Lawmakers Work on Fixing Shortfall," Deborah Baker, *Albuquerque Journal*, December 19, 2008.

152. "Police: Richardson not Tied to Hit and Run," Raam Wong, *Albuquerque Journal*, January 11, 2009.

153. "GRIP Contract Probed," *Albuquerque Journal*, August 29, 2008 and "David Rubin's Empire of Advice," Martin Braun, *Bloomberg Markets*, November 2006.

154. *The Forever War*, Dexter Filkins, Vintage, 2008.

155. See "Science Violated: Spending Projections and the Costing Out of an Adequate Education," in *Courting Failure*, Stanford Univ. Press, 2006.

156. Kreskin was a mind reader popular on TV. "New Mexico Politics: Today's Budget Deficit Predicted Four Years Ago," Walt Rubel, *Las Cruces Sun-News*, October 4, 2009.

157. "New Mexico Deficit Soars," Dan Boyd, *Albuquerque Journal*, October 10, 2009; and "Deficit: Governor, Lawmakers at Odds," Barry Massey, *New Mexican*, October 15, 2009.

158. "School Spending Cuts Fought," Dan Boyd and Sean Olson, *Albuquerque Journal*, October 21, 2009.

159. "Legislators Getting Closer to Deal," Dan Boyd, *Albuquerque Journal*, October 22, 2009.

160. "Pay to Pay Inquiry Derails Cabinet Post," Mike Gallagher, *Albuquerque Journal*, January 5, 2009.

161. "New Pay to Play Claim," Mike Gallagher, *Albuquerque Journal*, January 15, 2009.

162. "Richardson Confidants Played Key Roles on Both Sides of GRIP Bond Deals," Colleen Heild and Jeff Jones, *Albuquerque Journal*, January 8, 2009 and January 11, 2009.

163. Trip Jennings, *New Mexico Independent*, May 12, 2009.

164. "New Mexico Investment Advisor Caught up in NY Scandal," Mike Gallagher, *Albuquerque Journal*, March 22, 2009.

165. "Unwinding Swaps a Costly Proposition for State," Thom Cole, *Albuquerque Journal*, May 12, 2010.

166. "Shaking the Money Tree," Thom Cole, *Albuquerque Journal,* January 15, 2012.

167. "New York Probe Continues to Boil Over in New Mexico," Mike Gallagher, *Albuquerque Journal,* December 13, 2009.

168. "Rising Legal Fees Spark Criticism," Mike Gallagher, *Albuquerque Journal*, January 9, 2010.

169. "SIC Legal Expenditures and their Budgetary Impacts," Presentation of LFC economist Dan White to Senate Judiciary, January 25, 2010.

170. "Aboard the Good Ship Richardson", Thom Cole, *Albuquerque Journal*, September 12, 2009.

171. "Landeene Discussed Ranch Deal with Spaceport Lawyer," Heath Haussamen, *New MexicoPolitics.Net*, June 14, 2010.

172. "20 Months and Counting in Scandal," Thom Cole, *Albuquerque Journal*, November 24, 2010.

173. "Foes Lash Back Over Martinez Tactics," Sean Olson, *Albuquerque Journal*, February 24, 2011.

174. "Governor, APS Spar Over Budget," Hailey Heinz, *Albuquerque Journal*, February 28, 2011.

175. "Martinez Aims for Economic Growth," Deborah Baker, *Albuquerque Journal*, July 11, 2011.

176. "Mixed Results for New Governor's First Session," Dan Boyd and Sean Olson, *Albuquerque Journal*, March 20, 2011.

177. "Governor Signs Budget Bill," Dan Boyd, *Albuquerque Journal*, April 9, 2011.

178. "Downs Lease Ok'd Despite Opposition," Charles Brunt, *Albuquerque Journal*, November 22, 2011.

179. "Downs Lease Delay Triggered Tirade," Mike Gallagher, *Albuquerque Journal*, January 12, 2014

180. "At the Roundhouse: Spun, Spooked," John Robertson, *Albuquerque Journal*, January 21, 2012.

181. See report to the financial community, Michael Zavelle, NMFA Chief Financial Strategist, December 4, 2012.

182. "House committee deadlocks on educators' pension bill," Dan Boyd, *Albuquerque Journal*, February 21, 2013.

183. "Dems, Gov in Showdown Over Budget," Dan Boyd, *Albuquerque Journal*, March 14, 2013.

184. "Session Smoke Clears", John Robertson, *Albuquerque Journal*, March 19, 2013.

185. See also "Apology Given for Tax Bill Info," Dan Boyd, *Albuquerque Journal*, May 15, 2013.

186. "Center pushes Left Agenda," Thom Cole, *Albuquerque Journal*, June 15, 2013.

187. "GRT Reform May Have Shot in 2014," Win Quigley, *Albuquerque Journal*, December 20, 2013.

188. "Legislators Question Health Audit," Deborah Baker, *Albuquerque Journal*, July 3, 2013.

189. "Seeking Better Ways to Protect Vulnerable Kids," Leslie Linthicum, *Albuquerque Journal*, February 16, 2014.

190. "Keep an Eye on Session's Likely Movers and Shakers," Steve Terrell, *New Mexican*, January 19, 2014; and "Bregman takes Heat for Comments About Fellow Democrat," Deborah Baker, *Albuquerque Journal*, January 24, 2014.

191. "Budget Bill Fails in tie vote," Dan Boyd, *Albuquerque Journal*, February 8, 2014.

192. "Key Legislative Committee Faces Roadblock," Thom Cole, *Albuquerque Journal*, March 31, 2013.

193. "Governor Clarifies Policy on Info requests," Dan Boyd, *Albuquerque Journal*, April 6, 2014.

194. "Session Ends with Acrimony, Gridlock," Dan Boyd and Jon Swedien, *Albuquerque Journal*, March 22, 2015.

195. "State Needs to Weigh Tax Increases," Winthrop Quigley, *Albuquerque Journal*, March 27, 2016.

196. "House Gets Started on Budget Fixes," Deborah Baker and Dan Boyd, *Albuquerque Journal*, October 2, 2016.

197. "Exodus: New Mexico's Population Stagnant as People Leave in Unprecedented Numbers," Michael Coleman, *Albuquerque Journal*, January 29, 2017.

198. "Active Permian Shale Area Rife with Potential," Kevin Robinson-Avila, *Albuquerque Journal*, January 16, 2017.

199. "State of the State speech focuses on budget," Dan McKay, *Albuquerque Journal*, January 18, 2017.

200. "Cash Crunch is Real Says Budget Official," Dan Boyd, *Albuquerque Journal*, March 31, 2017.

201. "Governor Faces a Menu of Options on Budget," Dan McKay. *Albuquerque Journal*, April 5, 2017.

202. "Veto Pen Sets Stage for Legislative Showdown," Dan Boyd, *Albuquerque Journal*, April 8, 2017.

203. "Legislature sends new budget package to governor," Dan Boyd and Dan McKay, *Albuquerque Journal*, May 25, 2017.

204. "Analysis: Tax Overhaul Would Slash Revenue," Dan McKay, *Albuquerque Journal*, June 13, 2017.

205. "UNM, NMSU: Ladders and Labs," Jessica Dyer, *Albuquerque Journal*, July 29, 2017.

206. "Holding the Line," Kent Walz, *Albuquerque Journal*, July 1, 2018.

207. "Oil Production Still Booming in New Mexico," Kevin Robinson-Avila, *Albuquerque Journal*. November 26, 2018.

208. "Next Stimulus Round Offers Flexibility for New Mexico: Governor, Lawmakers still at Odds over $1.75 billion," Dan McKay, *Albuquerque Journal*, May 22, 2021.

209. "Two Lawmakers Go to Court over Governor's Federal Aid Spending," Dan Boyd, *Albuquerque Journal*, September 21, 2021.

210. "Looking Back at 40 Years on the Beat: Criminal Justice and Corruption Were Staples of His Career", Mike Gallagher, *Albuquerque Journal*, December 26, 2021.

211. "Senate Leaders Ousted in Monumental Primary," Dan Boyd, *Albuquerque Journal*, June 4, 2020.

212. "Biden Eyes DC Veterans for Key Posts," Alexandra Jaffe, Associated Press, *Albuquerque Journal*, November 10, 2020.

213. See LFC website, Public Education, for example, "Public Education and Policy Issues," LFC staff, August 2021.

214. "Leaders, Districts Must Stanch New Mexico's Big Learning Losses," Editors, *Albuquerque Journal*, November 4, 2020.

215. "New Mexico Students Likely to Suffer Learning Loss," Shelby Perea, Albuquerque Journal, October 29, 2022; and "Fewer Schools Taking Part in Extended Learning, Analysts Say," Esteban Candelaria, *Albuquerque Journal*, July 22, 2022.

216. "Experts: New Mexico to Face Prolonged Economic Pain," Dan McKay, *Albuquerque Journal*, July 16, 2020.

217. "State's Plan to Rescind Remote Work Policy Draws Criticism," Dan Boyd, *Albuquerque Journal*, December 1, 2022.

218. See LFC Appropriation Recommendations for General Services Department, Volume 2, January, 2023.

219. "Tax Rates Climb Amid Code-Revision Debate," Dan McKay, *Albuquerque Journal*, July 16, 2021.

220. LFC Spotlight: May 19,2021; "Governor: Pandemic Spending Justified," Dan Boyd, *Albuquerque Journal*, August 6, 2021; "New Mexico Submits Incomplete Stimulus Info, Report Says," Dan McKay, *Albuquerque Journal*, October 30, 2021; LFC Progress Report, "Challenges at Some DOH Facilities Deepen," September 2022.

221. "Opportunity Knocking as State's Revenue Spike Continues," Dan Boyd, *Albuquerque Journal*, December 13, 2022.

222. "David Abbey, director of the Legislative Finance Committee, to retire this summer," Dan McKay, *Albuquerque Journal*, March 28, 2023.

223. For a similar presentation of New Mexico metrics see presentation of Dale Dekker to NAIOP New Mexico, August, 26, 2024.

224. "Why is New Mexico's Labor Participation Rate So Low," Data Focus, Workforce Solutions Department, April 2022.

225. See memorandum, Cally Carswell and Ryan Tolman to LFC Chair Lundstrom, January 17, 2022.

226. "The American South is Booming: Why is Mississippi Behind?" Cameron McWhorter, *Wall Street Journal*, December 31, 2023.

227. *New Mexico: A History*, Joseph Sanchez, Robert Spude and Arthur Gomez, University of Oklahoma Press, 2013.

228. "Habits of Thought and the Process of Economic Development: Remarks on Receiving the Veblen-Commons Award", James Peach. Coincidentally my college studies included Myrdal's *Asian Drama: An Inquiry into the Poverty of Nations*, Pantheon, 1968, about development in India and China.

229. *Journal of Economic Issues*, 2020.

230. New Mexico's Options for 21st Century Economic Growth and Prosperity," New Mexico First.

231. *New Mexico 2050*, editor Fred Harris, University of New Mexico Press, 2015.

232. *The Myth of American Inequality: How Government Biases Policy Debate*, Phil Gramm, Robert Ekelund, and John Early, Rowman and Littlefield, 2022.

233. Mark Moore, *Creating Public Value: Strategic Management in Government*, Harvard University Press, 1977.

# INDEX

www.ingramcontent.com/pod-product-compliance
Lightning Source LLC
Chambersburg PA
CBHW050626280326
41932CB00015B/2537